Fighting Fire

ONE HUNDRED YEARS OF THE FIRE BRIGADES UNION

Dedication

To all firefighters and emergency control staff who have served their communities with distinction while belonging to the Fire Brigades Union.

Acknowledgements

Thanks are due to all those who have been interviewed as part of this centenary publication, along with all those who read and commented on early drafts. The authors are grateful to Dave Smith for carrying out interviews with a number of FBU members and reps.

Fighting Fire

ONE HUNDRED YEARS OF THE FIRE BRIGADES UNION

SIAN MOORE, TESSA WRIGHT & PHILIP TAYLOR

FOREWORD BY MATT WRACK

Fighting Fire
One Hundred Years of the Fire Brigades Union

First published in 2018 by
New Internationalist on behalf of   The Fire Brigades Union
The Old Music Hall   Bradley House, 68 Coombe Road
106-108 Cowley Road   Kingston-upon-Thames
Oxford OX4 1JE   Surrey, KT2 7AE
newint.org   fbu.org.uk

Cover photo © Mark Thomas.
Other photographs © as individually credited.
All weblinks referenced were accessed between September 2017 and
April 2018.

Design: New Internationalist

Printed by TJ International Limited, Cornwall, UK, who hold
environmental accreditation ISO 14001.

British Library Cataloguing-in-Publication Data
A catalogue record for this book is available from the British Library.

ISBN PB 978-1-78026-492-9
ISBN HB 978-1-78026-494-3

Contents

Foreword

Matt Wrack, general secretary of the Fire Brigades Union

The centenary of the Fire Brigades Union (FBU) is a highly significant moment for the trade union movement. The FBU is an organisation built by and for firefighters. We use the term 'firefighter' to cover all those working in uniformed roles in the fire and rescue service. It includes firefighters on fire stations, those working in emergency fire control rooms, those working in specialist departments (training and elsewhere) and those in managerial roles. It is a useful word for the entire 'team' needed to deliver the prevention, protection and intervention work of the modern fire and rescue service.

The FBU is relatively small compared to the big general unions. But to have lasted a hundred years as an industry-specific organisation is some achievement, especially in light of the long history of union mergers. We have much in our past and our present that FBU activists and others can learn from. We have also made mistakes that we should reflect on.

The FBU's Executive Council has invested significant time and resources in our centenary year. We concluded that it should be marked and celebrated. However, we are also taking the opportunity to re-state and re-assert our case for the type of fire and rescue service we want to see. This role – of setting out a better way for our trade and our industry – is one that has been a part of our culture for several decades (although it was disputed in the earlier years of the FBU). We have battled to ensure that we are not simply boxed into a narrow remit of pay, terms and conditions. Not least, we recognise the inevitable link between *what our members do at work* and *what they are paid*.

We approached this book in a spirit of openness and pluralism. We felt that different voices and opinions should be heard. Some parts may make uncomfortable reading and might provoke sharp debate. In places the recollections and perspectives of contributors differ about the same events. We won't necessarily agree with all the conclusions of the authors or with some opinions expressed in the various chapters by different FBU people. But a commitment to open discussion and debate is essential for progress. This book concentrates on the past three decades, but there are themes that have emerged and re-emerge during and prior to this period that stand out. I take this opportunity to raise issues that I believe FBU activists, as well as those involved in the wider labour movement, should debate and study further.

We need to think about how this should be done. One issue of concern in the modern labour movement (and in wider public discussion) is an often high-handed and dismissive approach to debate. All too often, arguments (especially on difficult and controversial issues) are approached on the basis of one side saying to the other 'You can't say that'. Yet even the most scant examination of the history of working people will show that the struggles for freedom of speech and for democracy have been central, and essential, to building any movement that challenges those in power. To address the huge challenges our movement faces today, we need to build a culture of debate and democracy which accepts that there will be different views and sometimes sharp differences of opinion. Democracy must include the right to express those differences. It also includes mechanisms for making decisions based on the conclusions of the majority. Democracy does, of course, mean the rule of the majority. It is a powerful force, and one which is essential in the labour movement and in wider politics. If we are confident in our arguments, confident in our case for change, then we should also be confident that we can win the battle of ideas and convince the majority. There is no organisational shortcut or manoeuvre that can avoid the need to engage in this challenge of winning the case for change.

Our centenary will hopefully give FBU members past and present, as well as others interested in building a labour movement fit for the challenges of the 21st century, an opportunity to reflect on the lessons of the past and discuss the ways forward. Indeed, this occasion has led me to ponder on the mistakes I have made at various stages of my time in the union. We should all take time to similarly reflect, and to assess and re-assess issues that may have become clearer as time has passed.

Several themes of particular note emerge for me as I examine the first hundred years of our union. These include the vital importance of strong rank-and-file organisation rooted in the workplace; the relationship between pay, terms and conditions and the functions the fire and rescue service undertakes; how best to challenge and address issues of racism, sexism, homophobia and the other divisions that exist both in wider society and within working-class organisations; and the relationship between trade union organisation and wider working-class politics. And as we enter our second century, it is vital that FBU activists address issues of strategy and tactics, to put our members in the best position for future struggles.

Workplace organisation

While the FBU is not the largest trade union in the UK, we do enjoy one of the highest levels of membership density of any union. For me, this is largely because we have remained an industrially based union: we are focused on the fire and rescue service and on organising those in 'firefighting, rescue or related services'. For the past decade or so, we have addressed this issue head on in internal discussions and, so far, have made the decision to maintain an independent fire and rescue service union. That gives our members a strong sense of identity, which is very clearly a feature of both the fire and rescue service and of the FBU.

We also focus our efforts on organising in the workplace, encouraging the building of our union around workers *organising themselves*. It contrasts sharply with, for example, a 'servicing' model of trade unionism that sees members as consumers buying a series of services from the union. Of course the FBU does provide members with a wide range of services (financial, legal, representative, etc) but that is not the primary purpose of the organisation. Rather the aim is to enable workers in our industry to be self-organised. Therefore a key strategic aim is constantly to create new generations of activists – union members who will represent workmates and also endeavour to organise them industrially and politically. These are *leaders* at a local level.

Key to this approach is the need to build organisation within the workplace. Our model is not based on passive union members who simply call some remote office for advice, assistance or representation (although that also happens of course). Rather we aim for the workers in a fire station or other workplace to represent and organise themselves. In this context the workplace branch, as set out in the FBU rule book, is the essential building block of an active and membership-based structure. Of course, things are never straightforward. The FBU, like every workers' organisation, has its ups and downs. We have gaps in the structure. We have periods of anger and demoralisation. But the strategy of the union should be based around the permanent need to build and re-build a democratic and campaigning organisation at workplace level and to develop the new layers of workplace organisers and leaders.

The FBU and the fire and rescue service

This book highlights, once again, the central role the FBU has played in developing the modern fire and rescue service. This was most clear in an earlier period – the years of the Second World War and its aftermath. Previous FBU books, such as Victor Bailey's *Forged in Fire*, highlighted firefighters' work in tackling the mass bombing of the Blitz and their efforts to limit the damage to the civilian population. At the same time, the extremely difficult but strategically correct decision to recruit and organise members of the Auxiliary Fire Service (AFS), gave the FBU a much larger membership and a truly national structure. After the war, these factors combined with other shifts in the political situation following the election of the 1945 Labour government. Trade unions were accepted as having a 'seat at the table'. The FBU made the case for new structures and ways of organising the service, as it had done in the run up to, and during, the war. The union, led by general secretary John Horner, did not always get its own way but it was increasingly listened to as the credible voice of the profession and it was able to exert greater and greater influence on the direction of travel. The FBU was firmly at the heart of the new fire and rescue service structures established by the 1947 Fire Services Act.

Before the war the FBU clearly linked the need for a modern and professional fire and rescue service with the case for better pay, conditions and pensions for FBU members. In the 1950s this meant new campaigns for better equipment and safety procedures. In the 1960s the union campaigned for firefighters to take on a new and broader fire safety role, inspecting workplaces and other premises rather than simply responding to fire calls. In the 1980s, the FBU was central to the campaign for greater fire safety in the home, with the campaign on foam-filled furniture. So, for most of our history, we have sought to be the professional voice for our trade as well as an advocate for better pay.

This approach by the union has been challenged by others within the fire service and by politicians of varying hues. This centenary book covers the period of so-called modernisation following 2003, when central government, local fire and rescue services, politicians and numerous chief fire officers made considerable efforts to put the FBU 'back in its box'. The aim has been to sideline the voices of those on the front line and to promote a new type of managerialism in the service as an alternative to genuine negotiation with the workforce. Some have done very well out of this agenda. The biggest pay rises for many years went to those at the top of local fire and rescue services. They essentially made the case that the more they cut, the bigger their pay rises should be. Disgracefully, many local politicians have fallen for this time and time again. This period has also seen numerous cases of very well-paid principal officers 'retiring' only to be re-employed the very next day on almost identical terms. These decisions have been a shocking embarrassment for the fire and rescue service, yet there has been nothing but silence from those who claim to lead and who claim to be the 'professional voice'. They have stood aside and allowed corrupt and self-serving practices to continue, only responding when government has intervened to stop such blatant abuse of the system.

The vision of the FBU for the fire and rescue service has always evolved and developed as the risks facing our communities have changed. The firefighters of the 1940s fought fires. By and large that was it. Much of the rest of the time they were drilling, cleaning floors and toilets, and polishing brass. (On my first station we still used to apply boot polish to the rims of wheels of the escape ladder.) Over decades since the 1950s, the FBU has argued for fire inspections, familiarisation visits, an acknowledgement of (and funding for) the new role of attending road traffic collisions, proper planning for major floods, adequate preparation for responding to terrorist attacks and for a similar approach on a wide range of other issues. When others have sought to limit the union's role, we have resisted. This approach by the FBU has also faced opposition internally, perhaps well summed up by conference comments along the lines of 'We're firefighters. We do exactly what it says on the tin; nothing more, nothing less.' I recognise that view is born out of the immediate frustrations of the time. However, it is a view that stands in contrast to the main direction highlighted by much of our history.

Our centenary is an opportunity for us to look back and reflect. Where would we be now if those who went before us had simply been content with the status quo? What kind of service would we be providing to the public and how much would we be paid for delivering it? Throughout most of our union's history, we have taken a more strategic approach to the development of our members' profession and to improving their pay and conditions. I would strongly argue it is more important than ever that we continue in that tradition today if we are to best serve the long-term interests of our members.

Building workplace and working-class unity

A central theme addressed in this book is the efforts by the union to tackle discrimination, bullying and harassment. The fire and rescue service remains a male-dominated industry, and the workforce and therefore the union reflect this. The service also remains overwhelmingly white, even in communities (such as big cities) where the local population is far more diverse.

All workforces will inevitably reflect, to some degree, the prejudices and outlook of wider society. I joined the London Fire Brigade in 1983, having been active in anti-racist and anti-fascist campaigning as a teenager. The blue watch on my first station had one of the tiny number of black firefighters who had joined the London Fire Brigade before the 1980s, and he told me just some of the things he had been through over the years. I well remember the shock I felt at some of the open racism I heard about in those early days. Such issues pose sharp and difficult challenges to union activists. How to challenge such ideas? How to win support among workmates? What is the best approach to take? These are questions FBU activists have been grappling with for many decades. Let's remember that women were recruited in large numbers into the service and into the union during the

Second World War, immediately raising for the FBU the issue of differences in pay. The same period saw the first (recorded) black firefighters in the UK. So the equality debates of the past 30 years were prefigured by the earlier attempts of the FBU to address similar challenges more than 70 years ago.

The starting point for any answer is to remind ourselves what our organisation is and what it is supposed to be for. Trade unions, by their very existence, are based on the idea that an individual worker alone cannot achieve anything: only through collective action can progress be made. That means we aim for all workers to be members of the union and for union members to act together. Hence the famous trade union slogan 'Unity is strength'. If we start from here, then anything that undermines unity stands in opposition to the collective interest; so if a union allows discrimination against any of its members or if it fails to confront harassment, it weakens and undermines the unity that is the very basis of its existence.

This approach is a far cry from the stance taken by those who, when asked why we need to discuss equality issues, answer 'Because we need to comply with the law'. Compliance with this or that law is not an argument – or certainly not a very convincing one. It does not make the case for anything and it is unlikely to motivate people to do very much at all. And, of course, laws can change. So while it is important that union reps appreciate and understand relevant legislation and how they might use it, that is not the same as making the case for *why* the union should take up such issues. Convincing people of *why* such issues are important provides a much firmer foundation for campaigning.

Politics

Most unions engage in politics. The legal and political framework they operate within makes it essential to lobby and campaign for government policies that favour the members of the union or trade unions more generally. This campaigning activity is addressed in this book. But the issue of how our union engages in politics also touches on more fundamental matters, questions about the sort of society we want to live in.

The period since the economic crash of 2007-08 has seen a sustained attack on workers, on our wages, pensions and conditions at work, and on the public services that provide the basic elements of a civilised life for millions. Firefighters and the fire and rescue service have not escaped that attack. While the position varies in different countries and in different regions across the globe, the austerity drive of the past decade has been international. Gains that workers won through their unions and through earlier political decisions (pay levels, pension rights, employment rights, staffing levels and the like) have come under sustained attack. The idea that the next generation will be better off than the current one – an idea that has been common for decades – has been called into question. This (potentially at least) challenges all politicians, political parties and strands of political thought: What has gone wrong? Is there some fundamental flaw in this society? Is there an alternative?

The FBU is seen as a political union and regarded as being on the left of the trade union movement. But the opportunity for reflection and debate our centenary provides should make us think about what this means – including whether or not it makes sense today. After all, a hundred years is a long time and the ideas that motivated Jim Bradley might not be relevant to the early 21st century. Bradley was a socialist, highly involved in the broader labour movement both politically and industrially. John Horner, who played such a key role in shaping the union during and after the war, was also a committed socialist. His approach, in many ways, set the tone for the political development of the FBU for much of the period since 1945.

The foreword to our rule book sets out succinctly – and beautifully in my opinion – the case for political trade unionism and for a commitment to socialism. It begins by outlining the basic role of a union as winning better conditions for its members. It then makes clear that firefighters are workers and thereby in the same social position as other workers 'however employed'. It states that for all workers only *self-organisation* can win improvements. It concludes that the FBU is part of 'the working class movement', which is international and that the ultimate aim of the union is to bring about 'the socialist system of society'.

In the past, many trade unions had similar clauses. When rule books were 'modernised', some unions got rid of such 'old-fashioned' ideas and rules. The FBU is one of a minority that has kept our version in place. In my opinion at least, it is the correct approach. The ideas set out in the foreword may originate in the past but they are still relevant to the political, social and economic reality our organisation operates in.

Firefighters, like most members of society, do not have the means by which to produce their needs – homes, food, clothing, cars, TVs and the like. They can only obtain these things (in other words, they can only live) if they obtain income from someone else. They obtain this by agreeing to exchange their ability to work for money (wages) – by getting a job, doing work and getting paid. Firefighters undertake a particular form of work and in the UK it is undertaken in the public sector. But differences in the *form* of work do not alter what different types of workers have in common; that they cannot survive unless they work. So the fundamental social and economic position of the members of our small UK trade union is the same as that of hundreds of millions of other workers across the globe, despite the differences of geography, language, pay levels and in the actual work undertaken. We should also remember that while the fire and rescue service in the UK is currently a public service, we cannot take that for granted. There are other (worse) ways of delivering fire and rescue services in other parts of the world.

The reference in the rule book to 'the socialist system of society' is also worth considering. It means a society different from the one in existence today, i.e. capitalism. Capitalism is a system in which wage labour is exploited by capital. It is based on the private ownership of the means of production (the means by which we produce all the various things we need to live) by a small minority. In general, production is carried out for profit – i.e. for the few rather than for the many. In turn, the ceaseless search for profit drives the entire global economy, shapes the world and creates the political environment in which trade unions operate and try to win improvements for their members. As we have seen over the past decade, when the world economy is not functioning it becomes very hard for unions to win such improvements. Indeed, employers and governments seek to take back the gains that were won in the past. It is often said in the current labour movement that 'austerity is a political choice' but the truth is more complex. History demonstrates that this capitalist economy has been subject to frequent and recurring periods of crisis, leading to phenomena such as inflation, unemployment, industrial bankruptcies, bank failures and the like. History also suggests that *every* time capitalism has suffered such a crisis, the response from governments and employers has been austerity – attacks on wages, pensions and public services. That suggests something more fundamental than a simple choice.

So 'the socialist system of society' was clearly seen as something radically different from the existing society. Socialism is presented in the foreword as an *alternative* to capitalism. That is an important assertion, which should be discussed since it differs from the approach taken by many on the left today. Some would argue that being a socialist is simply about striving for greater fairness in politics, increasing taxes here and there, and trying to improve public services, pensions and wages and the like. However, such policies do not necessarily mean creating a different form of society. The fundamental question remains – is the basis of society production for private profit and therefore an economy dominated by the demands of the profit system? If it is, then society remains capitalist. Socialism means something different. This was reflected to some degree in the old Clause 4, part IV, of the (pre-1995) Labour Party constitution in its reference to the 'common ownership of the means of production, distribution and exchange'. For me, socialism, as a different form of society to the current one, means an end to the system of production for private profit and its replacement with a system in the interests of all and based on social ownership of the means of production. After a decade of economic crisis and stagnation, resulting in falling living standards across much of the world, we should be discussing what alternative we want to aim for.

Operating in a changed political environment

For the past four decades, firefighters and other workers have faced a regime that is very different from the 'post-war consensus' our predecessors lived through. Since the late 1970s we have been subjected to a neoliberal ideology, where politicians have emphasised the need for 'free markets', deregulation and privatisation. This period has dramatically changed the landscape trade unions operate in.

After 1979, the Thatcher government inaugurated a low-intensity civil war on workers in general and on trade unions in particular. Thatcher imposed savage cuts in central funding to local public services, privatised whole sectors and made major inroads into others. None of the great institutions of the welfare state were spared, not even the National Health Service. The fire and rescue service also came under the spotlight. Beginning in 1980 with the Home Office's review of fire policy, the Tory government mapped out an agenda of cuts, lower standards and deregulation for the fire and rescue service.

Thatcher imposed successive anti-union laws on our movement, making employment law in the UK the most restrictive in Europe. The Tories also used the mailed fist of the state during the 1984-85 miners' strike, at Wapping and in other industrial disputes. Union organisation was beaten down by deindustrialisation and unemployment, collective bargaining arrangements were attacked and union activists victimised. Further waves of privatisation were launched in the early 1990s, with Tory minister Michael Heseltine pushing deregulation right into the heart of the fire and rescue service.

The election of a Labour government in 1997 might have been expected to bring some respite. But Blair's so-called modernisation agenda continued the same trends. It was ultimately Blair's government that destroyed the post-war framework of the fire and rescue service, scrapping national standards of fire cover, dispensing with national consultative forums and creating a fragmented local free-for-all.

The situation over the last decade has been even worse. The financial crash in 2007-08 led to a worldwide economic downturn. Governments of all colours decided to cut public spending at a time when more public investment was needed. Austerity has meant real wage cuts in the UK of over 10 per cent – equal to Greece as the worst in Europe. The Trades Union Congress (TUC) has said the UK has endured the steepest decline in real wages in nearly 200 years. The UK is on course for the longest fall in living standards since records began in the 1950s.

The fire and rescue service has experienced the deepest central funding cuts in its history – 40 per cent over the decade if governments continue to get their way. Since 2010, one in five firefighter jobs have been cut, with an associated impact on the membership of the FBU. Firefighters' pay has been held down, pensions attacked and 'Victorian' duty systems introduced to pay for a crisis we did not create.

This is the context within which our union has had to operate for most of my time as general secretary. It is not the environment of our choosing, but it is the one we've had to face. The union has endured a hail of blows affecting every area of our work and threatening our very existence. As officials elected to lead, the Executive Council and the delegates elected to our conference have had to take some hard and sometimes unpopular decisions to ensure the union remains industrially and financially viable. We have consulted members and tried to avoid self-inflicted wounds – but we have not flinched from doing what is necessary to ensure the survival of our independent firefighters' union.

Strategy and tactics

Our current situation raises issues regarding the strategy and tactics adopted by this union at various times and in different political or economic circumstances. These issues are not discussed regularly enough in the labour movement. Or if they are, they are discussed in secret and among a select few. But since trade unions are voluntary organisations of workers (which nobody has to join), the only discipline that can be imposed is, by and large, a voluntary discipline. So it is essential that the broad approach of the union is discussed more widely than simply by executives.

Strategy refers to a longer-term plan, while tactics refer to the particular means used at various times to achieve an objective. Tactics *may* be part of a strategic plan but they may also arise in response to actions taken by others (e.g. by employers or government). We can best see strategy as the 'line of march' for our organisation. It can be developed after an assessment of threats and opportunities. For a trade union it should take account of economic and political developments, changes in technology and an assessment of the strengths and weaknesses of the various agents (the employers, workers, the union, government, other politicians). It is based on thinking about where we want to be in the future, where we want to be heading over the next 10 or 15 years.

One theme addressed in this book and in the comments above is the role of the FBU in seeking to argue for a better way to run the fire and rescue service. This is widely (but not universally) accepted today but this was not always the case. In the early years of the union, there was a strong view that we should only involve ourselves in negotiations on terms and conditions. Questions of how the fire and rescue service is run, what it does and how it does it, were seen as matters for management and politicians. The major turning point in this approach was brought about by John Horner and his allies. The FBU developed policies and views on the structure and organisation of the service. The strategy was shown to be successful by the creation of a post-war service that improved standards and set the basis for issues such as response times, crewing levels, appliances and equipment to be addressed through national structures, with a powerful role being played by the FBU (structures later abolished by the Blair government). These structures protected the public and improved conditions for those working in the service. The approach taken may seem obvious and logical to FBU activists today but we need to remember that it was contested at the time. There were other views and therefore other outcomes were possible.

Similarly, one of the most controversial campaigns Horner led, was the campaign to recruit AFS members into the union. He was advised against this by leading figures in the TUC and the approach was opposed by many FBU members, some of whom even resigned from the union in protest at this 'watering down' and de-skilling of the union's membership. A useful thought experiment is to imagine what might have happened if these two major, and controversial, strategic decisions had *not* been made. It is very likely that the FBU would not have survived the war at all or, if it did, it would have emerged as the tiny organisation it was in 1939. The pressures for merger with a bigger organisation (which have been there for much of our history) would have been greater. In other words the union may well not have survived had it not taken these decisions: decisions that at the time were not obvious choices and were challenged, debated and opposed by significant voices within the union.

As the FBU enters its second century, we face new and different challenges. Economic, political and technical change continues.

The way public services are delivered is not guaranteed – look at health and education to see how far things have already changed elsewhere. Our view, expressed through our conference, is that the public is best served by a separate, independent, publicly owned and accountable fire and rescue service. Those working in that service are best served and represented by an industry-specific trade union. Indeed a specialist union also provides a key protection for the wider public in terms of the battle to protect standards and work for genuine improvements in public safety.

The history of the Fire Brigades Union provides stories of struggle and heroism. It is the story of women and men who built an organisation against the odds. They had to campaign, fight and make sacrifices to build it. At times many of them were victimised for their stand. They also had to think carefully about, and debate, the challenges they faced at various times. We owe it to the previous generations but, above all, we owe it to those still to come to continue that work – to think, debate, organise and struggle – in the decades ahead: 'The past we inherit, the future we build.'

Glossary

2-2-3 shift system
Standard shift system for wholetime firefighters in the UK. Firefighters work a 'two days, two nights, three days off', which ensures comprehensive fire cover and necessary rest.

Action short of a strike (ASOS)
Form of industrial action workers can take following a successful ballot, such as working to contract ('working to rule'), refusing to cooperate with the employer by completing paperwork, or refusing to work overtime beyond contractual hours.

Aerial appliance
Term for appliances such as turntable ladders, hydraulic platforms or aerial ladder platforms.

Aerial ladder platform (ALP)
Appliance with extending booms, ladder and rescue cage.

Appliance
Fire engine (or 'pump') designed for fire and rescue operations.

Close proximity crewing
Duty system where full-time firefighters are expected work four consecutive day shifts. During the night after each day shift, instead of going home, these firefighters live in dedicated accommodation near or in the fire station. At night, they are on call to attend emergencies. This increases working hours, cuts pay, worsens pensions, cuts jobs and undermines firefighter and public safety. Also known as 'day crewing plus' or 'low level of activity and risk' (LLAR).

Continuous duty system
Early 20th-century duty system where firefighters were on duty for 24 hours a day, for 14 days and nights, 330 days in the year and confined to fire stations.

Control staff
Uniformed personnel who receive emergency calls and mobilise operational firefighters from fire control rooms.

Day crewing
Shift system where certain stations are staffed with full-time firefighters during the day and then by retained firefighters at night.

'Dear chief officer' letter
Instruction from the Home Office to the fire service during the last century.

Detached duties
Redeployment of firefighters on a given shift away from their normal watch and fire station, to cover a shortfall elsewhere.

Equality sections
The FBU's equality representative sections are: B&EMM (black and ethnic minority members) section; the lesbian, gay, bisexual and trans (LGBT) section; and the women's section.

Establishment
Staffing levels under the Fire Services Act 1947, which could only be altered with the permission of the Secretary of State. Abolished by the Fire and Rescue Services Act 2004.

Everest safety anchor
Metal ring attached to a building, which together with a harness gave firefighters some security at height while using a ladder.

Grassroots FBU
A rank-and-file network within the FBU around the time of the 2002-04 pay dispute.

Grey Book
Common name for the National Joint Council for Local Authority Fire and Rescue Services' Scheme of Conditions of Service. These are firefighters' UK-wide conditions negotiated between fire employers and the FBU through collective bargaining.

Hook ladders
Traditional ladders meant to hook onto window sills. Unstable, leading to falls from height.

Incident Response Unit (IRU)
Mass decontamination and firefighter decontamination unit provided by the government to deal with incidents involving chemicals and other hazardous materials.

Jump crewing
Arrangement where firefighters have to leave their usual appliance to crew a specialist vehicle, such as an aerial ladder platform. Could render their normal appliance unavailable because it is not crewed sufficiently, or lead to fewer firefighters than necessary at the incident.

Live rescue drills
Traditional training exercises where firefighters carried each other without a harness up and down ladders. The cause of falls from height, injuries and deaths.

Mixed crewing
Fire appliances crewed by a mixture of wholetime and retained firefighters.

National Joint Council (NJC)
The collective bargaining forum for operational firefighters and emergency control staff across the UK. Firefighters are represented by the FBU.

Officers
Firefighters whose rank or role is generally watch manager or above. Applies to wholetime, retained and control staff.

Operational staff
Wholetime and retained firefighters who attend fires and other incidents.

One-pump station
Fire station with only a single appliance.

Recall conference
The provision in the FBU's rulebook for the union's annual conference to be reconvened to discuss particular issues or developments.

Resilience contracts
Contracts awarded to private companies or existing firefighters to provide 'emergency fire crewing' in certain situations – in reality when FBU members take industrial action.

Retained firefighters
Part-time firefighters who work the retained duty system (RDS). They are paid a retainer salary, along with a call-out fee when they respond to an emergency call. Retained firefighters have set 'on-call' hours, during which they must respond to emergency calls from their location, which could be at home or at another workplace.

Ridership
Desirable number of firefighters crewing appliances mobilised to incidents. Highly important for the weight of response to a fire and for firefighter safety.

Role maps
Descriptions of competence set out by the National Joint Council for firefighter roles or ranks (firefighter, crew manager, watch manager, station manager, group manager and area manager).

Section 188 notice
The duty to consult, set out in section 188 of the Trade Union and Labour Relations (Consolidation) Act 1992. Triggered when an employer proposes to sack and re-engage workers as a way to enforce unilateral contractual changes.

Standby
Periods when firefighters have to be available to attend emergencies. Raises implications for firefighters' working time and pay.

Stand-down time
The agreed rest period for firefighters during night shifts, when they are on stations between emergency calls.

Tactical response vehicles (TRVs)
Small vans, 4x4s or similar vehicles mobilised instead of fire engines with fewer firefighters and less equipment.

Trade sections
The FBU's special representative sections for control staff, officers' and retained firefighters.

Trailer-pump appliance
Pump designed to be towed behind a motor vehicle. Widely used during the Second World War.

Watch system
Team of firefighters on shift together at a particular station. Generally four different 'coloured' watches operate: red, white, blue and green.

Wholetime firefighters
Full-time firefighters organised into shifts to enable 24/7 crewing of fire stations.

Wholetime pump
Appliance crewed by wholetime firefighters.

'Spit and polish' demonstration, 1951

Picket line during the national strike, 1977

1

Introduction: the Fire Brigades Union and the political economy of fire

The essence of firemanship is to work as a team – self-reliant but interdependent – as comrades. The strong bond of mutual reliance which characterised 'the job', could be a powerful element in forging a special kind of union for a special kind of service.

John Horner, 'Recollections of a general secretary', in Bailey, (ed)[1]

Background

This book celebrates the centenary of the FBU, focusing in depth on the last three decades of the union's history. It follows the official history *Fetch the Engine*, by Frederick H Radford, published in 1951, and Victor Bailey's edited book *Forged in Fire: The history of the Fire Brigades Union*, published in 1992. The ground covered by the centenary publication spans the tenure of three general secretaries: Ken Cameron (1980-2000), who sadly died during its writing; Andy Gilchrist (2000-05); and Matt Wrack (from 2005). In the 100 years since its formation in 1918, the FBU has continued to be at once part of the fabric of the fire and rescue service and a 'politically committed union'.[2] This book is based upon the testimonies of FBU representatives and members: control staff, officers and wholetime and retained firefighters from Scotland, Wales, Northern Ireland and England. Their accounts capture the lived experience of firefighters in a changing environment and the organisational, ideological and political roles of the union that have shaped this experience and influenced their perceptions. A distinctive feature, compared to previous histories, is the way that the dynamics of gender, race, sexuality and class are woven into the narrative.

The FBU is an example of a single industry union that, unlike many unions in the late 20th and early 21st centuries, has resisted merger. Since its formation in 1918 as a trade union for firefighters in London, the FBU has become a UK-wide union that, at its centenary, represented around 34,000 men and women in the fire and rescue service, including control staff and retained firefighters.[3] Historically, industrial union structures have tended to close the gaps between craft and unskilled workers[4] and accordingly the FBU has organised all the workers in the service, regardless of 'skill'.[5] In contrast to the overall decline in UK trade union membership, it had one of highest levels of union density of UK unions, at around 90 per cent for wholetime firefighters, 66 per cent for emergency control staff and around 60 per cent for those in the retained duty system (RDS).[6] The union has coordinated bargaining for all uniformed occupations under one national agreement, the Grey Book, which has provided significant protection for the conditions of work and employment for fire and rescue service workers. Crucial to the union's capacity to organise has been, and remains, its elected lay structure and the 'depth of the union's democratic culture'.[7]

The FBU has always embraced concerns that extend beyond the defence of members' pay and conditions. Historian Shane Ewen argues that the FBU has been 'pivotal in establishing, defending and diversifying the firefighter's professional role since its formation in 1918'.[8] Moreover, the union participated in the creation of the National Fire Service during the Second World War, the regional structures introduced afterwards and associated standard-setting bodies and bargaining machinery. Its emphasis on the interdependence of public safety and firefighter safety has underpinned campaigns to first establish and then defend national standards of fire cover, and it has argued consistently for the provision of adequate funding for this role. It has led developments in health and safety, particularly in pressing for the latest technology in breathing apparatus, personal protective equipment and appliances (fire engines), in addition to seeking the implementation of rigorous safety procedures on the fireground and at other incidents (Chapter 8). While advocating wholesale changes in how fires should be fought and in the technology that should be made available, it has also pursued an expanded service to include fire safety and prevention, emergency rescue from road traffic incidents and floods, planning for large-scale emergencies and, more recently, piloting emergency medical response.

The union has also taken a leading role in promoting equality and diversity in the changing fire and rescue service, alongside tackling discrimination and harassment amongst its own members. The FBU sections providing representation for women, black and ethnic minority (B&EM) and lesbian, gay, bisexual and trans (LGBT) members have played a crucial part in this work (Chapter 7). Further, the internationalist outlook of the FBU, established under John Horner's leadership, was strengthened by Ken Cameron, with a particular focus on South Africa, Cuba and Palestine. This legacy is explored in Chapter 9, together with the union's central position within the British trade union and labour movement, its shifting relationship with the Labour Party and its political engagement in Wales, Scotland and Northern Ireland.

This introductory chapter starts by providing an overview of the formation of the union from 1918, drawing primarily on *Forged in Fire*, which ended with the first national strike in 1977-78. The chapter then establishes a context for the book in terms of the wider economic, political and legal environment in which the FBU has operated since 1978. Primarily, this context is the ideologically driven reform of the public sector by Conservative governments under the guise of 'New Public Management'. However, the 'modernisation' of public services was championed by New Labour and contested by the FBU, culminating in the union's disaffiliation from the Labour Party following the 2002-04 pay dispute. As the book makes explicit, the union historically has led the way in articulating the genuine 'modernisation' of many aspects of the fire and rescue service, but for government this term has increasingly meant deregulation and flexibility at local level at the expense of national standards. The introduction then describes the research methods which have informed the book and the sources of data on which the narrative is based. It concludes with an outline of the ensuing chapters.

The creation of a national fire service and national union: 1918 to 1947

The origins of a separate union for firefighters date back to 1918, when the London firemen's[9] branch of the National Union of

Corporation Workers (NUCW) broke away from the parent union to form the Fireman's Trade Union (FTU), a move led by branch secretary Jim Bradley, not himself a firefighter but a park keeper, socialist and union activist. George Gamble became the union's first general secretary, with Bradley as assistant secretary. The first rule book shows the date of foundation as 1 October 1918, with legal registration under the Trade Union Act completed on 31 December 1918.[10]

The union sought recognition from the London County Council (LCC) amidst growing unrest over pay, 'continuous duty' and the social isolation of living in fire stations. Firefighters' wages were below those of mechanics at the start of the First World War, and at the level of industrial labourers by 1917. By 1918 many groups of workers were protesting against wages inadequate to meet rising costs of living, with threats of strike action among sailors and even a police strike in August 1918, both of which rapidly resulted in pay increases. Union recognition had been resisted by the LCC, which believed that allegiance to a body outside the fire service would be a threat to the discipline required of a uniformed, hierarchical service operating under the naval traditions of drill and discipline. The majority of London Fire Brigade recruits were former members of the Royal Navy, the Merchant Marine or the Army, with the language, rules and culture of the organisation 'redolent of salt water'.[11]

After threatening strike action and following arbitration, London firefighters gained partial recognition through a 'representative body' to be chosen by firefighters, but whose 'spokesman' could be from outside the brigade, which enabled Bradley to continue in his role. However, the agreement contained a no-strike clause and 'created a most unsatisfactory framework of trade unionism in the London Fire Brigade',[12] in which the FTU had no official recognition, although its officials in practice were also members of the Representative Body. Bailey noted that although the compromise had disadvantages, it had the benefit of leaving the union free to recruit outside London, saying 'a link with the outside, however tenuous, was the obvious choice'.[13] This subsequently provided the platform for a national union.

By mid-1919 the FTU represented around 1,000 firefighters from 35 brigades, predominantly the London Fire Brigade and brigades around London. Firefighters in some of the larger brigades outside London, such as Aberdeen, Edinburgh, Glasgow, Birmingham, Manchester and Belfast, were represented in various municipal and general workers' unions, including the Municipal Employees Association, the NUCW, and the Workers' Union (forerunner of the Transport and General Workers Union).[14] However, more than half of those in the professional fire service outside London were police-firefighters and were banned from joining a trade union after the 1918 police strike. After the end of the First World War, the London firefighters had continued to press for improvements in pay and reductions in hours. This campaign came to a head in early 1919. Faced with the threat of serious disturbance, the LCC agreed to end the continuous duty system and tied accommodation on stations, to be replaced by a two-shift system of 72 hours, with revised pay scales based on those of the police. The first national inquiry into the pay and conditions of professional firefighters was established under Sir William Middlebrook, with pay, hours of duty and pensions the main issues. Bradley gave evidence on behalf of the FTU, calling for the same pay and conditions for brigades outside London, including better pensions in recognition of the dangers of the job. Although Middlebrook's recommendations could be considered a 'checklist for a new fire union keen to spread its reach' – formalising the link to police pay, providing a pension scheme, full sick pay for three months, and compulsory retirement at 55 – implementation was left to local brigades.[15] The consequence was that despite some gains on pay and pensions, implementation of the recommendations was patchy.

Post-war austerity saw the Lloyd George government seeking to cut public spending. In 1923 the LCC demanded a 20 per cent reduction in firefighters' pay, a cut that was not demanded of the police. This reduction was successfully challenged by the Representative Body at the Industrial Court, with a ruling in favour of retaining police parity. However, in other parts of the country councils succeeded in cutting pay and costs.

In 1922 Jim Bradley became general secretary of the FTU and continued to lead the union until his death in 1929. Although never a firefighter, Bradley was born at Marylebone fire station, the son of a station officer. He became active initially in the Municipal Employees Association, then helped form the NUCW and began recruiting firefighters to the branch which subsequently split off to become the FTU. He was active in the Labour Party and stood unsuccessfully as a Communist-supported candidate for the LCC in 1928, but he is best remembered as champion of the FTU for a decade. Following Bradley's death, former president Percy Kingdom succeeded as general secretary, a 'dour, blunt, gladiator' lacking Bradley's wider political and labour movement links.

In 1930 the union was renamed the Fire Brigades Union, to end confusion with railway and ships' firemen (stokers). Austerity continued during the depression of the 1930s and firefighters suffered pay cuts, finding that parity with police pay meant reductions as well as increases. Kingdom's demands for parity with the police in terms of hours were unsuccessful until, in early 1939, the Representative Body was offered a 60-hour week, based on two shifts. However, the Second World War intervened, and the continuous duty system was reinstated.

Preparations for war concentrated minds on the improvements to fire cover necessary to civil defence. The Riverdale Committee was set up in 1936 to reform what Bailey termed the 'ramshackle and archaic organisation' of fire authorities across England and Wales, and it recommended that fire protection become a statutory obligation of local authorities. This was implemented for the first time in the Fire Brigades Act 1938. The Act also established a Fire Service Inspectorate to standardise operations. Although Bailey noted that the FBU did not participate in the Riverdale Committee, at the time wanting no part in setting national fire service policy, the changes the Act instituted benefited the union by assisting its recruitment outside London.[16]

FBU membership had grown during the 1930s, amounting to 3,000 by the start of the war. Two-thirds of members were in London, where there had also been successful recruitment of the majority of sub-officers. Just months before the outbreak of the Second World War, Kingdom resigned and the 27-year-old John Horner was elected to lead the union. Horner had joined the London Fire Brigade in 1933 on his return from the Merchant Navy, and was earmarked for accelerated promotion at HQ, where he described being known as a 'big-headed bugger'.[17] It was his 'bolshie' nature and willingness to challenge injustice that led him to FBU activism. He recounts reading Marx and going to meetings of the Communist Party in order to explain 'the collapse of world capitalism', which he had 'recently witnessed at first hand' while travelling the world as a seafarer and on his return to Britain.[18]

Horner campaigned vigorously to include members of the Auxiliary Fire Service (AFS) – set up in September 1939 – in the FBU. With 89,000 men and 6,000 women, the AFS vastly outnumbered firefighters in regular fire brigades. Horner firmly believed that recruiting AFS members was the only way to ensure the survival of the FBU during wartime, but he faced fierce opposition from many in the union, who saw them as 'dilutees who threatened to depress the pay and conditions of regular firefighters'.[19] Horner's view prevailed and membership of the FBU leapt from 3,500 in 1939 to 71,500 by 1941, made up of 5,500 regulars and 66,000 auxiliaries (of whom 4,000 were women). New members included regulars from previously unorganised brigades in the Midlands, the North and Scotland.[20]

The FBU won the right to negotiate on behalf of AFS members in 1941 and sought to reduce the wide differences between the pay and conditions of auxiliaries and regulars in the hope that this would avoid dilution. It was the Blitz, though, that dissolved the differences between the two groups. According to Bailey, 'in that baptism of fire volunteers and regulars merged into one citizen army, discovering a camaraderie that laid the base for a single united union'.[21] The exhausting and dangerous work endured by firefighters during the Blitz also increased their standing in the eyes of the public, and, according to fire service historian GV Blackstone, they were 'cheered by passers-by in the street, [while] cinema audiences applauded when firefighters appeared on newsreels, [and] strangers stood them drinks in public houses'.[22] The Blitz also destroyed the FBU's newly leased premises in Chancery Lane. Horner recalls returning after a night spent at Millwall fire station in 1940 to find 'Fleet Street impassable with unexploded bombs, and half of Chancery Lane gone – our half. Nothing could be saved.'[23]

The extension of aerial bombardment from London to other cities, ports and industrial centres exposed the weaknesses of a fire service made up of more than 1,400 local fire authorities and led to the National Fire Service being created in 1941, organised into around 40 regional fire forces. This structure provided an opportunity for the FBU to press for widespread recognition, a national minimum rate of pay and greater consultation about how the fire service was operated. These demands were set out in the Fireman's Charter, which was followed by a Firewomen's Charter which recognised the contribution of women firefighters during the war. While women primarily occupied administrative and control roles, FBU historian Terry Segars has documented women's active role in firefighting, as drivers and operating pumps during raids[24] (see Chapter 7).

The union publicly intervened in the debate about the post-war fire service. Its 1943 pamphlet 'What kind of fire service?' proposed a regional structure, with large brigades covering urban and industrial areas, and was linked to calls for national minimum pay rates, a pension scheme and an improved discipline code. While the previous home secretary, Herbert Morrison, had resisted concessions to the FBU, the new home secretary in 1945, James Chuter Ede, was more sympathetic to working with the union over the shape of the future fire service. In the event, many of the union's demands were conceded. Under the Fire Services Act 1947, control was transferred from the National Fire Service to counties and boroughs. The Act established the Central Fire Brigades Advisory Council (CFBAC), with union representation, to advise the secretary of state on fire policy and standards. The National Joint Council (NJC) was also constituted in 1947 for England and Wales, with support from central government (although a non-statutory body), for national bargaining between local authority employers and trade unions over pay and conditions. The NJC would cover both officers and junior ranks, securing union recognition at last for all the FBU's officer members. The Act also unified the various pension schemes into the Firemen's Pension Scheme, broadly in line with the police pension scheme. Bailey noted that these changes 'marked the union's accepted role in building a professional fire service'.[25]

The battle for pay and recognition: 1947 to 1979

Despite the new negotiating machinery, the union did not succeed in winning pay increases from local authorities who were keen to curb costs and, according to Bailey, wished to 'clip the wings' of a union that had increased its power and influence.[26]

By 1951 discontent with declining pay led to a further claim for police parity, which was rejected by the NJC and resulted in the union's first industrial action, known as the 'spit and polish' demonstrations, in which crews responded to fires, but refused to perform drills, scrub floors or polish brass. The first 48-hour demonstration was unofficial action called by the London Action Committee in October, which spread to 70 per cent of the service. Official 'spit and polish' demonstrations then took place in November and were described as 'sabotage' by the LCC, causing members across the country to be put on disciplinary charges. The union pledged to defend every charge and received huge support from across the labour movement. The employers only withdrew the disciplinary charges after a tragic fire in the City of London, in which three firefighters were killed; Horner wryly noted that 'yesterday's "saboteurs" became London's heroes'.[27] Although the demonstrations did not result in improved pay, Bailey commented that they had revitalised the FBU, producing an effective new form of industrial action and showing that firefighters were part of wider working-class struggles. President John Burns told the 1952 Annual Conference:

> For the first time firemen on a national scale have played their part in a working-class manner. Members came to feel that they were part of a far greater movement than they had ever visualised. That there is another world outside of their stations, and that they were not some peculiar animal with no connection with the rest of the workers.[28]

In August 1952 a special arbitration board, chaired by Sir David Ross, rejected the principle of automatic parity between firefighters and police. The FBU therefore needed to find a new means of determining firefighters' pay – a challenge that would not be resolved until the settlement of the first national strike in 1977-78.

Demands for improved pay were linked to the union's campaign for a 'transformed, modernised fire service in which modern conditions of employment are granted for the men therein'.[29] The union's proposals, 'A service for the sixties', were presented to the annual conference in 1960, and called for pay scales that reflected the skilled job of firefighting, a proper system of training at all levels and an end to routine chores, or the 'mop and bucket' mentality of the service, as president (and future general secretary) Terry Parry termed it.[30] The demand for change had been given impetus by several notable incidents that exposed woefully inadequate procedures and the absence of fire precaution regulation, including the death of two firefighters at London's Smithfield meat market and the loss of 19 firefighters in an explosion at a bonded whisky warehouse in Glasgow.

The Holroyd Report on the fire service in 1970 recommended comparison with the earnings of skilled craftsmen, endorsing the emphasis in 'A service for the sixties' on the replacement of menial chores by fire prevention duties. The Cunningham Inquiry in 1971 accepted the FBU's key case equating a firefighter's job to a band of semi-skilled and skilled manual occupations. It also recommended a reduction in hours to 44 hours a week.[31] However, the restrictive pay policies of Conservative and Labour governments during the 1970s meant that real earnings declined by over 15 per cent between 1974 and 1977.[32] Membership dissatisfaction with the acceptance of government pay guidelines by the TUC and the union leadership grew. In 1973 an unofficial strike in Glasgow set the Area Committee against the union leadership, but, according to Jim Flockhart's account, it was ultimately successful in pushing the NJC to resist the Heath government's pay policy of £1 a week plus 4 per cent.[33] Part of the background to the Glasgow strike, according to former Scottish regional chair Ronnie Robertson, who joined the fire service in Glasgow in 1961, was resistance to 'the militarisation, the "spit and polish" atmosphere inside the fire service'. Robertson recalled that the Glasgow strike also represented the end of the subservient '"yes sir, no sir", tip your cap' culture within the union. Further unofficial local disputes occurred in 1976 and 1977, including those in South Yorkshire and Essex – evidence of mounting rank-and-file discontent over pay.

In 1977 the union put a pay claim to the NJC for adult male earnings plus 10 per cent, a pay rise of 30 per cent in the context of Chancellor Denis Healey's announcement of a 10 per cent limit on pay increases. Demonstrations took place in support of the pay claim, and Executive Council members from some regions called for strike action. At a recall conference in November, members rejected the Executive Council's proposal for continuation of negotiations and passed a motion from Strathclyde and Merseyside for strike action by a two-to-one majority. This vote was a major blow to general secretary Terry Parry, who had believed that firefighters would never take industrial action that put the public at risk. According to John Saville in *Forged in Fire*, he accepted the democratic decision, but found himself leading a strike that he did not support.[34] Many members believed that the threat of strike action would be enough to bring about a resolution. London fireboat crew member Paul Kleinman recalled:

> As 9 o'clock approached I still could not believe it would happen. Like most men who joined at the time I did, I came from a military background and just could not see firemen striking or the government allowing it. I was wrong. On the stroke of nine, Red Watch walked off the station, the boat was chained up. We refused to take up our positions. The strike which I never thought would happen... happened.[35]

The strike began on 14 November 1977, with solid support from wholetime firefighters, control and most retained members. Public opinion was generally with the strikers, but prime minister James Callaghan told the union's executive: 'Your strike will not win. You cannot be allowed to succeed.'

Several factors weakened the union's position during the strike. The refusal of the TUC to back the dispute, despite support from some union leaders, was a major blow. The acceptance by council workers' unions of rises within the 10 per cent guidelines, having originally claimed 30 per cent, hardened the government's line on pay. Additionally, officer members of the National Association of Fire Officers (NAFO) helped to train troops to fight fires, while some retained firefighters crossed picket lines.

On 8 December the Home Office proposed a two-stage implementation of a formula to link firefighters' pay to 'the adult male manual upper quartile',[36] but with no more than 10 per cent immediately. FBU members initially felt that this was insufficient to warrant a return to work after a month's loss of pay. However, after a bleak Christmas on strike, at a recall conference on 12 January 1978 members voted three-to-one to back the executive's recommendation to accept the offer and call off the strike.

For many the return to work after nine weeks was a sickening defeat, with opinion on the outcome sharply divided. Ken Cameron described it as 'one of most traumatic periods' in the union's history.[37] However, the crucial outcome of the strike was the long-term pay formula that linked firefighters' pay to that of skilled manual workers. As Chapter 3 shows, with the passage of time, members came to realise the significance and value of the pay formula, which secured pay levels for over 20 years. The agreement also reduced the working week from 48 to 42 hours. It introduced procedures for dealing with disputes, with failure to settle at brigade level leading to referral to a disputes committee of the NJC.[38]

Although some felt that Terry Parry sold out to the politicians,[39] his legacy in negotiating the pay formula should not be under-estimated. When he retired in 1980, he was given a 'splendid send-off' by the annual conference.[40] On Parry's retirement, former Executive Council member for the West Midlands and national officer, Ken Cameron, was elected as general secretary.

Conservative governments and New Public Management: 1979 to 1997

The 'Winter of Discontent' of 1978-79, marked by public sector strikes, was seen to contribute to the defeat of the Callaghan government. The succeeding Conservative government of 1979 unleashed three decades of public sector reform, motivated not only by a desire to reduce public sector expenditure, but also by the discourse of New Public Management, which emerged in the 1980s, originating in New Right public choice theory. This drive for 'efficiency' sought to shrink the state and to marketise public service delivery, with competitive tendering an alternative to direct public provision.[41] The Private Finance Initiative (PFI) would allow the construction of new public infrastructure to be financed by the private sector and leased back to the public sector (later realised in the construction of regional control centres; see Chapter 5). New Public Management favoured private sector management models and enshrined a shift in authority from professionals (seen as part of the problem) to managers accountable for individual and organisational performance, and driven by incentives, targets and results rather than delivery processes.[42] The move away from professional hierarchies (bureaucratic processes subject to democratic accountability) towards the imposition of direct 'performative control' (managerialism) was seen as making the public sector worker into a labour commodity, with work rationalised and intensified.[43]

For the FBU the first warning bells were sounded in the early 1990s with increased benchmarking of brigades through output measures and performance indicators[44] and then in 1995 by the Audit Commission report, *In the Line of Fire: Value for money in the fire service – the national picture*. While it praised the performance of the service generally, the report highlighted the national framework within which brigades operated as limiting their scope for assessing and responding locally to fire risk, and identified national terms and conditions of service as constraining brigades' flexibility. It proposed reductions in the high level of early retirement, which exacerbated the 'pensions problem'; more effective management of absence; and an increase in the efficiency of support services through the extension of the use of non-uniformed staff. The Audit Commission wanted to reassess fire cover standards 'to allow better targeting of scarce resources' and wanted fire authorities to be given statutory responsibility to promote fire safety. The report pointed out that previous reviews, such Holroyd and Cunningham in the 1970s, had recommended a change in emphasis from firefighting to prevention (which had also been a feature of the FBU's 'A service for the sixties' proposals), but that insufficient progress had been made. The move towards prevention was to be implemented through reorganisation of existing duty time rather than the provision of additional resources.

New Public Management promoted organisational and managerial decentralisation at the operational level, with stricter strategic control by government, and accordingly was accompanied by the removal of state support for national collective bargaining. As the Audit Commission report suggested, national collective bargaining was perceived as a barrier to promoting the flexibility of labour. However, the collective machinery for the fire and rescue service proved more resilient than that in other parts of the public sector, which was devolved and fragmented during this period.

The FBU, and in particular the officers section, has been

highly proactive in influencing the regulatory framework in relation to fire safety, and in 1996 the union launched its Fire Safety Bill in response to frustration over government delays in determining which agency should have responsibility for fire safety requirements. The Bill proposed consolidation of a range of legislation covering aspects of fire safety into a single statute, but while attracting support from MPs, it did not become law.[45] Instead, fire safety law was consolidated by the Regulatory Reform (Fire Safety) Order 2005 (see below).

Cuts in fire and rescue service budgets saw the loss of 3,500 full-time equivalent firefighter jobs in England from the early 1990s, a seven-per-cent fall between 1991 and 2000.[46] While Ken Cameron's leadership is associated with a period of relative industrial peace, secured by the pay formula, during this period and beyond the union was firmly committed to a policy of pursuing national strike action in the event of any redundancies of wholetime firefighters. A number of hard-fought local disputes in the 1990s (Chapter 3), effectively staved off compulsory redundancies and resisted cuts that would have worsened fire cover by reducing firefighter numbers.

New Labour, public sector 'modernisation' and deregulation: 1997-2010

The New Labour government initially invested in the public sector, but on the basis of 'modernisation', which was seen as a successor to the New Public Management model[47] and as being 'at the heart of the New Labour Project'.[48] The project required deregulation, not least because 80 per cent of central funding depended upon prescriptive criteria for national fire cover, including uniformed establishment.[49] Proposals for changes to national standards for fire cover were developed by the CFBAC, which established a Joint Committee on the Audit Commission Report (JCACR), with FBU representation. Its 1998 report, *Out of the Line of Fire*, outlined a response planning process based on brigades specifying the 'worst case planning scenario' for which they would plan a routine response in order to determine necessary resources. A CFBAC Fire Cover Review Task Group was then established to examine the implementation of this approach and set up 'Pathfinder' trials in 11 brigades. Recognising the growth in non-fire emergency response by the fire service, the review was broadened to include all emergency cover. However the Task Group would not publish its report (the 'Pathfinder Report') until December 2002, during the national pay dispute. On the basis of the Pathfinder trials, the report found that an increase of around 50 per cent in the workforce was needed and that the risk-based approach could be implemented without changes to national conditions of service.[50] The findings were conveniently superseded by the Bain Report.

Prior to the conclusions of the Fire Cover Review, the employers had made proposals to the NJC on greater local flexibility over certain conditions, including disciplinary procedures and promotion. These were rejected by the union's 1999 annual conference as an attack on the Grey Book, and in response the FBU launched its 'Smash and Grab' campaign, involving thousands of firefighters in lobbying politicians and fire employers. Following the employers' withdrawal from the NJC because of the union's refusal to discuss local flexibility, the Labour government set up an inquiry into the procedures determining the terms and conditions of service (other than pay) and for the resolution of disputes, led by Frank Burchill, professor of Industrial Relations at Keele University. The Burchill Report, published in 2000, was seen by the union as a vindication of its Smash and Grab campaign, rejecting unilateral changes to conditions of service and national bargaining arrangements.

At this point Ken Cameron retired as general secretary after 20 years. The incoming general secretary, Andy Gilchrist, said of his predecessor:

> Ken has safeguarded the future of the FBU by leaving a healthy lay democracy in place and a union committed to the principles of peace and progress. He has steered us through some tough times. We have spent the last 15 years being reviewed, investigated, monitored – you name it, it's happened to us! And every time we are found to be providing an efficient, effective fire service, which gives the public what it deserves – value for money. Over the past 20 months we have run the Smash and Grab campaign to stop our employers smashing our national agreement and grabbing our hard won conditions of service. The FBU survived the Thatcher and Major years relatively intact

compared to many of our brother and sister unions. All of us
in the FBU know that our survival is due in no small part to the
leadership of our general secretary Ken Cameron.[51]

Andy Gilchrist, a former Bedfordshire firefighter and a national
officer from 1996, was to lead the union through even more
turbulent times. As he noted, the drive for public sector
'modernisation' reached the fire service later than other parts
of the public sector, primarily because of its relatively low cost,
its effective performance and the existence of a pay formula that
avoided overt conflict.[52] The impact of local campaigns to ensure
public support for the service must also be factored in. However,
the FBU's second national strike over pay, in 2002-04, became
inextricably bound up with New Labour's 'modernisation' agenda
and as Chapters 3 and 4 show, there is considerable debate as to
how far the dispute facilitated this agenda by 'opening Pandora's
box'; or whether modernisation as signalled by the Audit
Commission was inevitable.

In 2001, the HM Fire Service Inspectorate report, *Managing a
Modernised Fire Service: Bridging the gap*, added to the pressure for
cultural and managerial change, particularly in the leadership
of the fire and rescue service, proposing the introduction of
'alternative recruitment and progression'.[53] In September 2002,
seeking a way to avoid conceding to the union's claim for annual
pay of £30,000, deputy prime minister John Prescott, at the request
of the employers, ordered an inquiry into pay and modernisation
in the fire service, to be chaired by Professor Sir George Bain. The
FBU refused to participate in the inquiry, which it did not believe
was independent. Bain's three-month *Independent Review of the Fire
Service* was published in December 2002, and once again identified
the Grey Book as a barrier to modernisation and recommended
demand-led shift patterns, variable crewing and mixed crewing
by wholetime and retained firefighters. It reiterated most of the
recommendations of the Audit Commission's 1995 report. Bain
urged changes to terms and conditions, to reduce the scope of the
Grey Book to four core areas – pay, total hours, overall ranks and
basic leave – allowing local flexibility on shift patterns, crewing
levels, overtime working, family-friendly working practices and
appointments and promotion. It also proposed 'a comprehensive

modernisation' of the Firefighters' Pension Scheme, which it considered to be inflexible, costly and poor value for money, foregrounding the major battles over pensions in 2005-06 and 2011 onwards.[54] It reiterated earlier proposals to move to risk-based assessment of fire cover and advised structural changes such as the replacement of the body dealing with professional standards and guidance, the CFBAC.

The majority of Bain's recommendations were incorporated into the government White Paper *Our Fire and Rescue Service*, published in June 2003. This paper became law as the Fire and Rescue Services Act 2004 (with related legislation in Scotland, Wales and Northern Ireland). It represented comprehensive legislation covering the functions and responsibilities of fire and rescue authorities and negotiating frameworks and replacing the Fire Services Act 1947. The legislation required fire authorities to produce Integrated Risk Management Plans (IRMPs) as mechanisms to address and identify risk in the community and based upon risk to life rather than risk to property. Bain had identified IRMPs as the key lever with which to change the fire service, entailing the repeal of Section 19 of the Fire Services Act 1947, which insisted on the secretary of state's consent to reductions in fire stations, appliances or crewing levels. Importantly, this change involved the abandonment of national minimum standards of fire cover that specified how many firefighters should attend 999 calls to fires and how quickly they should do so. In addition to scrapping national standards, the Fire and Rescue Services Act 2004 abolished the CFBAC and the Scottish CFBAC. These bodies were replaced by the Business and Community Safety Forum and the Practitioners Forum, led by the Chief and Assistant Chief Fire Officers Association (CACFOA), representing, for Ian Fitzgerald, 'a major consolidation of power for senior management'.[55] Abolition represented the loss of national forums that enabled professional experience to be shared and provided channels of communication with government.[56] For the union the removal of the CFBAC 'eliminated a key element in the development of professional standards in the FRS [fire and rescue service]', leading to increased fragmentation of the service and to a 'postcode lottery' in relation to levels of service, including equipment, training and planning for emergency response.[57] Professional standards were further diminished when Her Majesty's Fire Service Inspectorate (HMFSI) in England and Wales was dissolved and replaced in its role by the Audit Commission, which took responsibility for 'performance inspections' until its abolition by the Conservative-Liberal Democrat coalition government in 2010 and replacement by a 'deregulated performance improvement environment'.[58]

The 2004 Act looked to extend firefighters' duties to other emergencies (flooding and terrorism were mentioned) and provided the legislative basis for the regionalisation of control rooms to be embodied in the disastrous FiReControl project (see Chapter 5). The Act established a new equalities agenda, while a national framework of skills and competencies was introduced to map job roles along firefighters' careers, with common standards of competence across all firefighters, including non-uniformed and part-time workers, allowing for mixed crewing. The system was part of the settlement of the pay dispute and effectively reduced the 12-rank structure to seven roles. It was also the subject of prolonged local negotiations over pay protection for those in existing roles. Further local flexibility was enshrined in the replacement of the long-service increment by continual professional development after the employers suggested it was potentially discriminatory. Once again implementation was protracted and provoked grievances at brigade level.

Deregulation continued under New Labour with the 2005 Regulatory Reform (Fire Safety) Order, which ended certification by fire authorities and transferred responsibility for safety to a combination of employer, employee, occupier and landlord. While the union welcomed this consolidation of fire safety law, it raised serious concerns regarding the delegation of risk assessment to the 'responsible person', namely the employer or building owner. Shane Ewen commented that 'this was part of a government-wide shift away from direct enforcement, towards contracting out compliance to non-governmental bodies'.[59] Concerns about the delegation of risk assessment were raised following the 2009 fire at Lakanal House in Southwark and again in the wake of the June 2017 Grenfell Tower fire.

The protracted 2002-04 pay dispute left many members feeling dissatisfied, and, as occurred after the 1977-78 strike, it resulted in criticism of the union leadership and tactics from parts of the membership. In 2005 Andy Gilchrist lost the general secretary election to Matt Wrack, who gained 64 per cent of the vote on a 40 per cent turnout.[60]

The FBU in an age of austerity: 2010-18

The global financial crisis in 2008 brought large-scale cuts in government spending. Following the formation of the Conservative-Liberal Democrat Coalition in 2010 and its comprehensive spending review,[61] an ideologically driven programme of 'austerity' led to a 30 per cent cut in central government funding to the UK fire and rescue service, with the loss of 11,000 firefighter jobs between 2010 and 2015. More than 500 emergency control posts, a quarter of the UK total, were lost, resulting in serious staff shortages and a failure to maintain minimum staffing levels on some occasions.[62] FBU research carried out in 2017 revealed a reduction of more than a quarter of specialist fire safety staff in English brigades since 2011. FBU analysis found that a similar proportion had been lost in Northern Ireland (24 per cent) between 2013 and 2017, with a 12 per cent decrease in Scotland and 10 per cent in Wales.[63] Response times to fires were at their slowest for 20 years, according to Department of Communities and Local Government figures released in December 2015. The Home Office admitted in August 2016 that the number of people who died in fires had increased by 15 per cent in the previous year,[64] a figure which is likely to rise significantly in the light of the unprecedented number of fatalities in the Grenfell Tower fire. Further cuts in central government funding of 20 per cent or £137 million were to be made to fire and rescue in England in the four years to 2020.

At the same time as the number of firefighters was being reduced, FBU research in 2016 suggested an increased need for firefighters to intervene in emergencies. It found that firefighters had carried out more rescues over the previous year than at any time before, with over 40,000 people rescued in incidents attended by the fire and rescue service between April 2015 and March 2016, equating to roughly 100 rescues each day and representing a 7 per cent increase in rescue activity across UK.[65]

Consistent with New Labour's commitment to a mixed economy in service delivery, including the PFI, the Fire and Rescue Services Act 2004 allowed for fire and rescue authorities to outsource or contract out certain fire service functions. Subsequently, the FBU has perceived creeping privatisation. In London, training was transferred to multinational support services provider, Babcock, with those staff undertaking training removed from Grey Book conditions. In 2012, Specialist Group International (SGI) signed a 12-month pilot contract with Surrey Fire and Rescue Service to provide a diving service, and confined space and swift-water rescue capability. As part of this contract, SGI would provide fire cover during industrial action; the pilot was subsequently extended. Cambridgeshire Fire and Rescue Authority used private contractor Serco to provide cover for shortages of firefighters. A private provider of fire services, AssetCo, negotiated multi-million-pound PFI asset management deals to run the fleets of two fire authorities, London and Lincolnshire, followed by a deal to supply casual contract staff to break industrial action in the London brigade in 2010.[66] The company subsequently went into administration. The Coalition government's Localism Act 2011 gave local authorities powers to meet their legal responsibilities by any chosen method, opening local public services to a competitive market. Its preference for independent or voluntary sector providers was reflected in Cleveland, where proposals for mutualisation and the first 'John Lewis style brigade' in 2012 were successfully defeated by FBU members who believed it was, according to union president Ian Murray, 'a foot in the door and a precursor to potential privatisation' – privatisation by 'organised stealth'.

In May 2013 former English chief fire and rescue adviser Ken Knight published his review into efficiencies and operations in the fire and rescue service in England, *Facing the Future*. A key conclusion was that the long-term trend of decreasing fire deaths justified cuts in expenditure and firefighter numbers. In its response, *Facing Reality*, the FBU argued that this trend had occurred precisely because of the successful work of firefighters: 'Firefighters have been the active agent in bringing about this progress, although there is still a long way to go. It would be irresponsible to decimate precisely the active force that has catalysed these improvements. Such folly will put lives at risk.'[67]

The Knight Review called for greater collaboration and sharing of services across the fire brigades, as well as with other emergency services. In control there has been increased sharing of networked services and systems and some consolidation of control rooms, involving the further loss of UK fire control operators and local control rooms.[68] In Scotland, where responsibility for the fire and rescue service was devolved to the Scottish government, the existing eight fire services were brought together in April 2013 as the single Scottish Fire and Rescue Service. The FBU supported the move in principle, subject to the protection of the service, jobs and conditions. It believed it could provide uniformity across the service in Scotland, although it recognised that cost reduction was one of the motivations for the change. Scottish government figures showed a 10 per cent reduction in firefighters five years after the merger, with the closure of five control rooms (out of eight) cutting control staff by almost a third.[69]

The Thomas Review of conditions of service for fire and rescue staff in England was announced by fire minister Penny Mordaunt in August 2014, to 'investigate further the barriers to change' indicated by Knight's review.[70] Adrian Thomas, a human resources professional, was selected as an outsider to conduct the review. The FBU was critical of the review's timing, seeing it as a politically motivated attack on firefighters, as it was announced immediately prior to the union taking strike action over pensions. The union's submission to the review also challenged its independence, rationale and methods.[71] Publication of the review's findings was delayed by the Home Office until November 2016, when the report painted an 'unrecognisable picture of the fire and rescue service', in the view of assistant general secretary Andy Dark, failing to acknowledge the enormous changes in the industry, including developments towards expanding the role of firefighters to areas such as emergency medical response and flood rescue.

Thomas's review stressed the need for the service to rebuild 'culture and trust, including addressing the concerns around bullying and harassment'. However, the union described this charge as 'a pre-conceived notion... which is far from the truth', and emphasised the findings of its own survey of more than 10,000 firefighters, which it had submitted to the review. The union's research found that 'bullying was a factor of working life, but the majority of it was being inflicted on firefighters by fire service management, which is something the review avoided totally'. As home secretary, Theresa May restated concerns about bullying and harassment in parts of the fire and rescue service in a speech in May 2016, calling also for a transformation in the 'diversity of a firefighter workforce that is 96% white and 95% male'.[72] Matt Wrack responded by pointing out that 'it was her government who in 2010 chose to remove the diversity targets that were in place' and had cut recruitment.[73]

The Thomas Review supported proposals for police and crime commissioners (PCCs) to run fire and rescue services, opposed by the union on the basis that there was no evidence to suggest that the change would bring any improvement to the service, and because it would result in further fragmentation. Nevertheless, the legislation introducing PCCs in England was passed in 2012. Subsequently, the Policing and Crime Act 2017 represented a further change to the governance of the fire and rescue service by placing a statutory duty on all three emergency services to collaborate where improvements in efficiency or effectiveness would result, and enabling PCCs to take over fire and rescue services in their area. The legislation provided for two options: a 'single employer' or a 'governance' model. Under the governance option the fire and rescue service and the police service remain distinct organisations with separate management structures, whereas the single employer model enables a PCC to establish a single chief officer for policing and fire, and to harmonise conduct and complaints systems, as well as terms and conditions.[74] The FBU particularly opposed the single employer model, as a threat to collectively negotiated pay and conditions. In addition, it feared that closer association with the police would undermine fire prevention and safety work in communities. Wrack warned:

> Firefighters need to be seen to be neutral within the communities they serve. Police are law enforcers, while fire and rescue is a humanitarian service with a very different remit and culture. Firefighters rely on the public's trust to gain access to homes and buildings for fire safety work and, of course, to put out fires and we are concerned that this will change if firefighters are associated with police.[75]

In a further move towards integration and following discussion at the NJC, the fire and rescue service collaborated with the ambulance service in trials of emergency medical response for some categories of suspected cardiac arrest. There were mixed reactions to the trials from within the union and in September 2017 the union withdrew its participation following lack of progress on pay, alongside the failure of some brigades to address the operational, safety, training and welfare concerns raised by firefighters during the trials (Chapter 5). Nevertheless, over a century the work of the fire and rescue service has expanded and changed in nature. FBU research found that 90 per cent of the roughly 100 daily rescues undertaken by the fire and rescue service were at non-fire emergencies, including flooding, chemical spillages, road traffic collisions and lift rescues. In a press release, Wrack noted: 'The modern day fire and rescue service is an all-hazard emergency service – one that needs to be funded properly.'[76]

Research methods

This book draws upon a range of FBU sources, mostly published, including Executive Council reports, conference proceedings and decisions and union circulars. It also cites the excellent *Firefighter* union journal and the sectional magazines or bulletins *Alerter* (retained members), *Response* (control members), *Siren* (women members), *Advisor* (B&EM members), and *Flagship* (LGBT members). The FBU's online resources and digital archive at Warwick University have been invaluable. These sources are supplemented by government reviews, statistics, policy documents, and fire and rescue service reports. However, the book consciously privileges the testimonies of union activists and members, while locating their recollections, reflections and reported experiences in the social relations of work and the wider political and ideological frames which shape and are shaped by these relations. It thus reflects the tradition of oral history and a belief that oral sources are highly relevant to historical analysis.[77] There is a profound bond between public history and personal struggle[78] and histories are made through active processes rather than overly determined by structures.[79] FBU reps in their narratives emphasise collective and social (rather than individual) identities, producing collective history in the tradition of industrial sociology based on the workplace – for example, Anna Pollert's *Girls, Wives and Factory Lives*[80] and Huw Beynon's *Working for Ford*.[81] Oral histories are evidently based on recollection and there are tensions between individual and collective memory. The book reflects these tensions and presents sometimes conflicting interpretations of events in the union's history, a characteristic that is particularly true of accounts of the 2002-04 dispute and the question of representation for the equality sections within the union. In departing from a chronological and top-down approach focusing exclusively upon senior officials at the expense of lay activists, the book seeks to avoid the limitations in the writing of trade union histories highlighted by Eric Hobsbawm and reflected upon by Dave Lyddon.[82] Lyddon highlights that it is not possible to deal with every aspect of a union's history and that value judgements have to be made on what to include and exclude, as has been done in the case of the FBU.

This centenary history draws on almost one hundred in-depth interviews with key figures in the FBU, past and present. They were carried out between January 2016 and June 2017 and include national officers, regional and brigade officials, local reps and representatives of the equality and trade sections (Table 1). The interviewees represent all 12 FBU regions, the three trade sections and the three self-organised groups and a small group of 'key informants' with long-term relationships to the union. An interview with Ken Cameron was conducted shortly before he died in 2016.[83] Interviews were with few exceptions conducted face to face, although in a minority of cases via telephone or Skype. Interviewees were asked about their history in the service and the union and to recall the major changes and events that they had experienced. When referred to in the text, in the majority of cases, the interviewee's position at the time of the interview is given, as in Table 1; where appropriate to the context, their position at the time of the event discussed is given. The intention is to reproduce the words of the respondents, with limited editing in the interests of clarification. At no point has the meaning or sense of the testimonies been altered.

Outline of the book

Chapter 2 assesses the structure and organisation of the FBU, focusing on it as an industrial union which represents all employees in the service and highlighting the role of its three trade sections. The chapter argues that this structure, rooted in the workplace, the collectivist nature of firefighting work and the key role of workplace activists, have combined to create the basis for the resilience of the FBU over the century of its existence. Social relations at work and the organisation of work forge an occupational community that underpins collective organisation and solidarity. The chapter considers how the FBU has responded to challenges to recruitment and organisation, including through the use of social media. It explores routes to activism and the important role of union education, particularly political education, in the transition from membership to activism, looking at debates over the role of political leadership.

Chapter 3 examines the legacy of the 1977-78 national strike and its outcome, the pay formula. It highlights the subsequent industrial quiescence associated with Ken Cameron's general secretaryship. The chapter documents the series of local disputes that emerged in the last decades of the 20th century in response to cuts in local authority funding and threats to jobs and the service, in particular the conflicts in Merseyside, Essex and Derbyshire. It traces employer attempts to introduce local flexibility at the expense of national standards and the identification of the Grey Book as a block to 'modernisation'. The FBU's Smash and Grab campaign was launched to defend national pay and conditions, and firefighters in Merseyside, Northern Ireland and London successfully reasserted the terms and conditions upheld by the Grey Book. The chapter closes with signs of increased questioning of the usefulness of the pay formula, signalling that the stage was set for a further national battle over pay.

Chapter 4 examines the second FBU national strike in 2002-03 and the wider dispute, which lasted until 2004.[84] It looks at the rationale behind the claim for £30,000 annual salary (referred to as £30k), which led to industrial action, and documents the dispute against the backdrop of the Bain Review and the constellation of oppositional employer and political forces. The chapter records the organisation of the strike at national and local level. It presents conflicting testimonies on the dispute and its outcome, discussing the eventual acceptance of the three-year deal and how it shaped subsequent working conditions. The chapter finishes by tracing Matt Wrack's path to election as general secretary in the aftermath of the dispute.

Chapter 5 focuses on the period following the 2002-04 dispute under Matt Wrack's leadership, in which the union fought a series of local battles against fire authority attempts to use IRMPs as cover to deliver cuts to jobs and services and to downgrade fire cover. It documents the battle over FiReControl led by the union's control section against the regionalisation of control centres and against cuts to the control workforce and service. The chapter proceeds to document employer attempts to change shift patterns and crewing levels, including through the introduction of the notorious close proximity crewing, which resulted in a legal challenge under the Working Time Directive. Finally, it examines the expansion of the firefighter role through attempts to introduce co-responding and emergency medical response.

Chapter 6 discusses how the defence of members' pensions has played a significant role in recent FBU history, within the wider context of government attacks on public sector pensions. It examines the emergence of a two-tier pension scheme in 2006 with a new pension age of 60 for new entrants to the fire and rescue service. The chapter documents the union's legal victory in 2008 over employer moves to withdraw pensions after retirement on the grounds of ill health. It then considers the Hutton Review of public service pensions and its proposal to increase normal pension ages for all firefighters and emergency control staff. The chapter shows how the union pursued a combined industrial, political and legal strategy not only to defend, but also to promote, members' pension rights. Legal channels were used both to ensure that firefighters who work the retained duty system have access to the same pension rights as wholetime FBU members, and to challenge age, gender and race discrimination in pension provision.

Chapter 7 documents how the FBU was at the forefront of promoting equality and diversity in the fire and rescue service from the 1990s, with its role commended in the Home Office's 1999 Thematic Review. Aside from the years of the Second World War, women's presence in the fire and rescue service was largely confined to control rooms until the equal opportunities policies of the Greater London Council in the 1980s prompted efforts to increase the number of women and ethnic minority firefighters. However some women, B&EM and LGBT firefighters faced appalling instances of harassment and the union was forced to look at its own procedures for representing members accused of harassment. Women, B&EM and LGBT members of the unionbegan to organise themselves first informally and then more formally through committees of the union. Chapter 7 charts the development of equality structures within the union, which were strongly supported by Ken Cameron and national officer Andy Gilchrist. It also marks their achievements in promoting equality and diversity in the fire and rescue service. It documents dissenting views over the voting rights gained by the equality sections and the controversial decision to remove these in 2012.

The FBU has championed the health, safety and welfare of its members over the century. In Chapter 8, FBU head of research Paul Hampton highlights the commitment of the union to ensuring that the dangers of the job are minimised through the adoption of the highest standards of equipment, clothing and professional training, and via the most effective procedures. Mental health has increasingly become an issue of concern for the FBU, with recognition of post-traumatic stress disorder following incidents such as the 1984 Kings Cross fire. Chapter 8 shows how firefighters have long dealt with environmental hazards, ranging from grassland fires to floods and storms. Flooding has become a more significant part of the work of the fire and rescue service, with the 2007 summer floods marking a turning point in FBU policy. The union demanded that fire and rescue services should have a statutory duty to respond to major flooding, and be provided with the associated resources. The Scottish government had already made such provision, while FBU pressure led to devolved legislation in Northern Ireland and Wales, with the campaign continuing in relation to England.

Chapter 9 examines the union's wider role, reflecting on the FBU's political alliances within the TUC and as a Labour Party affiliate. It examines the decision to disaffiliate from the Labour Party in 2004 and to re-affiliate in 2016 in England and Wales and its support for the leadership of Jeremy Corbyn. In Scotland the union developed a close relationship with the Scottish government led from 2007 by the Scottish National Party, on matters of common interest, and similarly in Wales the union developed a relationship with the Welsh government that was not possible in England. The non-sectarian character of the FBU in Northern Ireland allowed the union to play a role in the Peace Agreement. Chapter 9 also highlights the significant involvement of the FBU in national campaigns for social justice, and considers the union's long history of internationalism, including ongoing support for and links with firefighters' unions across the globe. Finally, it considers the FBU's position in the 2016 referendum on whether the UK should remain in the European Union and its subsequent stance on Brexit.

Lobbying at Westminster, 2014

© Hazel Dunlop

March against the cuts, 2015

© Cameron Matthews

2
An industrial union: organisation, activism and education

I'm always struck by the power of having a single industry trade union and the loyalty that the Fire Brigades Union can inspire in firefighters and I think it is because we're a single industry union. I think that sense of being has really kept the union together in the way that perhaps others haven't done. The fabric of the fire service is the fabric of the Fire Brigades Union. When I joined, the union was part of going to work. There was no separation.

Gary Spindler, brigade chair, Avon

The FBU is an industrial union that historically has represented and organised all uniformed employees in the fire and rescue service, including emergency fire control staff, those on the retained duty system and officers.[1] While the union has latterly broadened its membership, at its centenary three-quarters were wholetime firefighters, over one-fifth retained firefighters and 3 per cent control staff. In the context of declining union membership and reduced collective bargaining since the 1980s,[2] the FBU has maintained high densities (Chapter 1). Notwithstanding different interpretations of the outcome of the 2002-04 dispute (Chapter 4), the FBU did secure equal pay for retained firefighters (equal to that of wholetime firefighters) and established the principle of equal pay for emergency control room staff. The union secured a rate of pay of 95 per cent for control staff. While retained firefighters may once have been regarded as second-class firefighters, the union has pursued legal cases to ensure rights to pay, sick leave, annual leave and, crucially, pension entitlement that are equivalent to those of full-time staff (Chapter 6). Control staff and retained firefighters have active national committees and regional representation,[3] which play a full role in the democratic process and provide key activists.

The FBU has negotiated for all uniformed fire and rescue service employees under the Grey Book, with the exception of principal managers, although it recruits up to chief fire officer level. Consequently, when national and local industrial action is proposed, members in all sections can potentially be balloted.[4] However, in 2015, in response to structural changes in the fire and rescue service that removed some workers from the remit of the National Joint Council (NJC), the FBU determined to broaden the scope of its membership,[5] reinforcing its status as an 'industrial-type' union. It changed the rules governing membership, enabling it to organise all those employed in the provision of firefighting, rescue services or related services. In the context of debate within industrial relations about so-called 'core' and 'periphery' workers and the problems trade unions have in organising the latter, the FBU is attempting to overcome fragmentation in workers' terms and conditions and representation.[6]

The FBU's resilience results from three combined factors: firstly, its structure and organisation; secondly, the way the nature of firefighting generates collectivity among fire and rescue service workers; and thirdly, the leadership provided by lay union officers, underpinned by comprehensive union education. Accordingly, this chapter describes the union's emphasis on workplace-based organisation and the role of the three trade sections: the sections for control staff, retained firefighters and officers. It highlights how firefighters' work facilitates collective organisation, the challenges to this and the role of workplace reps in a changed working environment. The chapter then depicts union approaches to recruitment and organisation, including the use of new technology and social media. Finally, it traces the path from membership to activism, and looks at the importance of union leadership and union education in this transition.

Structure and organisation

The structure of the FBU is based on the organisation and representation of members at their place of work (branch); this feeds into the divisional, brigade, regional and national domains. Compared to other unions, branches are small, with a high ratio of reps to members.[7] In the 1970s a new national structure emerged, reflecting the establishment of large metropolitan authorities and brigades, which led to concentrated and large, politically active FBU regions. Workplace structures are complemented by the three trade sections, along with sectional representation for under-represented groups and other member categories. The latter includes ROOT – the retired and out-of-trade section – with a membership of around 6,500 former firefighters and control operators.[8] Unlike other unions, the FBU has a mostly lay structure, where three national officers plus the general and assistant general secretaries and president are elected and have been firefighters or control operators. This characteristic makes the union accessible to members, as Stewart Kinnon, ex-vice-chair of Strathclyde brigade, observed:

> The other important thing was that we were an accessible union. It was possible for a firefighter to phone up Kenny Cameron; you met them, if you were an official. You got to meet them all the time. Even as a branch official you got to meet them, you got to see them and they would have a chat with you.

For reps, the FBU's industrial unionism is crucial. Karl Wager, Cleveland brigade chair, commented: 'I think the strength of our union is the fact that we represent each other; we're all Grey Book employees, we're all under the same terms and conditions, and we all fight tooth and nail to keep the Grey Book.'

Bob Walker, former Devon and Somerset brigade chair, confirmed this important feature, observing that 'the principle of this union is that we mimic the workforce we represent'. Despite this premise, the fragmentation of bargaining, promoted by outsourcing, which has challenged public sector trade unionism in general,[9] led to the decision in 2015 to widen membership to include all those employed in firefighting, rescue or related services. While the decision meant the retention of single-industry status, the organisational shift was anticipated to include the increasing number of posts previously filled by firefighters on Grey Book conditions but now removed from NJC conditions of service. These included control members in the North West no longer directly employed by the local fire and rescue service and those employed by privatised training providers (for example, since the Fire Service College at Moreton-in-Marsh was privatised).[10] The FBU executive recognised that widening the membership would require organisational changes, including to membership contributions, internal culture, union structure and bargaining rights. The Executive Committee proposed varying contribution rates for those not covered by the Grey Book and a trainee/development rate. A key organisational challenge was that potential new members would not sit within the brigade committee structure rooted in the workplace while, in bargaining terms, new members might not be in recognised workplaces, which would mean the union having to pursue recognition. Notwithstanding this adaptation, the unifying struggle to defend the Grey Book has meant that the three trade sections have been stepping stones to wider and key roles within the FBU, and this is particularly true for women in emergency control rooms.

Emergency fire control

Historically, emergency fire control has provided a voice for women and, in some respects, pre-empted the creation of equality sections (Chapter 7). Ex-president Ruth Winters emphasised, 'There was no other avenue for women to have a voice.' The first woman and first control staff member on the Executive Council was Marion Gaunt in 1979. She had campaigned for a control member to be on the Council for over 20 years. On joining the service in 1956, she had found that control staff were 'second-class citizens in the FRS [fire and rescue service]' and were 'badly organised within the union' and she worked with others to change this situation.[11] The same conference resolution that introduced the Executive Council position in 1979 also established the Control Staff National Committee.[12] Lynne Harding followed Gaunt as Executive Council control member, and a later Executive Council member for control, Ann Jones, subsequently became a Member in the Welsh Assembly. The union's first female president (2002-07), Ruth Winters, came from the control staff national committee and Rose Jones was a control member who became West Midlands brigade secretary and the first female member to represent a region on the Executive Council. Sadly, Jones died shortly after being interviewed, but she recalled her determination not to be seen as solely representing control or women's interests nationally, while remaining loyal to her control branch:

> I was the first woman ever to represent a region from control, obviously not a firefighter. I think the person who stood against me at the time made a big mistake in saying, actually, you should always have an operational firefighter. People who don't normally vote in West Midlands popped into the office and said 'We are voting for you because he's actually saying that you're useless and we know through you being the brigade secretary that you're not useless', so in a way he did me a favour. That was the worst thing he could've said, really. I always said that if I went to conference, I would never go as control because I don't want to be classed as the control girl. I wanted to represent people, the whole spectrum rather than just control issues. You don't really know as a branch member what the Executive Council is and I always tried to portray that in every meeting. I might be on the EC [Executive Council], but I'm still a member of my control branch. That's where I come from, you know, and you have to keep your feet on the ground. I was a woman who'd come from control; they'd never had that before. I was very proud when I got it.

Danni Armstrong, the second woman regional Executive Council representative, elected in 2015, also started as a control operator, in Surrey. She referred to Jones's influence in mainstreaming control throughout the union:

> I took up the rep's job, and control wasn't really active within the brigade, and we were very much out of the loop and made to feel separate from the fire service and therefore didn't really have any input or any ability to influence anything within the service. I always feel I was quite fortunate arriving in Surrey because the union was very supportive to me as an individual through my progression. And also very supportive of control issues and I think it wasn't the members that saw control as a separate entity, it was very much management who tended to isolate control. I think we have done, within the national union, a lot over my time. When I attended my first annual conference,

which I think was 1996, I very much sought support from people involved with control, like Rose Jones – people who brought a control element to the mainstream within our union that then put us in a position of using that back in our own brigade. So, it has taken time. I don't think we're yet at a point where there are no differences, but I think we've definitely gone a long way to assist in that.

Between 2004 and 2010 the emergency control section led the fight against the government's abortive FiReControl project to regionalise control rooms, which control members knew would undermine the service they provided and threaten jobs (Chapter 5). Former West Midlands regional secretary Chris Downes recalled how the dispute increased the profile of fire control staff:

That actual dispute was good in the respect that it made firefighters sit up and take notice of what actually control did. They just said, 'Oh they're on the radio, on the end of a phone and that's it.' I said, 'Well, actually, don't you think they always fix everything?' And actually relationships changed then between firefighters at the station and fire control. It did us a real favour in the respect that they were more visible, because we'd have branch meetings and get fire control to come and tell us what was going on.

The emergency fire control section has always taken up members' work-related health and safety concerns, including hearing problems from the use of headphones and repetitive strain from computer work. In some respects, control staff have seen most changes to their work; technological innovation has introduced graphic information systems, call concentrators (touch screen), recording systems, radio telecommunication, mobilising systems, database retrieval and electronic mailing and PC-based programme use.[13] Control has increasingly been key to gathering information for central statistics and local management. Lynda Rowan O'Neill, national secretary for the control section, agreed that the representation of control members had improved and that their profile had been raised because of newly introduced mobilising systems that were not 'fit for purpose', following the abandonment of regionalisation in 2010:

> I think control issues had been put on the back burner; possibly as a committee our voices might not have been strong enough. We might not have been getting our issues out in the right way, whereas now we are. We're getting out the issues around the systems and the problems people are having with them and how dangerous they are for operational [firefighters] because of the delays. In the past few years since the FiReControl project was cancelled, brigades have got money to update their systems, and they're buying what I would call an 'off-the-shelf' system. And they're doing what it says on the packet, but that packet isn't enough for what we need. So they're being introduced, the control members have not had proper training, they have pointed out the inadequacies, but the systems have gone live before people are properly trained. They don't work. They cause control members stress because they're not mobilising the appliances [fire engines], they're endangering the public. At 2017 conference we asked that we should find out what brigades are actually asking for when they're tendering for these systems. I think we are now becoming relevant and people are realising, 'Oh, it's not controls with their little system that's going wrong, it's controls and they're warning us what the system failures are going to do.'

The stress generated by the job and the systems were graphically demonstrated by *The Operator*, a short film centred on an intense phone call between a control room operator and a distressed mother trapped with her sons in a burning house.[14] Rowan O'Neill confirmed:

> Stress is on the rise across the board in controls. You're taking a call, you've got somebody screaming at you that they're trapped in a room. You've got a system sitting in front of you – what happens is the screen produces a form to fill in and then you will get your appliances proposed and you mobilise them from that. So you're sitting with this and you know that at any time that screen could freeze. So that screen freezes and you're taking the information, you're shouting to somebody else to open another

screen to put the information into there. You're trying to stay calm with somebody who is in a life and death situation. Can you imagine the stress of that?

While the 2002-04 dispute settlement saw emergency control staff pay increase from 92 per cent of firefighter rates to 95 per cent, full pay equality remained an issue. In 2017 the control Annual General Meeting (AGM) voted to commission research on control job evaluation, which would explore equalisation. Delegates emphasised the reduced number of supervisors and expanded responsibilities of control staff, including emergency medical response (Chapter 5).[15]

Retained duty service

For the FBU, 'a firefighter is a firefighter is a firefighter. It does not matter which duty system you are working.'[16] The FBU is the predominant union for retained firefighters and the sole union recognised nationally for negotiation on the NJC. Historically, the non-TUC Retained Firefighters Union (RFU) was promoted by ministers and chief fire officers as an alternative among retained firefighters but has never managed to compete with the FBU.[17] In 2008 the NJC constitution introduced a mechanism for minority trade union representation; however, the RFU decided not to pursue a membership audit to evidence the threshold required for a seat on the NJC.

Residual tensions have endured over the boundaries between the wholetime and the retained duty system. The 1974 FBU Annual Conference agreed to seek an end to the wholetime retained system, whereby wholetime firefighters could take on extra retained cover. The successful reduction in working hours created 3,000 additional jobs. The 1977 strike achieved the removal of references to wholetime retained duties in the Grey Book. However, following unsuccessful attempts by the employers to re-introduce wholetime retained firefighters in the following decades, the settlement of the 2002-04 dispute conceded that there would be 'no barrier to any employee working on a combination of different wholetime, part-time and retained duty systems'. Tensions persist, particularly where retained hours are used to circumvent the recruitment of both wholetime and retained firefighters. However, the union has campaigned for increases in retained personnel in the face of recruitment difficulties, recognising the service's reliance on them. For example, in Cornwall two-thirds of firefighters are retained. In winter 2016 national secretary for retained firefighters, Peter Preston, told *Alerter* magazine that the retained duty system was in crisis, stating 'the long, anti-social hours coupled with the difficulty recruiting and keeping retained firefighters in the service makes me really fear for our future'. He reported that companies were more reluctant to release retained staff from their primary jobs at short notice to respond to emergencies. The concentration of jobs in large towns and cities made it harder to recruit new retained firefighters in rural areas. Increased commuting means that fewer prospective retained firefighters meet the requirement to be within accessible distance of fire stations (five minutes). Further, with the closure of some fire stations, retained firefighters have been asked to move to within the required proximity of another station, which inevitably has meant loss of staff. Tam Mitchell, former Executive Council member for retained firefighters, reported the greater demands being placed on retained staff and the strain on their work-life balance:

> Because a wholetime firefighter is a shift firefighter, they go to work at a certain time and go home at a certain time. Retained firefighters are basically slaves to a pager and if you've got a young family and things like that, it can be very, very tiring. You can't take the baby down the street because the pager could activate. You've always got to be within a certain distance of the fire station, normally five minutes. I would say that retained are in a far better place than when I joined. They've got to be treated the same now. We're better protected, the same as a wholetimer, in terms of fire gear. Everything's quite good for them, but the challenge will always be having people living within that five-minute radius of a retained station and being able to respond. And in most villages and towns now, people have to travel outside town for work, so you don't have as much of a catchment area.

As Mitchell indicates, the FBU has made huge strides in aligning the terms and conditions of retained firefighters with those of wholetime staff. In 1994 the union secured retrospective redundancy payments for retained firefighters who had lost their jobs as a result of the closure of their stations, following the House of Lords decision to grant redundancy rights for part-time workers. Former general secretary Andy Gilchrist was credited with pushing equal treatment. He argued: 'Retained firefighters are still treated by employers as second-class firefighters only entitled to second-class rights. Yet in many parts of the country they are the fire service.'[18]

A significant breakthrough was the settlement of the 2002-04 dispute, when equal pay was secured. Peter Preston suggested that this achievement led to improved recruitment:

> Securing recognition as a firefighter, now that sounds strange. It's just that historically we've always been viewed as second-class firefighters, as not really firefighters. And this probably stems from when we used to be paid a different rate of pay, because we were part-time and had a quite considerably lower rate of pay. Well, again this was the union campaigning on behalf of the retained membership. There was a big push in the early 2000s to actively involve the retained by Andy Gilchrist. He seemed to have a lot of drive, a lot of focus on getting retained and sectional involvement in the union at a higher level. It made a big difference, it very highly motivated the members of our committee. When they gave us a seat on the EC [Executive Council] – that made a huge difference. It was felt that the retained section had received more exposure and recognition and was quite valued as part of the union. It was quite a good time to be involved in the union.

Retained firefighters have an increased voice in the union that reflects FBU pressure for improved working conditions. In October 2001 Morris Butterfield became the first retained firefighter member of the Executive Council,[19] although this reserved seat was removed in 2015 alongside those for control staff and officers, as part of a wider union re-structuring. The next significant development came in 2006, when the House of Lords ruled in favour of equal pension and sick pay rights for retained firefighters, giving them access to the Firefighter's Pension Scheme (see Chapter 6). This ruling confirmed that retained staff were employed on 'the same type of contract' as wholetime staff and was a landmark judgement for all part-time workers. Interviewees believed that the union's principal focus on wholetime personnel had shifted, particularly since the equalisation of pay and conditions, the promotion of training and full access to protective clothing and equipment.

Cuts to wholetime posts mean fewer opportunities for retained firefighters to progress to wholetime roles. Cuts in services and the reduction in calls may mean lower earnings for retained duty system members, since they are paid only when called out. However, the FBU continued to pursue increases in the retention element of pay (with the aim of achieving 25 per cent of a wholetime salary) and reductions in the number of hours on call before the retention fee applies.

Retained firefighters may not belong to a union in their primary job and the FBU may be their only trade union. There are logistical issues in recruiting them to the FBU. Where there are dedicated retained stations, particularly in remote areas, firefighters might meet only once a week on drill nights. For example, 60 per cent of Scotland is covered by retained appliances[20] and Scottish regional organiser Seona Hart reported using officer members to help organise retained personnel:

> They're isolated on the islands and in communities. We have got retained members but it's getting access to them. So, for example, if we want to speak to retained members on one of the islands, it might be two boat trips and a flight. Of course, union expenses get scrutinised, and rightly so. So you've got to think, well what's the benefit of something like that? But what we do have is officer members in the union. They're obviously responsible for those areas. So we say to them 'Here's the information, can you take it while you're visiting them or doing a training night?' I've given loads of officer members direct debit forms for training nights. So it's about utilising your members just as much as your officials.

The union has promoted branch and regional structures amongst retained members that mirror the wholetime structures. At branch

67

level retained members may meet separately, or with wholetime members, or may attend a combination of separate and mixed meetings. All issues are discussed at brigade committees. Retained members have their own regional structure, in which regional retained duty system reps are a part of regional committees but may additionally take generic brigade officer posts. Gareth Beeton was a retained firefighter from Suffolk who became a wholetime firefighter in London and subsequently regional chair. He recounts how working alongside wholetime FBU members got him involved:

> They were very proactive within the FBU, the firefighters who were there, and the input from them spurred me to get involved. They were all instrumental really in encouraging us as retained firefighters. Back in the day, retained didn't have the same pay as wholetime firefighters, didn't have the same holiday benefits, didn't have the same pension, didn't have any pension rights. And the FBU fought for all of that. Unfortunately there was a certain amount of disparity between retained and wholetime in the older days. I never saw it because at my station, the wholetime would encourage us retained firefighters, would give us support, and actively encourage us to join. They'd say, 'The FBU can help you do this. They look after firefighters' health and safety, they negotiate and bargain on your behalf. The other union, the RFU, they've got no bargaining rights.' So the wholetime firefighters educated the retained crews. I was a butcher for my father and not union-oriented at all. I'd never been part of a trade union. But when I went into the fire service as a retained firefighter and the wholetime firefighters encouraged me and said, 'It's invaluable for you within this job', I built on it. I went on education courses in Eastbourne, and I liked everything I saw. I liked the movement, I liked the attitude of the people. And I liked it because of the fairness, the values of the FBU. It really got hold of me. I liked the ethos, the trade union movement, and I got more and more involved.

Officers

The FBU officers section includes watch managers and above, all the way to chief officer level. Victor Bailey recounts that a rival organisation, the National Fire Services Officers Association (NFSOA), 'to all intents and purposes a company union', was sponsored by the Home Office to represent officers between 1941 and 1942 to counter the FBU's growth[21] and to create separate consultative structures to prevent the FBU representing officers.[22] The NFSOA was renamed NAFO (National Association of Fire Officers).[23] Decades later, in 1990, NAFO merged with the electricians' union, the EEPTU. Following the EEPTU's merger with the engineering union AEU to form the AEEU and that union's admission to the TUC in 1994, some of the original NAFO membership seceded to form the Fire Officers Association (FOA).[24] The FOA initially met separately with the employers to discuss officers' terms and conditions, but the FBU remained the primary representative body and officer concerns were negotiated through the NJC. Following the 2002-04 dispute and a review of the NJC, the Fire and Rescue Service Middle Managers' Negotiating Body of the NJC was established in 2008 to cover station, group and area managers. The FOA secured one seat to the FBU's 13 employee seats on this body. While the FOA retained minimal national representation, such recognition was seen by the FBU as a reward for taking the employers' side in the 2002-04 dispute. Dave Beverley, former secretary of the officers section, saw the FOA as an insurance policy for officers unwilling to take industrial action:

> I think a lot of people miss that point of how important it is to be able to take part in some sort of industrial action because at the end of the day, we might be officers, but we're still employed, and if we're not happy with the conditions our employer is putting forward then we need to have a voice strong enough to be able to do something about it. I think that's where FOA slips up and if they did decide to take action, I'm pretty sure that their membership wouldn't uphold any action.

For Matt Wrack, 'the union is greatly strengthened by our officer members' and their highly professional knowledge and expertise is utilised on specialist committees at national level and when the union needs to deal with fire service issues with government departments.[25] Paul Embery, London Executive Council member, described the importance of officers being organised in the FBU:

> The truth is the further up the role structure, the less the membership density. But many people who move up from firefighter to crew manager, watch manager, station manager, group manager stick with us. We've got people in all those roles. And we want people in all those roles. There's been an argument, not by many, but some people in the past argued that the FBU shouldn't represent middle managers or officers – the term is used interchangeably – because there's a conflict. I don't see that. I think it is a real problem for employers and government that we can actually attract a layer of officer members who they expect to be running the fire service and taking us on, when actually in many cases those people have got loyalty to the FBU as well. So I'm all in favour of having as many officer member as we possibly can.

The Merseyside dispute of 2000 is one example of where industrial action helped prevent employer attempts to undermine appointment and promotion procedures for both firefighters and officers. Proposals included the introduction of non-uniformed personnel into officer posts (Chapter 3), part of New Public Management efforts to move away from internal professional hierarchies towards 'Human Resource Management' and reflecting historic attempts to break independent union organisation amongst officers. Subsequently, the officers' section has opposed employer moves to realign officer posts to contractual conditions of employment outside the Grey Book or to offer pay increases or allowances beyond those agreed for all firefighters through national negotiations.

Work and collectivism

In the previous history of the FBU, Victor Bailey linked the masculine solidarity of firefighters to the radicalism of the union: '[T]he shared workspace and male camaraderie together with the high level of team work enforced by a dangerous job all nurtured a strong group solidarity... the very consciousness of a separate identity from other workers, [which] disposed firemen towards industrial and political radicalism.'[26]

In a different period, with changed gender dynamics, firefighters confirmed that collectivism remains rooted in the labour process.[27] Avon brigade chair, Gary Spindler, suggested:

> I think without a doubt the job we do is dependent on each other. One of us can't do our job without someone else helping us. Everything we do is teamwork, whether it's in the union or in a fire or at a special rescue. Whatever it is, it's always with someone else. And I think that camaraderie and togetherness is fundamental to the union. The same as we fight fire together, we fight our bosses, we fight the government, we fight anyone who's trying to put the service down or make the job harder or more dangerous for us. So we're all tied into each other. Really, literally depending on each other for our lives. So that really breeds a sense of comradeship, of brotherhood and sisterhood that translates into the FBU.

Steve White, London regional organiser, considered that teamwork underpinned collective action:

> Once you've achieved that democratic mandate for whatever it is that you're going to do, whether that's taking strike action, action short of strike action, whether you're going to have a picket, what your picket is going to look like, everybody will throw themselves into it because we do teamwork like nobody else does teamwork.

Gareth Beeton, London regional chair and former retained firefighter, confirmed that comradeship rooted in work and the workplace was equally prevalent for retained firefighters:

> Retained stations are family as well and there is camaraderie. They are all your mates, they are all your brothers and sisters, and you all work together all the time. Every time the pager goes off, you work with those people day in and day out and the retained station I experienced was FBU.

The social processes underpinning collectivism at work are entrenched in the watch system, where loyalty and teamworking are for Ian Fitzgerald and John Stirling 'translated into a collective consciousness of the importance of the collective generally accepted by a management that remains a part of it'.[28] With workplace culture strongly influenced by fire brigade trade unionism, the introduction of new shift systems (Chapter 5) was seen as a management attempt to dislodge the fundamental building block of union organisation. Danni Armstrong reflected:

> It made us more militant having a red watch, a blue watch, a green watch and a white watch that was replicated within the control rooms. I think that gave us a sense of camaraderie. It's not gone totally, but I think it has been affected and we'll have different people working together with a different skillset doing additional things. We'll have wholetime and retained. It's mixed it up to a point where it's no longer a case that if you turn up to see a watch, it will be a watch. In lots of cases it will be a collection of people and I'm pretty sure that it would always have been a wish of management to squash the watch culture because it was something that was seen as a strength that caused them problems. I know there are still a lot of watches, but I just think the variety of work we do, some things being pushed down locally, means we have very different ways of working across the country.

Older firefighters like Scottish regional chair Gordon McQuade suggested that union membership had always been engrained within the service culture. He recounted how firefighters joined the FBU immediately on recruitment and generally at training school: 'I joined the Fire Service in September 1987. I didn't know anyone who wasn't in the FBU. It was sort of just automatic that you signed up to the FBU. In fact, I don't even recall having an option, but I probably would've had the option.'

FBU membership figures have been affected by cuts to the fire and rescue service and recruitment freezes, but full-time and lay officers also reported that the shift in political climate since the 1980s has meant that recruitment is not as instantaneous as previously. Former president Alan McLean perceived:

The way we do our business at grassroots is changing and has changed. I've personally seen the way society has changed towards trade unionists and unions, I see a difference in our ability to recruit. Not a difficulty as such, but challenges where once there were no challenges. It's being thwarted by management. At one time management would give us full access to recruits or new starters. Now we have to fight for access in many places to get to speak to them and join them up. So we have to wait till they get on the shift and hopefully there's an active branch representative to join them up. Everything's become a little bit more difficult.

Older reps recalled that monthly branch meetings were 'part and parcel of your working life'. Jamie Wyatt, Eastern region Executive Council member, described how meetings developed his politics:

Branch meetings were held at the beginning of the night shift at six o'clock, so you had the on-duty watch and the day watch would hang behind and others would come from home to attend. The expectation was that you would attend meetings, you'd become well informed quite quickly. And I think with that information and the activity going on, it was something that sat quite comfortably with my politics. I was 21 years old, had those socialist values and so you just ended up being drawn into conversations around the branch and taking on an active role.

Some saw calling branch meetings as more difficult with declining attendance, attributed in part to firefighters being less likely to live locally. There was consensus that attendance at meetings picked up during campaigns or disputes. Variation in branch activity inevitably reflects the ups and downs of industrial challenges and campaigning. Some recalled that after the 1977 strike it had taken time to rebuild the union and the same was reported after the 2002-04 dispute. In Chapter 3 Tony Maguire describes how the 1999 dispute in Northern Ireland over local allowances reinvigorated the union. Similarly in Chapter 5 Ian Murray, president and former Yorkshire and Humberside Executive Council member, reports how the 2009 dispute in South Yorkshire over 12-hour shifts led the union to revitalise union organisation, recounting, 'I saw the brigade go from on its knees to all of a sudden the membership rising up.' As evidenced in Chapter 6, the pensions dispute also generated activism.

Several reps reported using social media and new technology to organise, including Facebook, email and WhatsApp groups of reps and members sending out 'newsflashes'. Short films were uploaded on YouTube to share activity. There are differing observations on the implications of social media for union organisation. Essex brigade secretary Alan Chinn-Shaw highlighted some issues:

> You used to go to your branch meeting to be given information and to debate that information and then the next branch meeting would be debating people's views on it. Throughout our disputes we'd send out all-members circulars on Facebook and people constantly have information, information, information. It almost detracts from the requirement to go to a branch meeting and discuss views. It's a good thing that they've got the information, but if it results in activism dropping, that's a major concern.

Social media has been used to engage the public, particularly during anti-cuts campaigns. One example is the social media campaign initiated by East Sussex Fire and Rescue Service to secure compensation for the families of Brian Wembridge and Geoff Wicker, killed in the Marlie Farm fireworks disaster in 2006. *Firefighter* reported in 2016 that the FBU's national Twitter account had nearly 20,000 followers and its Facebook page had over 5,000 'likes'.[29]

The 30k website that emerged in the 2002-04 dispute strike generated ambivalence over the use of new technology and social media (Chapter 4). Despite the benefits of these forms of communication, FBU reps reported the disciplining of members for 'inappropriate' postings on Facebook. However, it was also suggested that such action was a consequence of a changed disciplinary climate, with the use of bullying and harassment policies ostensibly designed to protect firefighters being used against union members. Barry Downey, West Midlands Executive Council member, recalled:

I was hauled before the chief for re-tweeting something I hadn't read that had the word 'scab' in it and it's absolutely against the rules to say that word at work or in any connection with work. Where they're threatening our members with dismissal for using the words we've got little protection, they'll sack them and we end up at employment tribunal. We might win but they don't get their job back. We're having to say, 'Don't use the word, find something else – sausage, chips and beans.' There was a picture in Tipton station of a watch during the 2002-04 dispute that all went into work. And they were dressed as waiters because they'd done a charity night and on the board is 'sausage, chips and beans'. And it stayed there for about 10 years and everyone in the know laughed, but for every single member on that watch the penny didn't drop, so it made it doubly funny. And then all of a sudden someone went in and said, 'You know what that means, don't you?' The balloon went up! It was spirited away, the picture was.

Several reps report disciplinary proceedings over the word 'scab'. Consequently it was replaced by the term 'sausage, chips and beans', which was popularised by songs on YouTube clips. Reps also referred to CCTV in stations, which had the effect of censoring or policing firefighter behaviour by instilling a fear of disciplinary proceedings. Gary Critch, Essex brigade chair, was suspended on the basis of CCTV evidence for allegedly intimidating staff on resilience contracts (see Chapter 5):

I was carrying an axe on the fire ground. I had always carried an axe on the fireground because I used to use it in incidents, but I was accused of basically carrying it to deliberately intimidate resilience members. So I was suspended, they brought an external investigator in who'd already made their mind up that I was guilty of the charges. CCTV evidence was basically cut together to just show me walking around with the axe. When it was eventually realised that there was no case to answer, I still wasn't allowed to go back to work until I apologised for not doing anything wrong to them and had mediation with that entire element of the workforce on my own, but when they said they didn't want the mediation, I was allowed to go back to work.

Motions to the Black and Ethnic Minority Members (B&EMM) national committee AGM in 2009 highlighted a 'dramatic' increase in disciplinary investigations and/or actions against FBU representatives. Steve White discussed 'punishment postings' in the aftermath of the 2002-04 dispute:

> Taking people out of their watches and moving them somewhere else or disciplining them for relatively trivial things was starting to happen quite a lot. And if someone is going to discriminate against you, they're not going to tell you they're discriminating against you. So no one is going to say 'I'm disciplining you because you're the union rep', they will find something you did and exaggerate it and discipline you for that. And we found that happening a lot to key individuals who were particularly vocal during that dispute and subsequently.

There was a reported increase in the incidence of formal disciplinary proceedings against members, following the changes to disciplinary regulations after the 2002-04 dispute and the strengthening of local HR management. The removal of national standards of fire cover has meant reps at brigade level dealing with many more issues. One example is negotiating the rank-to-role restructuring at local level that followed the 2002-04 settlement. North East Executive Council member Andy Noble recounted:

> I mean, for the first two years as a brigade official, I just lived and breathed rank and role and it was the biggest poisoned chalice I've ever been handed in my life. It virtually took over my life because there were that many — actually there weren't that many — people adversely affected, but they were so strongly affected that they just would not let it lie and you couldn't blame them by the way.

Increased demands on local reps were made in the context of rigorous restrictions on facility time or time off for union duties, with staffing reductions making it harder for firefighters to be released. Employers have increasingly refused to bear the costs of full-time release of Executive Council members, and regional and sectional officials, with the FBU having to cover these at huge expense, a factor in the removal of Executive Council representation for the equality and trade sections (Chapter 7).[30] A particular challenge was the threat posed by the 2015 Trade Union Bill to end 'check-off' – the ability to collect membership fees through deduction at source. While the Trade Union Act 2016 did not entirely scrap check-off,[31] the FBU began a programme of transferring members to direct debit – a substantial organisational undertaking. The pressures on reps have a knock-on effect on the time available for recruitment and organisation. Assistant general secretary Andy Dark suggested:

> The amount of change locally has affected the time and resources that brigade officials have been able to put into organising. And if you've got a choice between making sure we don't get rubbish terms and conditions as opposed to making sure the branch is organised, I think I'd make the same unconscious choice. I've got to put time into always making sure that management doesn't take advantage.

An increasingly challenging environment for union organisation has necessitated a more conscious recruitment strategy, consistent with broadening FBU membership. A Brigade Organiser Toolkit provides guidance to those new to delivering regional recruitment and organising strategies. The Young Members Inclusion Framework recognises that young firefighters might have limited experience of unionisation and supports reps in informing, recruiting and involving young members.

Routes to activism

Tom Redman and Ed Snape's survey of operational fire service workers in northern England found that commitment to the union was associated with solidaristic pro-union beliefs rather than a more rational calculation of the benefits of membership, and that such commitment and beliefs influence participation in the union.[32] Accordingly, many reported how quickly they were propelled from membership to activism. Andy Findlayson, Basildon branch rep, recalled:

> If I'm honest, it started with a bit of social awkwardness. I was

at a branch meeting where the secretary was standing down, he was retiring. As is usual, I was told when I joined the Fire Brigade, 'Don't volunteer for anything'. So everyone was sitting quietly, with their hands down and because I was the new boy, they said all the job involved was opening the post, putting stuff on noticeboards. So under the social awkwardness I crumbled and put my hand up and it started there really. And you start doing a bit more, and start learning what unions are about and I got involved that way.

South West Executive Council member Tam McFarlane amplified this theme, reinforcing the influence of the FBU:

It's hard to get across to people who aren't in the fire service how fundamental the Fire Brigades Union is. When I joined in 1992, it was just taken for granted you joined. I remember going to training school and it was 'You sign that, you're in the Fire Brigades Union', that was it. In terms of the branch, the guys were retiring. They said, 'Well, we need somebody to hand over to. You're young, basically you're in.' And I remember thinking, 'I'm not sure I really want to do this'. I was at the branch a week and [thought] literally, 'Jesus Christ, I'm not even in the job a couple of years then you're the branch sec.' But to be honest, it wasn't as daunting as you might think because the watches ran themselves, the stations ran themselves and there was a lot of help from the old hands.

The mentoring of new members by established activists was crucial and would often entail political education. Former Scottish regional secretary Kenny Ross recalled:

They were all on our station and most on the same watch, the red watch. Alex Miller, John Paul McDonald, all these guys. So at one time we had a union official at every level of the union right up to EC in this station. So you couldn't help but be influenced by the people around you, learn from them, how you deal with politicians, how you deal with management.

Some activists came from trade union or Labour Party families, which informed their involvement. Secretary of Eastern region, Riccardo La Torre, had family roots in the Italian Communist Party but was also politicised by the strong culture of the Essex brigade:

I joined as a nipper. I was only 18 and still living with mum and dad. And my dad's side are a heavily, heavily politicised family. We're the only ones in England, but in Italy my uncle was a regional Communist Party secretary, my other uncle was in local politics. They've always been involved. And I don't think my dad would have let me back in the house if I hadn't had joined the union on the first day. Then I moved to Basildon and got politicised very quickly. It's got a history of trade unionism and has always been one of our strongest branches. It's produced brigade officials, national officials throughout its existence.

Other younger FBU members did not share this union background. Holly Ferguson, from Durham, describes becoming active during the pensions dispute:

I had an upbringing where I didn't know what a union was, so it was only in the job that I got to know. What got me interested was coming to annual conference as an observer two years ago. I was absolutely blown away. I thought, 'Right this is what the union does, this is what it's all about'. I was fascinated and ever since I've just been like, 'This is what I want to do'. I saw that picket lines weren't organised, people turning up as and when. Sometimes there were 50 people at the line, sometimes there was one. And I saw that people just needed a little bit of organisation, so I set up a sheet on the station where I said to people 'If you can come down, mark it on the sheet so I know that someone's on the picket line between two and four. I can be there when it's slack.' So we organised a really good picket line with people there every single hour. That sent a clear message to management that we were together and united.

For some, the impetus to becoming active was their experience in the workplace. Redman and Snape found that negative perceptions of industrial relations and pay equity were associated with intentions to participate.[33] Marcus Giles, a former West Midlands regional official, joined the union in 1986:

> I got fed up with draconian instructions from management. I felt they were wrong. Also, I used to go drinking with the brigade secretary and chair and they cajoled me. It opens your eyes to the injustices that you want to fight. I enjoyed the networking – you understood that you're not the only brigade going through all the crap, that there's other people out there.

Merseyside brigade chair Ian Hibbert became active during the pensions dispute. He described his politicisation:

> It started when the pensions dispute began. I found myself getting increasingly angry with the direction things were going, like a lot of people sat round the mess table, but they did little about it. I reached a turning point where I thought, 'You know, I either need to get involved and do something or just shut up and get on with it'. I joined the FBU because everybody just joined but I was very middle of the road to be honest. I was one of these people who thought that it didn't really affect me. Obviously, very quickly, you find out that every little decision that's made by them sat up on high affects every single one of us every day of our lives. So my politics now changed from being quite standoffish, not wanting to get involved, to taking it out to other people and saying, 'If you want to effect a change you must be involved, you must be organised, you must be motivated because they will not give us anything for free.'

Others reported how their increased involvement came from dissatisfaction with local organisation. Darren Lane from Cleveland brigade recollected:

> Basically I just wanted to get more involved. Some reps we used to have, I didn't feel we were getting enough from them. It was always the same answer if there was a problem; are you willing to strike for it? Are you willing to strike for it? I thought that can't just be the only option. I was only a member at the time but there was times when the picket lines were empty or full so

I tried to make sure that there was a few members to always go there and show support.

The testimonies show differing routes to activism. Reps from the control and retained sections reported how their sections provided stepping stones to activism in the wider union and Chapter 7 confirms this pattern for the equality sections. Fundamental, though, is the union's embeddedness in the workplace.

Political leadership and education

While the nature of work within the fire service provides the roots of mobilisation, the traditions of union militancy and left-wing leadership underpin the effectiveness of the FBU's counter-attack against employers in the 1990s and beyond. There is a debate on the importance of left-wing activists in the FBU. Fitzgerald and Stirling argue that the culture of collectivism generated by the nature of work is more important.[34] However, Ralph Darlington's study of the Merseyside Fire Brigade and the dispute of 1995-96 (Chapter 3) places more importance on the political affiliations of activists. These varied, but the common thread was commitment to strengthening union organisation through militant opposition to managerial intransigence. In Merseyside, the brigade committee included left-wing activists from the Socialist Workers Party and the Labour Party, who shared 'an adversarial ideology'.[35] In other regions, particularly Scotland, the Communist Party had been influential from the 1970s, though many younger militants, as elsewhere, were members or supporters of the International Socialists (from 1977 the Socialist Workers Party) or the Militant Tendency. In Scotland in the late 1990s and early 2000s the Scottish Socialist Party and then the Scottish Nationalist Party were attractive to several FBU activists (Chapter 9). Former regional chair Ronnie Robertson recalls being exposed to left-wing political militancy in the early 1970s:

The culture was that the officials were mostly members of the Labour Party, some members of the Communist Party. And I remember in the first years of my union membership you would attend a meeting and the squad at the back of the hall would be screaming their heads off, 'Sell out, sell out'. You didn't know if you'd been sold out or not, but anyway you had them sitting at the front pretending that everything was OK. That was my early memory of the union, you know.

Decades-long traditions were established. However, while there have been left networks, the FBU has not been marked by the bitter battles between different factions that have affected other unions. Keith Handscomb, former Executive Council member from Essex, discussed the advantages of not being identified with a particular organisation while engaging in political leadership:

> I became a fairly well-respected and popular official amongst the membership and I would have lost respect if I'd been a member of a revolutionary organisation – the level of debate I could have had with people. Likewise, being a Labour Party member would have compromised me. I was never quite comfortable with any particular party anyway, but certainly once I became a regional official and EC member, it would have reduced my influence with my members. So I've always tried to influence from a left-wing organising perspective. Essex in particular would be regarded as militant and left-wing, but they're not Socialist Worker Party members; they're not revolutionary politicos. I think if I'd had a tag of Labour or Socialist Worker it would have been harder. At every meeting I went to I said, 'I'm a socialist. I'm a socialist sympathiser. That's my politics.'

His profile fits with Darlington's leadership model and the ideological dimensions of trade unionism often missing in discussions of union representation.[36] Some FBU women drew on feminist ideas, or perceived other women activists to be feminists (even if they did not identify themselves as such). Lynda Rowan O'Neill, in paying tribute to Rose Jones, reflects on her own activism:

> She was strong. I think anybody that is a control rep has to be strong because you have to be. In fact anybody does that's a union rep. Most of the time reps come on because nobody else wants to do it. You take on the role reluctantly and it grows and you start to think 'Will I actually make a change?' And then it

becomes 'Well actually, you know what, I'm a bit good at this.' And that's what happens and Rose was very strong. Rose I would probably describe as a feminist – she had those values.

The relationship between class and gender and self-organisation within the union are explored in Chapter 7. In the case of control staff, activism may emerge from gendered experiences of work, rather than feminist ideas. While several reps brought committed political outlooks to the union, others were politicised through activism that was underpinned by the FBU's comprehensive education programme. This programme combines industrial and political approaches based on progressive adult education teaching methods, according to Trevor Cave, who joined the FBU in 2005 as director of education, having previously worked for the National Union of Mineworkers. He emphasises the aim of creating political activists and thinkers as well as well-trained union reps:

> The union's approach really sees the need for grassroots education and that's important in order to build union organisation. One reason why we're successful is that people know they can expect to get education to support them in the work they're doing at branch level, at brigade level and generally locally. So the education programme concentrates on skills and confidence and knowledge, but also we think it's important to have a wider approach because people need an understanding of the world in which the trade union and labour movement exists, if for no other reason than that they need some understanding when they propose alternatives and promote change. So we have a sort of parallel path. We concentrate on the grassroots skills education, training if you like, but we've also got a strand of political education. We mix them because, actually, politics is interesting and it's not much use if you don't understand campaigning. So it's bringing theory and practice together.

The introductory branch official's pathway is known as 'a ticket to ride'. It allows reps access to five three-day accredited introductory courses, firstly handling members' problems, with secondly a follow-on around disciplinary casework and representation. The third course introduces fairness at work and tackling bullying and harassment, with a follow-on concerned with promoting union policy. Finally, there is an introduction to health and safety. At its centenary, the union was putting 450-500 reps through the programme annually. Reps can also take local TUC education programmes. Once reps complete their introduction, further courses are provided on bargaining skills, time management, equality and employment law, tackling mental health problems and understanding public sector finance in the fire and rescue service. Reps are required to take courses on pensions and medical appeals and on providing representation in these areas. The introduction to political engagement includes understanding political issues and how the union influences political decision-making. A further national course 'Getting organised – Building union membership in the UKFRS' is designed to help brigade organisers and regional treasurers understand the importance of building a stronger union, in recognition of the need for all officials to participate in recruiting and retaining members. All courses are residential but reps reported increasing difficulties in getting time off for training, because of staffing reductions, so they sometimes have to take courses in their own time. Chris Downes reported:

> A lot of our members can't get time off to go on our training courses. There are shrinking numbers on watches and on appliances. If we want somebody off a watch of six to go on a three-day course, we generally ask them if they can do it in their days off and most of the time, if they're interested in the education, they'll do it. But obviously that's a big ask for a lot of people when they've got family commitments. To become an FBU rep you've got to go into it with your eyes wide open because it's going to be a massive demand on your time – and willpower.

The FBU stages a week-long annual residential national school, described as 'the flagship course of the union', which covers contemporary industrial and political issues with national and international speakers. Forty to sixty members or officials, put forward by their regions, attend each national school, which actively promotes political debate and education on labour movement history, politics and economics. In 2015 the programme was rewritten to reflect the political and industrial consequences of the 2015 general election, the new Conservative government and changes in the leadership and direction of the Labour Party. Topics and presentations included the importance of a political voice; the Trade Union Bill and the struggle for trade union rights; and the secret state and trade unions – surveillance, blacklisting and provocation. External speakers included shadow fire minister Liz McInnes, John Hendy QC and blacklisting author and campaigner Dave Smith.[37] Annual schools are also held for the B&EMM, the Women's and the LGBT sections and courses are offered for the officers' and control sections. Reps acknowledged the value of the political education they received, as a former branch chair in Hampshire, Simon Green, reflected:

> Trade union education is massively important. The first weekend school I attended created me. I went down there looking for answers but I didn't know what I was doing. It's like a real eye-opener. We'd always have political speakers. I remember that first weekend school, Dennis Skinner came. I'd never met a working-class MP; didn't really know they existed, to be fair. You know, he spoke about class, about equality, about fighting the oppressors as a class, those kind of things. FBU national school is legendary. It's like a socialist boot camp, just unbelievable. We'd buy books because there'd always be a bookshop at national school. So this was like a branch policy. It was unofficial, I don't know if anyone else did it, but in our branch we had a flipping library of political books. So guys watching football or TV in the mess room, they had books to read. So the idea is hoping that one person would pick out a book.

Trevor French, South West regional secretary, concurred:

> I tell you, honestly, the union gave me everything: my politics, my understanding of society, the ability to give voice to my own and my colleagues' concerns. The role of trade union education in FBU has been fundamental to protecting our members. It really has. I remember Wortley Hall and Tony Benn was there.

Now, I've come out of the Marines and joined the fire service and got involved in the FBU. So there's Tony Benn. What's this about? I heard the guy talking and I was absolutely transfixed. So it opened my eyes up. There's a different part of life here and it was fantastic. When I got further involved, I did different schools on equality and it made me understand a different political route. So yes, I owe not just my trade union career to the FBU and its education, I owe a big part of the person I am today to that as well.

Holly Ferguson also indicated how union education had politicised her:

Union education gave me confidence and knowledge because that's always what held me back before, so, like, I'm going to speak at this conference hopefully and that's the first time I'll have done it and I wouldn't have dreamed of doing that last year before I did this Employment Law Diploma. My parents are Lib Dems so I've been brought up that way. I didn't even know what Labour was or anything like that and now I love it, I love Jeremy Corbyn. I'm definitely more of a sharer now than I ever was, if you know what I mean?

This sense of politicisation was shared by Rod Barrett, a West Midland Brigade rep:

You know you're doing the basic branch reps course and then it just goes from there. Once you get involved, it's hard to kick it because you start seeing injustice and realising things that are happening. For me, it made me more aware politically actually. I took a lot more interest in politics. Look and understand things and question things basically.

With a different emphasis, FBU Union Learning, based at the National Learning Centre in Cramlington, northeast England, provides accredited courses delivered by distance learning to FBU members and their families. They include basic skills but also cover topics such as mental health and dyslexia awareness. In 2017, the National Learning Centre was placed on the Register of Apprenticeship Training Providers, which made it eligible to deliver accredited apprenticeship training. It began by providing fitness instructor apprenticeships for firefighters, initially tendering for 200 places with Leeds City College. These were quickly filled, and it subsequently expanded its provision to 500 places. Union Learning Fund project supporter Brian Hurst reported that the FBU aims to have a Union Learning Rep in every workplace and that several officials had started out as Union Learning Reps, which gave them the confidence to take on officer roles.

Conclusion

The resilience of the FBU in the 25 years leading up to its centenary relates to a wider debate over the relative importance of agency – the role of activists and officers – and structure – the broader economic, political and legal context in which unions operate. This context has been shaped by government attempts to restrict union power and attacks on collective bargaining, alongside changes in work organisation, particularly increasing management control, and expanding job demands and intensification. One consequence is the limited time and resources that workplace reps and members can commit to the union. Some commentators have suggested that unions have been ill equipped to deal with structural change because of the more difficult objective circumstances generated by neoliberalism.[38] While the innumerable hurdles facing unions cannot be ignored, the history of the FBU in the late 20th and early 21st century suggests that this view downplays the importance of the role that activists play in defending their union and their members' conditions. The crucial contribution of FBU activists is fully demonstrated in Chapter 3.

Demonstration during the Derbyshire dispute, 1996

Rally during the Merseyside dispute,1995-96

3

Pandora's box: Ken Cameron, the pay formula and the end of industrial quiescence

During a period when many unions came into bitter conflict with the government, the FBU managed to avoid national industrial action. Perhaps the most significant aspect of fire service industrial relations under Ken's leadership of the union was the maintenance of the pay formula throughout the Thatcher and Major governments. The formula was agreed in the aftermath of the 1977 strike, and the last pay formula calculation was in 2001, a year after Ken's retirement. Its survival for more than two decades was a remarkable achievement.

Matt Wrack, 'Farewell, Ken Cameron', *Firefighter*, June/July 2016

The 1977-78 firefighters' strike and its outcome, the fire service pay formula (the 'upper quartile pay formula') shaped the subsequent history of the Fire Brigades Union, and this distinctive legacy runs through the testimonies of firefighters. Particularly notable is the association of Ken Cameron with the relative industrial peace secured by the pay formula, which is captured in Wrack's tribute. Equally, there is much reflection on Cameron's insistence that to abandon the pay formula would open up a 'Pandora's box', with potentially unwelcome consequences for firefighters' terms and conditions. The durability of the pay formula was certainly debated, but by the end of the century the employers had made clear their desire for greater flexibility at local level and for modifications to the national bargaining framework and the Grey Book. In response, the FBU launched its 'Smash and Grab' campaign, and the last years of the 20th century are marked by local actions to defend national terms and conditions, alongside a myriad of fights against local authority cuts to the service and to jobs, most notably in Merseyside, Derbyshire and Essex.

The legacy of the 1977-78 national strike and pay formula

The FBU demands in the 1977-78 strike included a formula to bring firefighters' wages into line with average male earnings plus 10 per cent. The pay formula agreed in the settlement linked the earnings of a qualified firefighter to those of the upper quartile (the top 25 per cent) of male manual earnings and, thus, skilled workers. This link to the wider labour market ensured higher increases over the next 10 years than those that might have been negotiated, as evidenced by pay settlements over the period. This trend would have continued had it not been for the much faster growth of non-manual and female earnings.[1] Not only did the national strike deliver on pay and hours, leading to a reduction in the working week from 48 to 42 hours, it also reinforced national collective bargaining, and entrenched the Grey Book and a standardised duty system across the entire country. Former chair of the Scottish region Ronnie Robertson emphasised how the 1977-78 strike prepared the ground for Ken Cameron and Ronnie Scott's leadership:

> The 1977 strike gave us one of the best wage deals that we had ever got. In the fire service pay formula, the agreement gave us a platform to fight for the 42-hour week. The 77-78 strike gave us – shortly after – Kenny Cameron as general secretary, one of the best left-wing general secretaries. It was good because we also had Ronnie Scott as the president and they gave us backing within limits, they gave us our head. That dispute gave us the confidence and the platform through the pay formula and through the militancy and the activism established during that dispute to get involved in battles. Particularly in Strathclyde, when I became the Scottish regional chair, our main function was to see that Cameron's back was protected on the EC [Executive Council] because he was under a lot of attack from the right wing. But it was quid pro quo; it wasn't a 'We'll guard your back, Kenny, regardless'. It gave us the opportunity to fight a lot of other battles and lose a lot of battles as well. We lost a lot of them.

Former FBU president Alan McLean, who in 1977 was newly active in Tyne and Wear, conveys the gradual realisation within the union of how important the pay formula was in securing industrial peace:

> Well, firstly, I didn't see it as a victory. We voted not to accept the offer on the pay formula. Young angry men sometimes take some calming down and don't react in the way that they should. Within a year or two I realised that it was actually a fantastic deal. I realised that it might well have the ability to keep political peace in a service that, even though we'd been on strike, wasn't really conditioned to go on strike. It was a massive thing for those people to go on strike.

Keith Handscomb, former Eastern region Executive Council member, similarly refers to the status that the pay formula achieved:

> We'd had a pay formula that kept peace and of course the old guard who knew that, had been around then, or shortly after, and the watches that were created, were very, very protective of their pay formula, because that's what they'd achieved out of the '77 strike. Those of us who were younger were basically taught that it was sacrosanct. I don't suppose we even knew what it was because we just got a pay rise every year. There were those who said it wasn't worth the price, but I think they used to say that as a way of telling us, the younger ones, how much we ought to be respectful of them for having gone through that, because we were getting the benefits. I'm not sure they always really meant it, but they certainly treasured the pay formula and also the shift system – the 2-2-3 shift system came out of it. The 2-2-3 shift system, based upon 48 hours over an eight-day cycle, was to endure into the 21st century (Chapter 5).

The sanctity of the pay formula was consistently restated by Cameron, evoking an enduring image in the mind of activists, including Wrack: 'If you touch pay, you'll open a Pandora's box and you don't know what will come with it.' This was the phrase he drummed into conference every single time the matter was raised. Chris McGlone, Scottish Executive Council member, reflected on Cameron's role:

> I think the pay formula was the single most significant thing that emerged from the strike of '77. I don't know if people would have realised at that point the significance of it or even if Ken Cameron would have. I'll give him the credit; I think he was a smart, intelligent man. I think he would have realised, 'there's the key to industrial stability for the next 20-25 years, for the next generation of firefighters'.

The long-term settlement of pay allowed the FBU to focus on other aspects of the firefighter's job, as former Scottish Executive Council member Roddy Robertson recalled:

> The industrial peace over that time allowed us to concentrate on the safety issues within the job, on the job side of the industry, and we had a huge influence in the service because we were able to focus within the job and we weren't having to concentrate every year on negotiating for pay. And although the employers came back every year and tried to put forward conditions, it was an agreed pay formula and it wasn't subject to conditions. So they found it frustrating and we could see that and understand their point of view, but the trade-off that we put back to them obviously was industrial peace – you're not going to get an industrial dispute over pay so surely that's a good thing.

Alan Campbell, a brigade official in Glasgow during the 1977-78 strike, agreed that the pay formula allowed space for a wider union agenda, including equality:

> We would discuss other things besides pay. Health and safety was coming in, a bit to do with uniforms, with shift patterns, all the things that help to run a fire service. We could go into these areas of negotiation. The pay formula, we just waited to see what it threw up and we accepted it. So there was never any kind of conflict. You just applied the pay formula and that was it. And getting near the end of the 1990s, there were things

like equality sections within the fire service, a black and ethnic minority section, a gay and lesbian section.

Defence of the service

In 1981 the FBU annual conference unanimously supported a policy that conference would be recalled in the event of any wholetime firefighter being made redundant, with a recommendation for national strike action. In his foreword to Victor Bailey's *Forged in Fire*, Ken Cameron reported that 'this policy in conjunction with national and local lobbies and marches, has resulted, to-date, in all threats of physical redundancy being withdrawn.'[2] This outcome was in spite of a range of attacks by local authorities on the service in the 1980s. In November 1986, FBU members in Strathclyde took one-hour strike action over threatened job cuts, a strike backed up with a national rally in Glasgow. At the same time, Merseyside firefighters balloted for selective strike action after threats to 88 jobs. In September 1987, a national demonstration took place in Swansea to protest at West Glamorgan Fire Authority's dismissal of 360 FBU members after an 83 per cent vote on a 98 per cent turn-out in favour of one-hour strikes against proposals to reorganise the Brigade with the loss of 40 wholetime and 12 part-time jobs. Spontaneous emergency-calls-only action in several parts of the country supported the West Glamorgan brigade. Former Wales executive council member Mike Smith recalled:

> The dispute came about as a result of a fire cover review carried out by the West Glamorgan Fire Authority, the result of which was a proposal to close one fire station with the loss of 40 jobs. We balloted the members, who voted by a large majority for strike action. Following the announcement of the ballot result, the fire authority issued dismissal notices 'with immediate effect' to every member of the FBU. They were instructed by the fire authority not to attend their workplace and told that they had been instantly dismissed, and the Army was brought in to provide fire cover from suitable surrounding premises and not from the fire stations, because we instructed our members to ignore the dismissal letters and report for duty as normal. All the local officials, including the then EC member Peter Lloyd, had been sacked and the fire authority refused to

meet the sacked officials. I, along with the general secretary Ken Cameron, then spent the next 72 hours negotiating with the fire authority for their re-instatement and the withdrawal of the dismissal notices. The NJC [National Joint Council] got involved and, nationally, there were calls going out for national strike action in support of the West Glamorgan membership. In the end we managed to have everyone re-instated and the full extent of the fire authority's proposals were not implemented. It was a challenging time but we came out of the dispute richer and more informed than when we went in to it. I had only been regional secretary for four months. It was a baptism of fire and probably coloured my opinion of fire authorities for the next 24 years – the rest of my career.

The authority abandoned its proposals after talks involving Acas.[3] The 1988 annual conference condemned West Glamorgan and other Labour-controlled fire authorities that had taken action against the interests of the FBU and its membership.[4]

The first threat to the pay formula came in 1992, when the Conservative government imposed a 1.5 per cent pay freeze across the public sector. For the first time since 1977 the FBU had to mount a national campaign over pay, including a strike ballot. National officer John McGhee recalled the campaign:

During the Tory pay freeze I remember we were trying to defend the pay formula. They were looking to cut, give us less than what was in the pay formula and in fact we ended up fighting to get less – the pay formula gave less than the government pay freeze! The government pay freeze was 1.5 per cent and the pay formula gave us 1.4 per cent and we were fighting to get 1.4 per cent because we wanted the pay formula! I can remember standing outside, I think it was Belgrave Terrace, where they had an NJC meeting and thousands of firefighters were chanting 'You can stick your 1.5 per cent... '. We wanted the pay formula, we didn't know what the pay formula was going to give and Ken Cameron came out on the balcony pumping his fist, saying 'We've got the pay formula', and there was a huge cheer. And on the way home on the train we found out the pay formula had given us 1.4 per cent. It was like, 'Did we win?!'

Potential strike action was thus forestalled when the pay formula produced a 1.4 per cent increase that did not break the government's cap. In the same year a committee was established by the employers to review the Grey Book.[5]

Warning shots were fired and in 1995 the Audit Commission published *In the Line of Fire: Value for money in the fire service – the national picture*. This report recalled that there had been six major reviews of the fire service since 1970, which had made common key recommendations that had not been implemented. These included an examination of conditions of service, a switch of emphasis to fire prevention, better use of duty time and a review of standards of fire cover. The report stated that individual brigades were constrained from responding adequately to the pressures they faced by the national framework within which they operated and had little scope to depart from the nationally specified approach to assessing fire risk and the standards for responding to fires. Response standards were based on historical precedent rather than empirical evidence. The Audit Commission report predicted increased financial pressures, in particular the 'pensions time bomb' and foresaw that higher contributions would be required from the employers. National terms and conditions of service were also seen to limit brigades' flexibility. *In the Line of Fire* advocated modernising the national framework and increasing local discretion. It specifically recommended giving fire authorities statutory responsibility to promote fire safety, modify risk categories and attendance standards, simplify the rank structure and introduce greater flexibility into shift systems. The report identified 'perverse incentives' discouraging brigades from promoting fire safety, and said these should be removed. In total, it estimated that £67m could be saved at local level through efficiency improvements including effective absence management, reductions in early retirement, extension of the use of non-uniformed staff and maximisation of duty time within the shift system. The Audit Commission concluded that it would not be possible to implement the necessary changes in the national framework unless current terms and conditions of service were modified. Responding to the report, the Central Fire Brigades Advisory Council (CFBAC) established the Joint Committee on the Audit Commission Report, with FBU representation, to review the risk assessment process. It published *Out of the Line of Fire* in 1998, which proposed a response planning process based upon a 'worst case planning scenario'.[6]

In the same year as the Audit Commission report, Cameron warned that employers locally and nationally were intending to turn the clock back with regard to hard-won conditions of service. The employers had given the union 'a shopping list' they were seeking of alterations to conditions of service as part of a fundamental review of the Grey Book, including significant changes to sick leave and duty systems. The FBU agreed to a joint working party to consider the proposals. In September 1997, the NJC agreed changes to a number of conditions of service. The FBU conceded that these would have a detrimental effect on sickness provision but thought they were better than those that might have been imposed in the light of provision for local authority staff and the police, where there was no right to 12 months' sick pay. Under the agreement there would be no graded entitlement based on service, and the entitlement to 12 months on full pay would remain only for illness or injury arising out of duty. The agreement secured commitments on equal opportunities, including the promotion of positive action, with new arrangements on parental leave, career break schemes and childcare costs associated with attendance at residential training courses. Any change to duty systems would await the conclusion of the CFBAC Joint Committee on the Audit Commission Report. Barry Downey, West Midlands Executive Council member, reflected on the outcome:

> I think we lost a full 12 months' sick, pay didn't we? It went down to six months. But in exchange we managed to get in a whole raft of equality paragraphs and health and safety [provision] into the Grey Book that weren't there before. People argued we should never have given away the 12 months, but when your employers as a national group are looking to dismantle your national terms and conditions completely, I think we did pretty well at that point. Without having to actually take any action, ballot the members or anything like that.

Merseyside

The Audit Commission Report emboldened chief fire officers (CFOs) and fire authorities in the context of government reductions in local authority expenditure. Between 1995 and 1998 the FBU were forced into a series of ballots opposing cuts or threats to terms and conditions, and firefighters took strike action in Merseyside, Derbyshire and Essex. The first strike was instigated by Merseyside Fire Authority's attempt to undermine Grey Book national terms and conditions. In August 1995 the authority backed the CFO's proposed £700,000 budget cuts, to be achieved by cutting 20 jobs through natural wastage and reducing annual leave by three days. The FBU responded with a ballot, which produced an 81 per cent vote in favour of selective strike action. This action consisted of nine hours, with the first coinciding with a march and demonstration. For North West Executive Council member Les Skarratts, the strike took place against a background of conflict in Merseyside:

> I joined in an era of industrial unrest in the '80s and we were almost perpetually in dispute of one sort or another, usually what we called 'work to rules', which was removal of goodwill. So I suffered very early on in terms of industrial unrest. Our first strike in Merseyside, since I joined, was in the '90s – '95-'96 regarding annual leave – and that was a very long, very bitter industrial action, in which actually I ended up as the official that took the dispute to arbitration at Acas. It consisted of a lot of strike action over short periods. It was a dispute over annual leave so it was an important issue taking frequent but short periods.

Ten separate nine-hour strikes were held between August and October, with the authority stopping 24 hours' pay for each, followed by a second ballot, in which members voted by 90 per cent to escalate action to 24 hours. The dispute lasted over nine months, to May 1996, and comprised twenty-one 24-hour strikes, involving almost all permanent station commanders and officers below the CFO rank. The fire authority responded by bringing in the Army to run fire appliances on strike days, funded by central government. More than 300 soldiers from the Royal Regiment of Fusiliers were deployed at 10 centres in Merseyside, operating 24 Green Goddess fire engines. Over Christmas 1995 the authority issued members with 90-day notice, warning that if they did not accept new contracts of employment before New Year's Day they would be deemed to have dismissed themselves. FBU members returned these notices to the CFO unopened. The fire authority then unilaterally imposed the new working patterns.[7]

The dispute was settled following Acas talks in April 1996 with a provisional agreement involving the restoration of two of the three days' leave and a joint union-management working party chaired by Acas to review staffing levels. The FBU ballot on the offer delivered 68 per cent in favour. The settlement forced the authority to breach the spending cap and secured an extra £2.1m for the service, lifting the recruitment freeze.

At a national level it was clear that 'if Merseyside falls we all fall',[8] opening the way for locally determined terms and conditions. The dispute was marked by two large national FBU solidarity demonstrations in Liverpool. Delegates from Merseyside were sent across the country to appeal for financial assistance, resulting in enormous levels of support. While the deal fell short of FBU demands, it underlined the resilience of workplace union organisation.[9]

Derbyshire

Just as one local dispute was being settled, another emerged. This time it was in Derbyshire, which had a brigade that, unlike Merseyside, was not historically regarded as militant, although in 1991 branches had threatened strike action in the face of proposed redundancies, forcing the authority to back down. Since 1990 the fire authority had lost £6 million from its budget and a further £1.3-million reduction was proposed for 1996-97 through a package of 14 cuts, including: the removal of a turntable ladder from Derby; the downgrading of a day-crewing station to retained status; the removal of eight officers crewing fire appliances and four retained pumps; the conversion of four flexi-duty officer posts to day duty; the conversion of uniformed posts to non-uniformed; cuts to training and fire station budgets; a review of establishment levels in control; and changes in national conditions on dental charges and subsistence. In May 1996 Derbyshire members delivered a 75 per cent vote for nine-hour strikes on a 84-per-cent turnout. The dispute was characterised by the Labour council's willingness to use anti-union legislation to try to break the strike action, on the basis that it had changed its proposals for cuts prior to the ballot, a move defeated by the FBU in the High Court. The first nine-hour strike took place on 10 June followed by 11 nine-hour strikes, with a different watch called out each week on a four-week rota, so that most members took strike action once a month over five months. Marc Redford, branch official at the time and later regional chair, recalled:

> Derbyshire held a brigade-wide strike in 1996 based on cuts. So they got a list of 10 cuts and we took to the streets and we campaigned. We had more public support than ever because we weren't going there begging for money. We were going there as public servants highlighting the fact that the service that protected their communities was being cut. And this was before the days of having massive government-imposed spending assessments; this was about us actually seeking to protect the service. All the brigade was out because the brigade members felt so strongly about the cuts we were facing, and in today's money they were the smallest cuts. This was a brigade-wide strike, not just for one day, but for a number of days over a long time.

Several local rallies and marches were followed by a national rally of 3,000 in July to coincide with the fifth nine-hour strike. Facing employer intransigence, in August the FBU authorised a ballot for a series of two-hour strikes. The county council then determined that if union members took industrial action for part of a normal shift their pay would be stopped for the whole shift, effectively locking them out. FBU members remained united. Industrial action ended on 27 September, when a revised employer proposal was accepted by two to one, although a third of members wanted to continue action to protect the remaining jobs and appliances. Strike action had made significant inroads into the employer's original cuts package.[10]

Essex

For former Essex brigade secretary Keith Handscomb, 'Merseyside members found the confidence to break the mould and gave a lead to members in Essex and Derbyshire.'[11] He described how some of the most vigorous campaigners in the Essex dispute of 1996-97 had been amongst the two busloads from Essex who joined the march in Liverpool on the first day of the Merseyside strike. In fact, in December 1995, Essex took unofficial action in support of Merseyside, answering emergency calls only, in the face of employer threats to deduct pay. He recalled that Essex FBU drew on the Merseyside and Derbyshire disputes when considering the tactics for running their dispute and campaigning.

Simultaneously with Derbyshire, in February 1996 Essex County Council announced £1.3-million cuts to the fire and rescue service, to be achieved by running under-establishment plus an £80,000 reduction affecting four local conditions of service and the top-slicing of support budgets. The FBU immediately consulted on strike action, with a mass meeting mandating branch officials to reject proposals and to ballot for industrial action. The ballot delivered a 69 per cent vote in favour of nine-hour strikes on an 82 per cent turnout, with Essex and Derbyshire announcing a joint strike day on 10 June. At the end of May the employers made a second compromise offer, which was accepted by the brigade committee three days before the joint strike day. Whilst cuts were still on the table, Handscomb considered that the employer had been given a 'bloody nose', but that 'the rematch will be soon and the fight is far from over'.[12]

Handscomb's statement was prescient. In 1997 the County Council announced a £1.54-million cut in the fire brigade budget for 1997-98, with a cut in wholetime posts from 928 to 876 over the period, alongside cuts in the training budget and operational equipment. In response, 58 per cent voted in favour of strike action on a turn-out of over 80 per cent. Crucially, the ballot result came weeks before the 1997 General Election, placing the dispute directly in the political spotlight. A 24-hour strike on 19 April and a four-hour walkout on 21 April were to be followed by seven strikes before 1 May, the date of the election. The week before the first strike Cameron attended talks, at which he secured a deal and, under intense pressure from the Labour Party and TUC, who were on the verge of a Labour victory after 18 years of Conservative rule, he proposed suspension of the strike. However, the deal was rejected by the brigade committee, as Handscomb reports:

It was before the election. And that night, bearing in mind

58.2 per cent had voted 'yes' so about 500 people had voted 'yes' to take 1,100 of us out on strike, because a lot of people didn't vote, the brigade committee said, 'Shove it up your arse, Ken. We're on strike tomorrow at 10 o'clock. That's it, go back to the station.' So Ken got phone calls from Bill Morris then John Monks,[13] and they said, 'You're the general secretary. The laws are it's your strike. You call it. Tell them they're not having strikes until after the election', and Ken said, 'What kind of union do you think I run? They've voted. That's democracy.' I can't think of anyone else who would have done that – support the vote of a few hundred members in the face of huge pressures around the general election. His principles that night, I think, were remarkable.

The union selected those watches where union organisation was strongest to strike first. Alan Chinn-Shaw, then an Essex brigade rep, recalled the first day of the seven strikes:

I think there was a greater sense of unity then than I'd ever felt – even in the build-up and ballot and the information going out – and I was visiting watches and stations in my area, campaigning. But on that day, when it was time to walk out, it just felt [special] – because you've never been on strike before, you don't know what you do, you don't know how you're going to feel, what's going to happen. You've convinced all your comrades, all your friends, all your firefighters around, who are going to walk but... So we just lined up in the bays, the bay doors opened and out we went, and I think that sense of unity was as strong then as I've ever felt. So that was my first experience of strike action and you didn't really believe it was going to happen until you walked out of the door.

The union accelerated the frequency and duration of action and, drawing on advice from Merseyside and Derbyshire comrades, ensured that they actively picketed fire stations for a highly 'visible strike'. The dispute was settled when the County Council agreed to maintain a wholetime establishment of 928, with a recruitment process to begin imminently, and to ensure the existing number of fire stations and appliances remained. There was agreement to increase the training budget, with particular emphasis on retained and wholetime frontline personnel. No budgetary savings would affect the allowances and conditions of employment of uniformed staff, who were able to buy back pension entitlements lost due to participation in action. The settlement was accepted by 94 per cent in a ballot and described as 'a comprehensive victory'.

The effective action did not put the County Council off for long. In January 1998 a budget cut of £1.238 million was proposed, involving cuts to 20 jobs by altering the ridership factor,[14] moving two foam vehicles to retained stations and axing one aerial appliance. Overall, the Council proposed to cut 36 posts. Once again the FBU balloted for strike action and secured a 70 per cent vote in favour. Despite the union calling short duration strikes, the employer locked out strikers without pay for whole days in an attempt to force them back to work. There were 37 periods of discontinuous strike action taken overall, ranging from 2 to 24 hours, with members losing an average of 42 hours' pay per month.

Again Cameron proved himself to his members, when the Council threatened in writing to sack all 1,100 striking firefighters and control staff. Keith Handscomb wrote:[15]

Ken joined FBU members from around the country who had come to march around Chelmsford town centre in support of their Essex brothers and sisters. After he had spoken to the rally and the crowd was dispersing, Ken was confronted by a BBC TV news team about to broadcast live on the lunchtime news. The interviewer asked, 'Mr Cameron, the Essex fire authority say that unless you call this strike off, they will have no choice other than to sack your members, so what are you going to do now?' Ken replied, 'Well, I sincerely hope they won't do that or they will find themselves responsible for provoking only the second national strike in the history of the UK fire service.' Interviewer: 'But surely, Mr Cameron, that would be illegal?' Ken paused: 'So be it!'

As in 1997, fire stations, towers, forecourts and picket lines were festooned with banners. In one case the fire station hedge was clipped to convey the message and public-awareness car washes became regular strike-day events to build support and raise hardship funds. At the V98 concert in Chelmsford, bands Chumbawumba and All Saints both sported the Essex firefighters' 'Adinuff' T-shirts (with the Adidas three-stripe logo and FBU initials, inspired by the Merseyside dockers' 'Calvin Klein' T-shirts).[16] This was topped by West Ham striker Ian Wright's show of support after he scored during a match against Wimbledon, as former regional secretary Graham Noakes remembered:

> As part of our campaign, we had some T-shirts made where we mimicked the Adidas brand and adapted the logo to say 'Adinuff' and we got a local firm that a friend of a friend knew, they produced them for us – somebody always knows somebody – and being quite close to London, a lot of West Ham supporters were Essex firefighters. And somebody said, 'We're going to get Ian Wright to wear one of these', because they knew that he was quite supportive, and they gave Ian some shirts and as promised, he wore it on a match day. He scored a goal, pulled up his West Ham shirt and underneath he had his Adinuff T-shirt on and he did a lap of honour around the stadium. It was instant news across the TV on the night and the mainstream media.

Another initiative involved a member of the fire authority:

> We went to a negotiating meeting, and he was really spiky across the table. Not just the usual disputes way, bit strange, and he made some comment about a lawn and grass, and I thought, 'What the hell's he on about?' Turns out that he loved his front lawn and the year before somebody had put down nitrogen so the grass kept growing through thick and dark revealing 'NO CUTS' no matter how often he mowed it!

The dispute came to a head when the union called three two-hour strike periods straddling shift changeovers, challenging the Council to choose between locking firefighters out for 72 consecutive hours and backing down on their lock-out strategy. Stretching 'scab' cover over three whole days without a break was hugely problematic. Then, as the three-day lock-out loomed, the union announced two sets of seven two-hour strikes, raising the stakes and the stark prospect of two sets of seven-day lock-outs. The new tactic triggered hastily brokered talks.

The outcome was described by participants as 'the biggest victory ever'. All proposed cuts to jobs and appliances were reversed and recruitment programmes ensured the highest number of wholetime firefighters ever employed in Essex. Also agreed were extra training courses, with priority for retained and junior officers, and parity of operational equipment and uniforms for retained firefighters. Union negotiators reported that they had secured more in the settlement than they had asked for in the initial trade dispute and they were running out of concessions to ask for; the agreement eventually included progression of the retained staff pension scheme and the provision of crèche facilities in fire stations.

Campaigning in the community

These important strikes in Merseyside, Derbyshire and Essex were accompanied by a growing number of local battles over reductions to budgets. For example, 1995 saw anti-cuts campaigns in Devon, Gloucestershire and Tyne and Wear. Trevor French, subsequently regional secretary in the South West, recalled a lobby of Surrey Fire and Rescue service that aimed to prevent the downgrading of Haslemere and Walton fire stations to day-crewing only:

> That was a campaign, and looking back we used to run the fire brigade really. When I say we, the union did. It was a good campaign and we won it. So that is the reason I got involved – being part of that campaign and having a little victory. We had a mass lobby in Kingston and it was mobbed really. Basically, we were told we were going there. It was just my first experience of the power of people lobbying over firefighting and there must have been nigh on 700, 800 people. It was literally everyone. It was the thing, you had to go. It was just part of what you did as a firefighter.

Tam McFarlane, subsequently South West Executive Council member, described a local campaign against the loss of cooks at fire stations:

We had two cooks at Taunton. And you think about that fire station – 14 firefighters working long shifts – we needed someone there to cook meals because if the firefighters started doing it the alarms and the bells would go off [and interrupt them], and the cooks were such a big part of our fire service family. Somerset County Council decided to make cut-backs and it was seen as an easy option to remove the cooks. We arranged to meet at the station one morning because we were going to march to County Hall and make representations for the two cooks. I remember going to the station. I could not believe it – all the watches had turned out, all the retained crews had turned out. Crews had come over from neighbouring towns like Bridgewater and Yeovil and we got the union banner. The cooks were with us, God bless them, out onto the roads and we marched from Taunton fire station to County Hall. There were so many of us that the traffic stopped. And when we got to County Hall, they said, 'What's going on, all the firefighters here? What's happening?' So we said, 'They're cutting the cooks' and they were like, 'What? No, we're not having that.' There were so many of us they didn't have room to accommodate us at the Council meeting, so half of us were waiting outside. The brigade secretary made a speech in support of the cooks and you could hear the wave of applause from the firefighters rallying and they backed down. And that was an important part of trade unionism for me.

Suffolk Fire Service proposed a £430,000 cut in the 1995-96 budget, including the loss of 12 retained firefighters and eight wholetime posts. A mass meeting of the retained membership supported a ballot for action and the campaign saw 'a magnificent demonstration' outside Suffolk County Hall, preceded by FBU members taking 999 calls only. Given this total commitment to strike action, the Council found the money to reverse the retained redundancies, described as 'a significant and tremendous victory for the whole of the FBU'.[17] FBU retained membership increased from 190 to nearly 250, boosted by defections from the Retained Firefighters Union (Chapter 2).

In Greater Manchester a ballot for industrial action over job losses and the removal of three appliances was lost in August

1997. However, in Nottinghamshire, the FBU called a strike ballot against a 1.5 per cent reduction to the 1997-98 budget, which involved the potential loss of posts, special appliances and frontline pumps, and the running down of the establishment. The authority then relented on frontline pumps and retained ridership levels. While *Firefighter* maintained that most members would not class Nottinghamshire as a particularly militant brigade, in 1998 it asked if the union was 'in the throes of a Southern Revolution?'[18] It pointed to a strike ballot in Surrey in 1996 that forced the County Council to withdraw job cuts, while Kent was on the point of calling a ballot in 1997, with a 1,000-member protest outside County Hall against threats to remove a day-crew station. A further strike ballot in Surrey in 1998 aimed to stop the closure of two retained stations, which would have entailed 24 job losses, the removal of three wholetime pumps and a downgrading from wholetime to day crewing, with 70 full-time job losses and the introduction of wholetime retained firefighters. In the event the Council relented on one wholetime pump and the downgrading of crewing, saving 42 jobs.

Resisting local flexibility: 'Smash and Grab'

In 1998, during these local battles against service cuts, the employers wrote to Cameron, as the employee-side secretary of the NJC, indicating their desire for a more flexible framework agreement at national level.[19] In response, the FBU launched its 'Smash and Grab' national campaign to defend the Grey Book. The CFBAC had commissioned the Fire Cover Review Task Group to examine the practical issues that would have to be addressed if risk-based fire cover were introduced, as recommended by *In the Line of Fire* in 1995. The first meeting was June 1998, but the group would not publish its report (known as the Pathfinder Report because of the Pathfinder trials that took place over three years in 11 brigades) until December 2002 during the pay dispute (see Chapter 1).

The employers put their 10-point plan to the NJC meeting of 14 March 1999. Their main proposals were for local flexibility; the deletion of extra statutory annual leave, the loss of NHS reimbursement charges, the introduction of capability procedures and incremental progression dependent on acceptable performance and good conduct. The May 1999 annual conference rejected the employers' proposals. The employers were informed the FBU would commence a ballot for strike action if they attempted to impose changes to the Grey Book. The 'Smash and Grab' campaign intensified. Thousands of firefighters demonstrated their support for the union by lobbying the NJC meeting of 15 June 1999. Members wrote to politicians, visited MP's surgeries and lobbied fire board meetings to argue for retaining their conditions of service.[20] The employers then invoked the provision for unilateral arbitration where there was a failure to agree and referred their proposals to Acas.[21] They withdrew from the NJC, arguing that the FBU would not agree to their request for discussions.[22] In November 1999 the government announced an inquiry into the procedures determining the terms and conditions of service (other than pay) and working practices of firefighters with reference to procedures for the resolution of disputes, to be headed by Professor Frank Burchill. During the inquiry it was agreed that attempts to modify national terms and conditions and any industrial action would be suspended.

Burchill saw the inquiry as a way for the parties, including the government, to reconstitute the NJC without loss of face or threat of industrial action. He stated, 'The exercise was predominantly one of mediation – the key substantive changes and modernisation issues were on hold.'[23] For the FBU, the Burchill report, published in 2000, vindicated the 'Smash and Grab' campaign,[24] because it contained no unilateral changes to conditions of service, confirmed the status quo with regard to pay, annual leave and duty systems and ensured the union retained its right to strike over any trade dispute. Burchill reasserted national collective bargaining and joint regulation. However, the thrust of the report was to propose a means to promote peace by offering a way forward when differences occurred, enshrining conciliation by Acas and an acceptance that the decisions of the NJC disputes panel were binding. A key aspect was the appointment of an agreed independent chair to moderate the adversarial climate that characterised meetings.[25] Although the report recommended negotiations take place through sub-committees rather than the full NJC, Burchill subsequently reported that neither party supported this suggestion. A procedure for resolving local disputes with recourse to Acas, was, however, accepted. In the light of the report, a smaller joint standing sub-committee considered the replacement of the rank structure with new role descriptions assimilated into the NJC pay structure and an Integrated Personal Development System. Other issues discussed included retirement, sick pay entitlement, annual leave and family-friendly policies. The disputes procedure was amended and reviews into rank structures, pensions and the amalgamation of control centres were ongoing. The Burchill report was accepted by the employers and the FBU Executive Council and was endorsed at the FBU annual conference.

The new disputes process was soon tested, firstly in Northern Ireland and then in London and Merseyside. In Northern Ireland, in November 1998, the CFO proposed new employment contracts less favourable than those for existing firefighters and reductions in leave. The issues remained unresolved until September 1999, when the authority recommended the removal of the Northern Ireland allowance. The Northern Ireland situation coincided with disputes in Greater Manchester, London and West Yorkshire over employer attempts to impose job losses and inferior contracts. In West Yorkshire, the employers intended to remove five days of annual leave. In Manchester, brigade restructuring would have meant the loss of 21 jobs. In both cases successful strike ballots were held and the employers removed the proposals in the light of the impending Burchill Inquiry report. Contrary to expectations that the Northern Ireland authority would also shelve its proposals, it persisted with the implementation of less favourable contracts. An overwhelming yes vote for strike action forced the authority to back down, with an agreement that new recruits should be placed on the same contracts and conditions as other staff, backdated to the start date of their employment. The then regional secretary, Tony Maguire, described how the dispute strengthened the union in Northern Ireland:

The difficulty we had was involving retained firefighters, who were not directly affected by these changes. But we went on a very intensive campaign, going round and meeting these people individually and getting them on board. Anyway, they were balloted and I think returned something ridiculous like 97.5 per cent in favour of a strike. We knocked Merseyside off the number one position for the biggest ballot mandate! And we won – we didn't have to activate the ballot. I went to the meeting with the fire authority as it was at the time, expecting there to be blood on the walls. And the chair said, 'The authority has caved in.' That's how he opened the meeting and I had to do a double take – did he really say that or did I imagine it? Andy Gilchrist, who was the general secretary at the time, came over and addressed the meeting here and said, 'You know sometimes we're not good at recognising the victory', and he was right. So we were cockahoop about ourselves – we thought we could do no wrong. We ran a very well-oiled machine here and the chief and the fire authority had the greatest respect for us in terms of what we were capable of. So that put us on a good footing for the pay dispute because we were at the top of our game then, in my opinion.

A further defence of the Grey Book came in London in 2000, resulting in the case of the Homerton 11. Here union members refused to break the national overtime ban that had been in place since 1974 as a means of ensuring that working hours were reduced and staff shortages were dealt with by recruitment not overtime. As former FBU president Mick Shaw wrote in *Firefighter*, 'The London Fire and Civil Defence Authority spent most of 1999 attacking our national agreement and attempting to impose second-class contracts of employment. They decided to end the year by trying to break our overtime ban.'[26]

At Homerton fire station in Hackney, 11 FBU members were suspended for allegedly refusing to work with personnel who had agreed to work overtime on New Year's Eve and New Year's Day 2000 – during the millennium celebrations in London. In fact, the suspended members reported that they did not actually refuse to work with anybody, because nobody working overtime came to the station, and the FBU argued that the only time that the public was placed at risk was when the green watch was ordered by management not to attend a call as they were about to be suspended from duty. A large public campaign placed pressure on management, with a day of action for each watch involved and London FBU members wearing stickers on their uniforms. A march of over 1,000 firefighters from Hackney Marshes to Hackney

Empire, with delegations from brigades including Merseyside and Essex, ended in a rally that filled the Hackney Empire, addressed by the London Mayor, Ken Livingstone. One tactic used was the mass submission of form 10s, as Khaled Haider, group and branch secretary, described:

> We said, 'What happens if everyone writes a form 10 – form 10 is like a letter, a memorandum to your officer in charge – stating that if I was put in that situation myself I would do exactly what the Homerton 11 have done?' So *en masse*, we did a *pro forma*. Everyone, right across London. So we had thousands of letters coming in now and obviously getting filtered upwards, clogging the system, because they had to respond. It's like a very old antiquated way of working, but if you sent a form 10 they had to respond to it. So they've got these thousands of letters all saying the same thing, saying that they would do exactly the same. So if they can do something to the Homerton 11, they would have to do something to these thousands basically. If they sacked them, they've got to sack these guys. And they didn't know what to do, management, and they got the shock of their lives, didn't they? Then on the day of the hearings, there was a national demonstration and march in support. And that was great. We were in the hearing room and the window was open and we could hear the bagpipes and the drums and all that coming down the street.

The campaign forced the employer to lift the suspensions and at subsequent disciplinary hearings in March 2000, the majority of charges were not proven, all those suspended kept their jobs and the overtime ban remained intact until after the 2002-4 dispute. The action was widely accepted to have galvanised union organisation in London. Matt Wrack, alongside Andy Dark, played a central role in organising the campaign and defending victimised members. In terms of building branch and watch organisation, the dispute marked a key turning point in the level of activity and laid the foundations for how the national pay dispute of 2002-04 unfolded in London. For Joe McVeigh, former London region secretary and one of the Homerton 11:

The response was incredible; once you explained the facts and the guys could hear what had gone on, they were absolutely angry. And at that time in London our trade union activity was, I've got to say, woeful. The rest of the country looked at us as southern softies – I think that was probably the term they used, 'southern softies' – not really up for any fights, we're being walked all over by senior management. But on this particular thing, in London our members responded magnificently.

The key test of the Burchill Report came in Merseyside. Over the 2000-01 Christmas and New Year period FBU members were balloted for all-out strike action over control room staffing levels, acting-up payments, reduced attendances at automatic fire alarms and the use of postings as a disciplinary tool. The membership voted by 69 per cent in favour. A resolution to the dispute was achieved through meetings brokered by the joint secretaries of the NJC. At the time it was acknowledged that the resolution had been assisted through the installation in May 2001 of a local joint secretarial arrangement, as a result of the Burchill report. However, later in the year two associated disputes arose, in which the commitment of the authority to the new dispute resolution process was thrown into question. The Merseyside authority proposed, firstly, to employ Ministry of Defence firefighters in the Merseyside Fire Service, in contravention of equality measures, and to use a four-week assessment course rather than the nationally agreed method of training entry-level firefighters stipulated in the Appointment and Promotions regulations. Secondly, it announced an intention to employ non-uniformed personnel in officer posts, meaning they were not required to have operational experience, again outside the regulations.

The two disputes were registered and referred to the NJC disputes panel, which voted unanimously in favour of the union's position, with the employer and union sides voting together. However, the authority re-interpreted the decision of the disputes panel and pursued their plans, in defiance of the Burchill Report recommendations and in breach of national conditions of service. This triggered a call for a brigade-wide ballot for strike action from the officers' section. The authority attempted to thwart a legal ballot through a High Court injunction, claiming it had fulfilled the terms of the trade dispute settlement. A four-day hearing ended with the fire authority withdrawing, to avoid a damning and embarrassing judgement from the High Court judge; the injunction cost £70,000. Members voted by 83 per cent for discontinuous strike action beginning on 13 July 2001 to coincide with a national rally. After negotiations failed 100 per cent of the membership walked out, taking eight days' discontinuous strike, with a return to work for two and a half days, before embarking on a further eight-day strike. A third wave of strikes was to take the form of a return to work of one day, followed by eight days out. A special FBU Executive Council meeting was called to discuss national strike action, which pressurised the authority into making an offer, which was accepted, and included immediate compliance with the status quo as per national conditions of service. In *Firefighter* Andy Gilchrist argued that the entire basis of the national agreement reached after the 'Smash and Grab' campaign had hung in the balance because a local authority had flouted the authority of the NJC and the national agreement, with the national union again having to defend national bargaining.[27]

Just prior to the Merseyside dispute, Berkshire FBU secured a significant victory in a dispute over the fire authority's proposed reduction in the number of special appliances and their planned cuts to wholetime fire station establishment by 24 posts. A mass meeting in January 2001 gave a clear mandate to the brigade committee to ballot and in April an 82 per cent yes vote for strike action was secured on an 81-per-cent turn-out. In response, the authority offered a settlement, which was rejected, and the committee called a first day of action. A second offer was rejected on 26 April and a further three strike days were called. Within a day the authority made a revised offer, so the brigade committee suspended the first two strike days and consulted the membership, who confirmed acceptance. The authority conceded all demands, with a commitment to recruit to full establishment and to reintroduce local collective bargaining.[28]

The Merseyside dispute had raised concerns among control room staff, particularly in the context of a report released in 2001 called *The Future of Fire Control Rooms and Communications*, which placed intense pressure for control room mergers to provide shared 999 services. Cleveland fire control staff had refused to move from their previous location into the proposed Teeside emergency control room, where fire, police and ambulance control services would be shared. There had been no consultation or guarantee of job security. The Cleveland control branch voted overwhelmingly to ballot on industrial action; the fire authority subsequently withdrew its proposals.

Conclusion

The final decade of the century saw the fracturing of consensus on the joint regulation of the fire and rescue service, as a result of an employer offensive backed by government pursuit of public service reform. At the end of 2000 the Local Government Association Fire Executive agreed to pursue changes within the NJC that would entail modifications to terms and conditions, with the retention of a pay formula and shift system dependent upon modernisation and best value measures. The spate of local industrial action in response to the assault on jobs and local conditions had certainly strengthened union organisation in several brigades. However, by the end of the century the employer agenda had become clear and, in retrospect, a number of FBU activists reflected that an attack on the pay formula was inevitable. For assistant general secretary Andy Dark:

> In 2000 the chief officers with a section of the employers had an agenda which was modernising the fire and rescue service. So they were going to bring the fight to us. Three or four years before we'd fought off the 'Smash and Grab' attack on our pensions and the Grey Book terms and conditions, we fought that off. So the employers were coming and the chiefs were coming again and it certainly wasn't appreciated. I think it's one of those things where for 25 years we've had a pay formula which even in its latter years paid quite significant pay rises. But of course what wasn't known, understood, appreciated, never can be, is that the formula was going to get bashed up by the employers anyway.

It is highly questionable whether the dispute over the pay formula could have been avoided, as national officer Dave Green comments:

> Ken Cameron's basic view was, 'Don't open that can of worms,

because if you open that can of worms, you know, all sorts of things start coming to play'. He was right, but, by the same token, you couldn't have carried on like that ad infinitum. I think we pre-empted it and we probably accelerated everything that happened, but I suspected it was going to happen. Even through the 1990s and into 2001-02 there was conference resolutions about pay, asking us to do something about the pay formula and to open up negotiations. The problem we had was at that time there was a number of attacks on us from employers, there was a review of fire cover which could lead to a vast amount of job losses if it went ahead as we saw it. There was rank-to-role restructure, which meant a loss in numbers. So a number of attacks were seen by the union as coming together. The members had been angry about pay for a long time and it made sense at that time to basically say 'Well OK, if we're gonna do that, we understand everything will be up for negotiation and everything up for grabs.' So although the dispute was about pay, it was ultimately about, in my opinion, the relevance of the FBU and the influence of the FBU going forward. So an argument was put – rather than fight these individually, which would weaken us – that the strongest thing to do is to basically have the fight of all fights. So in order to have a trade dispute it was pay, but it was about influencing all these other things that were going on as well, it wasn't just about pay.

Across the union a perception had emerged that the pay formula had outlived its usefulness, particularly given the changed structure of the labour market, the reduction of skilled manual employment and thus the dilution of the pay comparator that historically had delivered significant pay increases. While the need for its replacement was not universally accepted, the increasingly dominant narrative was for a stronger settlement in an altered employment context. Further, with the inevitable assault on the Grey Book, should the union take pre-emptive action that might forestall the worst of the offensive and shape developments more favourably? While the inevitability of a second national dispute is debatable, what is certain is that the scene had been set for it.

FBU members walk out on strike, Birmingham, 2002

Picket line at Homerton fire station in the 2002 pay strike

4

Pandora's box opened: the pay and modernisation dispute 2002-04

The politics beat us in the end. Not the politics of the strike but the politics of the country, the bigger politics - we were never going to outflank them on the Iraq war.

Jim Barbour, Executive Council member for Northern Ireland

If the 1977-78 strike profoundly changed industrial relations in the fire service and the character of the FBU for a quarter of a century, then the 2002-04 dispute was no less transformative. Similarities between these dramatic episodes of industrial conflict are compelling, not least because they were the first two instances of national strike action in FBU history. Both were precipitated by grievances over pay, both were driven by claims for substantial increases, justified, in large part, on comparability grounds, and both gave rise to powerful campaigns and the impressive mobilisation of members in strike action,[1] though the difference between the all-out strike in 1977-78 and discontinuous action in 2002-04 is notable. A common aspect is that the strikes took place under, or more accurately *against*, Labour governments. Both witnessed the uncompromising hostility of a national government committed to pay and incomes policies and both saw the marshalling of state forces in extensive strike-breaking.

The broader political, economic and industrial relations' contexts of the respective conflicts contrasted sharply. The 2002-04 dispute followed almost 25 years of neoliberal economic and social policies set in motion by the Thatcher governments, which included an array of anti-union legislation designed to curb unions' ability to act democratically and to resist employer injustice. The firefighters' strike of 1977-78 occurred against a backdrop of generalised union strength, albeit that unions were, arguably, less powerful than a few years earlier, when the Tory Government was turfed out on the back of the 1974 miners' strike. Moreover, the firefighters were not alone in the late 1970s, as other groups of workers fought government pay policy. In contrast, in 2002-04, while the FBU had emerged from the previous decades of hostility relatively unscathed (Chapter 3), it entered the fray at a point when the trade union movement was generally weaker than in 1977-78.

Rather than signalling a rupture with Thatcherism, the New Labour government from 1997 with, arguably, some qualifications (e.g. the Employment Relations Act and the National Minimum Wage), accepted the nostrums of neoliberalism. Its re-election in 2001, immediately preceding the 2002-04 dispute, confirmed the emphasis on marketisation, privatisation and so-called modernisation of the public sector.

While evidently the FBU were up against 'big politics' in both strikes, the nature of political opposition had a qualitatively different dimension in 2002-04. If, to paraphrase Marx, the past weighs like a nightmare on the brains of the living,[2] this unfortunate legacy was most pronounced in the mentality of New Labour. The myth of the Winter of Discontent of 1979 – that it was union action rather than Labour's failure to deliver better pay for its working-class support base that paved the way for Thatcher – was deeply entrenched in its psyche. A Blair government would not deliver favours to unions and would strenuously resist union action that apparently threatened its political position. The 'demonstration effects' for the public sector of any potential victory for the FBU was a particular menace. Any dispute would inevitably have serious political consequences. Yet no political calculator could have foreseen the causal chain stretching from George Bush's militaristic imperialism, through Blair's unconditional support for illegal war in Iraq,[3] to strikes by firefighters, which would be viewed as challenging the British state. This constellation of political forces was ranged against the firefighters. Big politics indeed.

The first part of the chapter presents the detail of the claim and its justification, followed by an overview of the dispute. Care has been taken to present a factual account and to minimise the danger of misrepresentation through the wisdom of hindsight. This section provides the framework for evaluative sections based on FBU members' testimonies in the second part of the chapter. To achieve pure objectivity is impossible, given differences in work experiences, personal histories, political inclination, union position, degree of involvement and geographical location. It is in the nature of the testimonies of participants, who are not disinterested observers but engaged actors and activists, that a certain and welcome subjectivity will often prevail.

Formulation of the claim and chronology of the dispute

The 2002-04 dispute was a slow train coming. By the 1990s, firefighters' pay had emerged as an issue at the FBU conference. In 1994, the conference had committed the Executive Council to conducting a 'review into potential improvements to the fire service pay formula, with a view to negotiating improvements with the employers'.[4] However, it was a convergence of other political, organisational and professional drivers for change, and the determination of the national leadership that meant it was increasingly likely that a significant pay claim would be launched.

The Whitehall agenda for the fire service was committed to dismantling 'restrictive' national bargaining and removing 'inflexible' national standards in pursuit of even more efficiency savings, as set out in the 1995 Audit Commission report *In the Line of Fire*. Additionally the report laid the foundations for a radical change in the planning and provision of fire cover. It recommended a shift in emphasis from firefighting (response) to fire safety (prevention), more local flexibility in determining emergency response and more emphasis on saving lives (Chapter 3).

In 1997, the New Labour government and a new prime minister were committed to the reform and modernisation of public services. In 1998 the government announced that it would review the 1985 standards of fire cover, commissioning its own research into speed of response and intervention standards to be operated by brigades. Originally called *Review of Standards of Fire Cover*, it was retitled *Review of Standards of Emergency Cover*, to more accurately reflect the expanding role of the fire service as the primary UK rescue service. In March 2000, speaking at the Local Government Fire Conference, the fire minister, Mike O'Brien, envisioned a future UK fire service based on three strands, with equal emphasis on *intervention* (emergency responses to fires and other emergencies), *protection* (enforcement of fire safety legislation) and *prevention* (community fire safety initiatives).

In May 2000, the FBU leadership changed when Andy Gilchrist was elected general secretary,[5] replacing the retiring Ken Cameron. Although sharing the same broad left background as Cameron, Gilchrist was open to moving away from the pay formula, to which his predecessor had been steadfastly committed. It had long been known that Tony Blair would call the general election for May 2001 and was preparing a Labour Party manifesto that would include the promise of large increases in public services employment, especially for teachers and nurses. Gilchrist saw the opportunity to add firefighters' pay to Labour's agenda. He also saw the risks of not doing so, namely that significant changes might be made to the service without improvement in pay. So, in early 2001 Gilchrist and the Executive Council undertook to organise a series of mass meetings in every brigade, to secure membership support for a pay campaign to be agreed at the FBU annual conference. The foot-and-mouth crisis delayed the general election until June 2001, but, by the FBU annual conference in May, all three major political parties had made manifesto promises to reform and expand public services. Some tentative optimism suggested that the call for improved firefighter pay might fall on sympathetic ears.

Gilchrist informed conference it was time to review the fire service pay formula as it no longer reflected the complexity and demands of the modern role of firefighters and control staff. While acknowledging a debt of gratitude to members whose long strike had won the formula, Gilchrist insisted it would be unwise to return to annual collective pay bargaining. However, he concluded it was time to look for change that would reflect the modern service and the new technical skills required. He forewarned delegates, 'We must not be fearful of the employers' position but all members must be prepared to see this through to the end – with a Recall Conference if necessary.' Conference supported the position.

Following the Labour government's re-election in June 2001, a draft White Paper set out a vision of a modern fire service with 'a well-equipped, skillful and highly motivated workforce', chiming with the union's view that firefighters' pay needed to properly reflect the modern service and the new technical skills required.

The proposed White Paper, which was never published, stated:

> The Fire Service is one of the most consistently high-performing services in local government. It has already made considerable progress towards modernisation. This 'succeeding' service is highly effective in its work of responding to fire and other emergencies and widely admired by the public. Certainly the Audit Commission Performance Indicators for 1999-2000 published in January 2001 fully bear it out. At the same time, the role of the fire service has begun to change, essentially from a reactive to a proactive one; and the next few years will see a major transformation in the way fire brigades deliver services.[6]

Subsequently, the terrible events of 11 September 2001 highlighted the bravery and sacrifice of firefighters, increasing their public regard. The event also triggered a step-change in planning for terrorist incidents and the provision of central-government-funded resources for deployment by fire and rescue services.

In spring 2002, the preliminary findings of the government's *Review of Standards of Emergency Cover* were presented to the Central Fire Brigades Advisory Council (CFBAC) and recommended additional investment of £1.6 billion. The final report was expected in the autumn of 2002. All the ingredients were there to support a significant pay claim – the only questions were when and how much?

The claim

During early 2002, Andy Gilchrist undertook another national tour of campaigning rallies. His message prefaced the Executive Council motion to the May conference,[7] saying, essentially, that the pay formula had 'served us well', but that the devastation of manufacturing industry had significantly undermined the value of the upper quartile comparator. Moreover, pay levels had failed to take account of the expanding demands on firefighters, changed control room technologies and the broader realities of modernisation. Nor was there justification for pay differentials between emergency control operators and wholetime firefighters or lower rates for retained firefighters. Expecting the employers to agree in principle to their case, Gilchrist nevertheless anticipated that 'the crunch will come when the Treasury says "No"'. He stressed his strong desire to avoid having to take national strike action for the first time since 1977-78 but was not convinced it would be possible. Gilchrist's clarion call was 'We will provide the leadership – I am clear about that. Are YOU up for it?'[8]

Increased communications with members, including personal appeals from Gilchrist, further prepared members for the campaign.[9] At the Bridlington annual conference of 14-15 May the Executive Council presented its unanimously agreed recommendation for a four-point claim, known as the 'four pillars'. While conceding that the pay formula had delivered 'a reasonable level of wages', the Executive Council acknowledged it was 'less effective' than it had been.[10] The Executive Council decided to implement 'a vigorous campaign in pursuit of a fair wage for firefighters and emergency control staff'.[11]

First, it committed the union to seek an increase in firefighters' basic pay to £30,000. Second, in view of its commitment to equality and fair treatment for all members, and in recognition of the 'pivotal role' of emergency control staff, it recommended that these staff be paid the same wages as firefighters of the equivalent rank. Third, acknowledging job equality, it stated that retained firefighters should be trained to the same standard as wholetime firefighters and should receive the same pay and conditions. Fourth, in committing to modernising the fire and rescue service, an 'appropriate National Pay Formula' was required to reflect the highly skilled and motivated workforce.

The figure of £30,000 derived, it was claimed, from several sources. A commissioned Labour Research Department (LRD) report[12] produced detailed analysis of the limitations of the 1978 pay formula, gave details of alternative linkages to earnings based on New Earnings Survey data, wage drift, distinctions between manual and non-manual earnings and the upper earnings range, and argued for a redefinition of what constituted a skilled workforce. As a result of labour market changes, the upper quartile earnings of *all* full-time workers (manual, non-manual, male and female) now stood at 20 per cent more than the upper quartile of male manual workers, which justified a new method of calculation.[13] The 2001 New Earnings Survey showed that the majority of 'associate professional' groups, the nearest equivalents, earned more than firefighters. Several appendices[14] provided a wealth of data on trends and comparators but, while the LRD report did not actually recommend £30,000, it concluded that a figure of this order was consistent with the changes in male manual earnings. A job evaluation exercise was undertaken by an independent consultant, Sue Hastings,[15] and reliable calculations of relevant labour market data were produced by Incomes Data Services.[16] Complex pay data was distilled into a two-sided leaflet ('What others earn') with easily digestible evidence of the comparators underpinning the claim.[17]

Passed unanimously, the 'four-pillars' resolution formed the substance of the claim to the employers at the NJC of 28 May. The last section spelled out the union's approach, essentially that it would negotiate in good faith and would only take strike action as a last resort . The employers' initial response insisted, in a five-page letter ('Employers' modernising agenda'), that pay improvements must be inextricably linked to imprecisely defined modernisation and changes in working practice. The Executive Council rejected this overture, arguing it was not a framework for negotiation, but a rehash of the 1995 Audit Commission Report (see Chapter 3), which the union had opposed.

In response, an enthusiastic campaign was launched to a receptive membership. The first *Pay Campaign Special* was issued in May 2002, with the emblazoned headline: 'Professionals get professional pay... so we're demanding £30k. Y... Because we're worth it'. These bulletins translated the claim into straightforward demands ('Pay parity means: £30k for emergency fire control staff and firefighters; a £7,500 retainer and £13.74 for every hour worked by firefighters on the retained duty system'). The campaign featured vibrant rallies of members and supporters, which strengthened collective engagement and re-affirmed the legitimacy of a substantial claim.

Reneging on their promise to deliver specific proposals to the NJC of 9 July, the employers sidestepped the key element of the claim. Unknown to the union side and leaked months later, the employers had drawn up a 'position paper', which considered offering a phased increase over two years and raising a qualified firefighter's pay by 16 per cent to £25,000 per annum. The quid pro quo was FBU acceptance of changes in working practices.[18]

Early stages of the dispute

At this juncture, government ministers intervened, not directly and publicly, but through the employers, to thwart negotiations. This interference set a pattern to be repeated throughout the dispute and the agonising path to settlement. The parameters of what would be financially permissible were firmly established by the government through John Prescott, as deputy prime minister, and his office (ODPM), which included Nick Raynsford as minister for local and regional government, who had direct responsibility for the fire and rescue service. The overriding constraint was public sector modernisation and pay reform, and the sharp edge was pay restraint.[19] Government intervention made strike action unavoidable.[20]

The employers asked the union to participate in a joint approach to government to request an independent inquiry into modernisation and pay. The Executive Council rejected this proposal on the grounds that these issues properly lay within the NJC's purview and that any combined request should be for additional funding to finance the claim. Shortly thereafter, in a decisive development that signalled their abandonment of an NJC-determined settlement, the employers requested that the government establish an independent inquiry to make recommendations on pay and modernisation. Their press release exposed the *realpolitik*: 'The Government has made it clear that it will not bail us out financially if we negotiate a deal we cannot presently afford.'[21]

The impasse continued throughout the summer despite a private meeting between Prescott and Gilchrist and interactions with the employers, but positions hardened when the employers stridently urged the FBU to drop its claim. The union continued to build its campaign amongst members and the public in advance of the NJC meeting (2 September) and the recall national conference (12 September), at which strike action would be called if no acceptable offer were received. Significantly, the government's Civil Contingencies Committee began preparing strike-breaking operations by requisitioning Green Goddesses and planning the training of troops.

At that NJC meeting, lobbied by over 1,000 FBU members, the employers made an offer composed of three elements: a four-per-cent increase, an undertaking to increase that if recommended by the inquiry, and the repeated offer of a joint approach to government for funding.[22] Falling far short of the claim, the offer was rejected by the Executive Council. Subsequently, the recall conference unanimously voted for a ballot authorising strike action. Given the angry reaction to this 'miserly' offer, the Executive Council was convinced that the ballot would deliver a huge majority.

Following the abortive NJC meeting, Raynsford established the Bain Commission and its terms of reference (ToR). Prescott invited the union to give evidence and comment on the ToR, but the Executive Council declined on the grounds that participation would distract from pursuing a negotiated settlement and the inquiry could never be 'independent', given the government's influence and priorities. Involvement would compromise the union, conferring legitimacy on a partisan process.

The Bain Inquiry

The government announced its Inquiry team of Professor Sir George Bain, Sir Tony Young and Sir Michael Lyons,[23] all of whom had been knighted by Blair's government and none of whom had experience of, or expertise in, the fire and rescue service. The ToR included the requirement 'to inquire into and make recommendations on the future organisation and management of the Fire Service', which would first, 'enable it to undertake the full range of responsibilities that are appropriate to it'; second, 'enable it to respond effectively to all the operational demands that might be placed upon it'; and third, 'enable the responsibilities of the Fire Service to be delivered with optimum efficiency and effectiveness'. Recommendations should consider 'the pay levels that are appropriate, taking full account of the wider context of pay arrangements, levels and their affordability across the economy' and 'the most appropriate arrangements for determining future pay and conditions'.[24]

These ToR deepened union suspicions, because they were seen as too broad regarding the future management of the service, and too narrow regarding pay, as recommendations would have to comply with public sector pay policy. Further, additional pay increases had to be self-financing through 'modernisation'. Moreover, the three-month timescale precluded a genuine, thoroughgoing review of the service.[25] Directed by Whitehall, and produced by civil servants and ministers increasingly hostile to public sector trade unionism generally and the FBU specifically, the inquiry would be imbued with cost-cutting imperatives. The near-universal view was that Bain represented a trap for the union.[26]

The strike ballot

If the ballot result was never in doubt, given the effective union campaign, the size of margin (87.6 per cent on a 83.5 per cent turnout) delivered an overwhelming strike mandate. Members in Northern Ireland voted by an extraordinary 96.6 per cent in favour. Having taken soundings from activists, reportedly disinclined to indefinite action, the Executive Council decided on discontinuous strikes which, it was argued, had several advantages: they maintained pressure on the employers, permitted pauses for meaningful negotiations and ensured that lost earnings were not excessive. An additional influence on the strategic decision to adopt discontinuous action and, specifically, to start by engaging in two bouts of 48-hour action followed by an eight-day strike, was the positive outcome of similar action in Merseyside in 2001 and previously, in 1995 and 1997-98, in Essex. In 2002 a clutch of national officers had organised local discontinuous action and their direct experience informed discussions

Accordingly, the Executive Council declared six periods of action before Christmas, beginning with two 48-hour strikes and finishing with four eight-day strikes. Government hostility was evident in the attitudes of the ministers responsible. Prescott walked out of a press conference when questioned about the impending strike and Raynsford, infamously, described firefighters as 'criminally irresponsible'. Nor were the employers more encouraging, with the national chair (Ted George) condemning the claim as 'unrealistic, unaffordable, unreasonable and unjustified'.[27] Nevertheless, the strike threat compelled the employers to resume talks and the FBU leadership agreed to suspend the three strikes scheduled for 29 October, 2 November and 6 November.

The Executive Council rescheduled the first strike for 13 November, to give the employers sufficient time to compose a meaningful offer. Meanwhile, on 12 November, the Bain Inquiry delivered its interim report which, as expected, failed to recognise the claim's legitimacy, which was a precondition for negotiation. Bain recommended an 11.3 per cent pay increase over two years, dependent on thoroughgoing reform of working practices and employment relations. Essentially, it was a cuts agenda that would mean fire authorities paying increases only within the limits of their decentralised budgets. The outcome would be cuts to stations and staff, more overtime, increased rest-day working and firefighters assuming ever-greater responsibilities.

First strikes and government sabotage

The inevitable consequence was the first national strike since 1978 (lasting 48 hours), during which the government implemented Operation Fresco and mobilised 18,500 military personnel and 827 antiquated Green Goddesses.[28] Following this demonstration of union solidity, the Executive Council countered Bain by advancing its own case for fire service modernisation, deriving largely from the government's abandoned White Paper of 2001. The case rested on FBU acceptance of modernisation, not a cuts version, but based on the successful Pathfinder trials, which demonstrated how extra investment could save lives and benefit society by reducing NHS and insurance costs (see Chapter 1).

Talks resumed and developed into intensive negotiations. However, a sequence of dramatic events ensued, which assumed notoriety. Simply explained, the employers had prepared by 21 November another 'position paper', substantively similar to July's undisclosed paper, which could have produced a 16 per cent increase by November 2003, enabled the union to shelve its first eight-day strike and ensured that final negotiations might take place the following week. Though detailed accounts of the episode vary, the essential facts are indisputable. By the early hours of 22 November a joint draft had been agreed between the union and the employers, but at dawn the ODPM intervened, refusing to give employers the latitude to pursue the agreed proposal. Belief that a negotiated outcome had been achieved was hardly fantasy, given Prescott's statement to Parliament on 21 November[29] that reiterated the employers' offer. Government intervention, directed by the Treasury (under Gordon Brown) and sanctioned by Blair, subverted the possible deal. From that point there could be no pretence that the outcome could be determined by the NJC through the bargaining machinery. The government, committed to rigid public sector pay restraint, increasingly enmeshed in Bush's foreign policy and haunted by the spectre of the Winter of Discontent, made the scheduled eight-day strike inevitable.

Disappointment at the collapse of negotiations turned to fury following Blair's subsequent attack on firefighters. In a press statement (25 November), he dismissed the FBU leadership's contention that the government wanted this dispute as 'palpably absurd', but proceeded to describe why the government had blocked the negotiated settlement. In Parliament, Blair made the unfounded assertion that the cost of the aborted settlement would have been £500 million, disregarding the employers' calculation of £70 million. He fabricated the figure of £16 billion as the cost to the economy if the firefighters' increase was applied across the public sector. Then, he instructed Sir Jeremy Beecham, head of the Local Government Employers' Association, to form a negotiating team, accountable to Bain, on the financial parameters of any proposed settlement. The by now 'on-message' deputy prime minister explicitly linked job cuts to pay increases, not least because pay represented 85 per cent of total fire service expenditure.[30] Taken together, these actions amounted to a major offensive against the FBU. The extent of the repressive action Blair was contemplating is revealed by an entry in the diaries of Alistair Campbell, Blair's press secretary: 'TB was making clear we should move towards taking over the FBU negotiations, making a final offer and if it was not accepted making clear they would be fired and new personnel hired.'[31]

The first eight-day strike was impressively solid,[32] but the next one, planned for 4 December, was deferred to 16 December to enable Acas to facilitate negotiations. Meanwhile, a joint TUC-FBU demonstration on 7 December saw 20,000 march in London in solidarity. Pressure on the union grew when the full Bain Report was delivered on 16 December. Acas-brokered talks continued until the week before Christmas, when the employers indicated a preparedness to make an offer in early 2003. The deferred eight-day strike was again suspended by the Executive Council.

Beyond the pay dispute: politics and Iraq

The 9 January offer, constructed according to Bain's prescriptions, came nowhere near meeting union claims. Pay increases of four per cent for 2002 and seven per cent for 2003 were conditional on union acceptance of reform proposals,[33] including more than 4,000 wholetime jobs cut over four years. Deadlock persisted when the employers refused to accede to the FBU's request not to 'unreservedly commit' to Bain's agenda, to enable negotiations to continue. Consequently, the Executive Council called three 48-hour strikes to commence on 21 January, 28 January and 1 March. The first was solidly supported and prompted the employers to agree to further talks without precondition. Yet once again, the employers' deeds failed to match their words, and the union proceeded with the 48-hour strike commencing on 28 January.

At this juncture, intervention by Prescott revealed how a pay and conditions dispute had not only become transformed into a conflict over public sector 'modernisation', but also had assumed an explicitly and unanticipated political character. With the invasion of Iraq imminent, the government signalled its intention to introduce a Fire and Rescue Services Bill giving the secretary of state the power to enforce terms and conditions of employment and to redistribute resources within the fire and rescue service. This draconian measure was roundly denounced by trade unions, employment lawyers and human rights organisations.

Despite tabloid media vitriol, which fuelled an increasingly hostile political climate, firefighters demonstrated powerful solidarity in their 1-2 February strikes. So effective was this action that Prescott agreed that employers should enter negotiations through Acas without preconditions although, significantly, ministerial approval was required if additional funding was needed for any settlement. Subsequently, the Executive Council suspended the scheduled strikes and shortly afterwards (15 February) went further and agreed to a four-week cooling-off period. A recall conference was organised for 19 March in Brighton, at which, it hoped, an improved offer could be considered. Frustrated at the lack of progress and dismayed at the cancellation of strikes, some activists openly questioned the leadership and its tactics. Discordant notes were sounded through an internet forum, the 30k website, which became an important medium for criticism.

In this febrile environment, the employers delivered a further offer (6 March), consisting of a three-phase pay agreement giving

16 per cent by 1 July 2004 and a basic annual salary for a qualified firefighter. While guaranteeing a new pay formula for a minimum of two years, the proposal for new conditions of service was couched in terms of managerial prerogative rather than consensus. Predictably, the Executive Council recommended that members reject the offer at branch meetings preceding the recall conference. Raynsford reiterated the government's intention to repeal section 19.4 of the Fire Services Act, which would empower CFOs to reduce establishment numbers without complying with national fire cover standards. With some activists now calling for indefinite action, the Executive Council announced a further 24-hour strike for 20 March to rally the membership and increase union leverage before Iraq hostilities commenced and, as rumoured, before the government introduced a ban on strikes.[34]

Deadlock and Burchill

An attempt to break the deadlock was made by the NJC's independent chair, Professor Frank Burchill, who mediated discussions at Acas. The outcome was a new offer that, the Executive Council claimed, overcame objections to changes in working conditions.[35] The Executive Council recommended acceptance, but angry delegates at the Brighton recall conference in March overwhelmingly rejected this so-called 'final' offer.[36] Prescott then informed Parliament he was considering using his powers to enforce a settlement on terms inferior to those on offer. At a meeting with the FBU general secretary and president, Prescott indicated that he was being pressurised to ban strikes in the fire and rescue service.[37] The Executive Council met on 26-27 March and, on the basis of the decision at the March recall conference, recommended further rejection in advance of a second recall conference, to be held on 15 April in Brighton.

The Burchill proposals, delivered on 2 April, required that changes in working conditions be agreed with the FBU within Integrated Risk Management Plans (IRMPs) and, where failure to agree occurred, binding arbitration should apply. The Executive Council regarded these proposals as acceptable, protecting the union's position at local and national levels. At its 7 April meeting, it agreed to recommend that the recall conference accept them as a basis for negotiations. The government's response was far less encouraging. Raynsford claimed, without evidence, that the arrangement would cost an extra £100 million per year. Again, the Treasury's influence dominated. Although the employers were more conciliatory, their chief concern was a fundamental one: that change by agreement 'would make it too difficult to secure the changes necessary to modernise'.[38]

Delegates to the recall conference (15 April) in Brighton decided to consult members on Burchill and voted overwhelmingly not to strike for the duration of the Iraq war, although the mood for renewed strike action was growing.[39] Then, on 19 May, the employers tabled a new offer entitled, 'Fire Service Pay and Conditions Agreement 2003'. A reconvened Executive Council decided to recommend acceptance as the offer met 'many of the concerns expressed by members when rejecting previous offers', claiming that, on the stumbling blocks of duty systems and working time arrangements, it maintained existing Grey Book conditions. The Executive Council's assessment was that changed duty systems would have to be agreed by fire authorities and the union under IRMPs and could not be imposed. Failure to agree would mean referral to a Technical Advisory Panel, 'on which the union will be represented'. Though the long-standing overtime ban was to be lifted, a deeply unpopular concession amongst activists, the Executive Council strove to reassure members that this would not 'support shortfalls in establishments' and would 'only be on a voluntary basis'.

The government again played its hostile hand. Raynsford reprised the mantras of modernisation and New Public Management when pushing the Fire and Rescue Services Bill through its third reading in the House of Commons. The Bill provided for imposed settlements, in contravention of International Labour Convention No 151, which aimed to guarantee negotiated settlements in disputes over public employees' conditions of service.[40] A draconian anti-labour measure, it was subject to trenchant criticism in the House of Lords by the doyen of labour law, Lord Wedderburn, and by Lord McCarthy, who had drafted the 1978 pay formula. McCarthy appositely used an industrial relations metaphor, 'the ghost at the bargaining table',[41] to capture the extraordinary government pressure bearing down on the union in its negotiations with employers.

Debate, division and formal acceptance

In the week preceding the latest recall conference in Glasgow on 12 June, firefighters voted on the recommended proposals. Divisions had simmered amongst activists since late 2002 regarding the dispute's direction, particularly over leadership decisions to suspend strikes to facilitate negotiations, and rifts now became entrenched. The summary account presented in the Executive Council's document to the 2004 annual conference, albeit an invaluable chronological narrative, does not convey the intensity of debate and division that occurred at branch and brigade levels. The depth of feeling amongst a sizeable minority, including the London region, who called for further action, is understated.

The Glasgow conference voted three to one to accept the package, albeit with the proviso that 'this offer requires further detailed agreement within the NJC on a number of matters' and that members should be 'fully consulted prior to final agreement being reached'. The conference debate reflected real worries about the future strength of the union, the limited nature of the pay offer, the likely cuts and job losses, the consequences of local determination, the fate of long-service pay and the effectiveness of union tactics. Many expressed disquiet with, for want of a better term, the grey areas of a reconfigured Grey Book. Despite the emphatic vote, the mood was unenthusiastic acceptance by members, who expressed well-grounded fears that much remained undecided.[42]

The 'final' offer

From July to October talks occurred on the detail. Relatively swiftly, consensus was reached on a new pay formula tying future pay rises to average pay for Associate Professional and Technical (APT) grades in the annual New Earnings Survey, but only for two years. The formal record shows that by 20 October substantive agreement had been reached between the FBU and employers on a 'position statement' consisting of the following: a minimum of 7 per cent from 7 November 2003 on firefighters' basic pay; an additional 3.2 per cent for emergency control staff from 7 November 2002; pay parity for retained firefighters amounting to 17.74 per cent from November 2003; a new APT-linked national pay formula but crucially only for two years; a new 'non-discriminatory' scheme to be negotiated when continual professional development (CPD) replaced the long-service increment (LSI); competence/qualified pay after three, not four, years; opportunity to earn payments for additional responsibilities (4.2 per cent from 1 July 2004); and guaranteed minimum of £25,000 for all 'competent' firefighters and £23,750 for control members at 1 July 2004. Agreement was conditional on ending the longstanding overtime ban, which had underpinned the FBU's commitment to staffing levels and prevented excessive hours of work. Further, in conceding employers' demands for flexibility, wholetime firefighters would be free to undertake retained duties 'where appropriate', lifting another long-standing FBU policy (the ban on retained duties for wholetime staff) with 'no barrier to any employee working on a combination of different wholetime, part-time and retained duty systems'.

An all-members' circular (22 October) attempted to allay fears regarding the contentious replacement of LSI with CPD. On control room pay, the employers agreed a joint job evaluation exercise, which increased pay from 92 per cent to 95 per cent of that of a firefighter. The Control Staff National Committee and the Executive Council accepted the proposal, which the NJC authorised. Although the employers had earlier also conceded the principle of parity for retained firefighters, it took several meetings before the National Retained Committee gave their consent to the new structure, which included an annual retainer, an hourly rate and a call-out payment.

The employers renege

Leadership expectations that the employers would endorse these 'position' proposals at the 28 October NJC were confounded. Again, government intervention was decisive. The employers declared that the 7 per cent increase scheduled for stage two, due on 7 November 2003, should be 'phased', with 3.5 per cent payable but backdated to November 2002, only once negotiations on the Disputes and Disciplinary Procedure and on NJC structures were concluded, and the Audit Commission had confirmed that new working practices were being implemented. Seeking to exploit the bargaining advantage that union acceptance had conferred, the employers continued to negotiate a new disputes procedure and a revised Grey Book.

The employers' 'bombshell' brought an explosion of anger throughout the FBU. One account[43] suggests that 35 of 59 brigades took unofficial action, mostly responding to emergency calls only.[44] To legitimise its position, the Executive Council instituted a postal ballot asking members to accept this payment of the stage two increase. Going directly to members has been interpreted as a means to circumvent activist opposition,[45] and produced a three to one vote to accept on a relatively low turnout.

The bitter end

As the dispute limped into 2004, several issues fuelled firefighters' discontent. Senior managers were already implementing 'modernisation', re-organising control rooms and cutting the number of appliances. Modernisation was becoming a byword for cuts. Unavoidably, disappointment and frustration found expression within the FBU amongst a layer of officers, activists and members. Dissatisfaction coalesced around common positions and platforms (*Red Watch* as 'the voice of rank-and-file firefighters and control staff' and a rank-and-file network Grassroots FBU for a Democratic and Fighting Union); forceful opposition to New Labour and a determination to push for FBU disaffiliation; criticism of leadership tactics; the need for change in leading positions; and recommendations to vote 'no' in the ballot to proceed with implementation. Accounts of the dispute must acknowledge the extent to which the union was riven by contested positions. Without understanding this cleavage, subsequent developments, notably the proscription of Grassroots FBU and the election of Matt Wrack as general secretary and others to leading positions, are inexplicable.

The employers protracted the agonising end-game over the issue of stand-down. The Grey Book had stipulated 12am–7am as stand-down time so those covering the night shift (6pm-9am) would rest between these hours, except to cover emergencies and locally designated essential duties. The employers now moved to remove stand-down from the revised Grey Book, giving fire authorities unilateral freedom to arrange shifts. The FBU argued that stand-down was not part of the June 2003 agreement and should not be included in subsequent negotiations. Additionally, there were the contested issues of the payment of the third stage (4.2 per cent due on 1 July) and the outstanding 3.5 per cent from November 2003. Accordingly, the Executive Council ran a consultative ballot to test support for progress on negotiations (including a recommended rejection of the stand-down proposal). It delivered a 62.8 per cent yes vote. Yet this mandate failed to move the employers. Delayed payment was saving them money, the union was in a weak negotiating position and they saw no need to accommodate the FBU ahead of its May conference at Bridlington. The employers' intractability made renewed strike action a distinct possibility. The Executive Council decided to recommend to delegates that the union withdraw wholesale from the June 2003 agreement, a move tantamount to non-compliance with modernisation, and to consult members on how best to secure their outstanding claim. Further, the Executive Council decided to ask conference to support a resolution calling for strike action in the event of the government imposing a settlement through the proposed Fire Service Act.

Bridlington proved a dramatic affair. On the opening day, conference followed the Executive Council's recommendation and voted to block implementation of the modernisation programme and to prepare for a ballot on industrial action. However, the leadership controversially then suspended the week-long conference, preventing alternative resolutions on immediate strike action from being debated. Meanwhile, on the brigade frontline, conflict escalated following the suspension of 19 firefighters in Salford for refusing to cover a new Incident Response Unit without a proper agreement. Unofficial industrial action broke out in around a quarter of brigades.[46] Conflict intensified as the suspensions mounted (120 in Greater Manchester), amplifying demands for immediate strike action from members there as well as more widely. Industrial action prompted an employer climb-down, as all suspensions were withdrawn and national agreement was achieved on the delayed introduction of the Incident Response Unit vehicles. However, hopes were dashed of a broader settlement as the employers insisted on removing stand-down for public holidays.

In this feverish context, the reconvened conference took place in Southport (16 June). Yet, despite the enormity of the employers' betrayal and the government's sabotage, the Executive Council recommended only a consultative ballot on action, should the employers fail to honour the agreement. It was indicative of the conference mood was that an altogether tougher resolution, moved by Nottinghamshire, was carried by a large majority. If the employers had not paid stages two and three by 30 July, then a ballot for discontinuous national strike action would be implemented immediately.[47] The delegates' anger was also expressed in their momentous decision to disaffiliate from the Labour Party, against the recommendation of the Executive Council (see Chapter 9).

The dispute's concluding stages reprised, as farce as much as tragedy, the familiar actions and behaviours of its *dramatis personae*: the vacillating employers flitting between seeking settlement and reneging on agreement, in order to push through modernisation and minimise FBU influence; the New Labour government setting strict parameters on the substance of negotiations, and interfering in the bargaining process and its outcomes; and the determination of firefighters and control room staff to pursue their case for fair pay, but also uncertainty within the FBU leadership on the emphasis to be placed on action and negotiation respectively.

Only the strike threat secured the resumption of talks on the implementation of the June 2003 settlement. The TUC general secretary, Brendan Barber,[48] brokered talks on the thorny issue of stand-down, accommodating the firefighters' need for adequate rest and the employers' desire to utilise these periods more 'productively'. Union concessions did not compromise the principle of negotiation under IRMPs and did not permit unilateral determination by fire authorities. Yet, the reality of modernisation was kicking in, creating friction at local level. Nevertheless, following exhaustive talks, the widespread expectation was that agreement would be secured on all outstanding issues and that the NJC of 2 August would mean formal endorsement.

However, there transpired an act of sabotage comparable to 21-22 November 2002. A members' circular, written by assistant general secretary, Mike Fordham,[49] exposed the political conspiracy between government (the ODPM and Raynsford), the Chair of the London Fire and Emergency Planning Committee (Val Shawcross), leading civil servants and hostile councillors. The employers' side of the NJC voted 13-10 against the agreement, achieved by 'flooding the meeting with mainly Labour councillors from London on behalf of the LGA [Local Government Association]',[50] an 'unconstitutional wrecking move' without which the vote 'would have been 10-6 in favour'. In preventing the employers and FBU from exercising autonomy, while tooling-up senior managers for modernisation, the government had now divided the employers.[51]

The FBU leadership instigated a fresh strike ballot. Further talks, again under the TUC's auspices, produced a formulation on public holiday working. Then the Audit Commission Report,[52] in declaring excellent progress on modernisation, appeared to remove the final hurdle. Yet, the dispute took another tortuous turn with the astonishing leak that ODPM officials had been secretly negotiating with private security firm Securicor to discuss the requisitioning and operation of fire appliances and the crossing of picket lines in the event of September's strike. Members' wrath was unconfined and predictions circulated that a massive ballot turnout would deliver a 9-1 strike vote. The scale of this imminent mandate forced a reaction from employers and government, enabling final agreement at the NJC of 26 August.

Although the ink was dry on the agreement, the ramifications of this bitter, protracted conflict were only beginning. In concluding this narrative, brief accounts are given of two significant internal developments: firstly, the banning of Grassroots FBU and, secondly, the election of Matt Wrack as general secretary. As indicated, they are explicable only by reference to the cleavage between, broadly speaking, the leadership and those generally supportive of it, and many activists and members now critical of it.

In October 2004, following a six-month investigation headed by the assistant general secretary[53] the Executive Council proscribed Grassroots FBU, arguing it was 'an organisation contrary to union policies and interests of the union'. In rejecting claims that it was 'merely a loose grouping of activists', the inquiry concluded it was an 'unauthorised organisation' with its own officers, bank account, treasurer and 'the potential to become an alternative union'. The inquiry also believed that participation in Grassroots FBU breached Rule 26(1) (f) and (g) and concluded that 'sufficient evidence of significant involvement' existed in respect of four London region members: Paul Embery identified as treasurer, Andy Dark as convenor of meetings, Gordon Fielden as registrant of the website and Matt Wrack as recruiting and organising support. However, disciplinary proceedings against them were 'blocked' because they were not supported by the relevant (i.e. London) Executive Council member as union rules stipulated; this member concluded that no rules had, in fact, been broken. In response, the Executive Council additionally recommended a rule change (to be decided at conference) that would prevent 'relevant Executive Council members from adjudicating on questions of discipline'.

Dissatisfaction with the settlement was expressed through union elections. Having become London regional secretary in 2004, Matt Wrack was elected (February 2005) as assistant general secretary following Mike Fordham's declaration of retirement. Wrack won 45.5 per cent of the eligible vote, defeating John McGhee (40.1 per cent) and Dean Mills (14.4 per cent). Given that five years had elapsed since Andy Gilchrist had become general secretary, a fresh election was required. In May 2005, Wrack defeated Gilchrist, winning 63.9 per cent of the vote on a 40 per cent turn-out. With the assistant general secretary position vacated, Andy Dark defeated Geoff Ellis 61.3 per cent to 38.7 per cent in September 2005. These elections and others reflected a groundswell of discontent with the incumbent leadership.

The chapter now fleshes out this largely narrative account, drawing on the testimonies of participants as they recall their experiences, express their perceptions and present their reflections.

Roots of the dispute

The significant decline in real pay was recalled by many interviewees. Gordon McQuade, then stationed at Falkirk, remembered:

> I was aware that firefighters were losing money. You certainly did not seem to get as much as you were getting in the 1990s and more so in the 1980s. By the end of the 1990s and into the 2000s, there was continual talk about pay, and issues were increasingly raised at conference that the pay formula wasn't working and we had to do something about it.

For Steve Harman, a former North West regional official, pay, in both absolute and relative terms, had become a significant issue:

> I knew our pay had slipped behind because I was on £21,000 or something and that was working nights and weekends, and there was no shift allowance, nothing. And I knew people working in clerical jobs in the public sector who were on more than me just working a 37-hour week Monday to Friday. My sister-in-law was at the Borough Council so I knew we had dropped behind.

Alan Paterson of Grampian FBU succinctly summarised the two-sided perception of the pay formula held by many: 'I wanted the principle of the pay formula but I was not enjoying what it was delivering.' It had once been a bedrock of stability but its value was open to question. Mike Fordham, whose responsibilities included detailed attention to the pay formula, recalled:

> I had concerns about the pay formula as soon as I started to be significantly involved in its detail. Initially, the firefighters' comparisons were done from the NES [New Earnings Survey] and we knew that was way out and we couldn't get specific information that was weighted by the NES. So we started to do our own survey of firefighters, something that used to take a good few months of my time every year. And we did it with the employers in a joint arrangement, a totally neutral thing. In a way, I suppose we became statisticians… It brought home to me what I would call inequality within the pay formula. The people we were being compared to no longer represented us and that was the male manual worker, because what we had created through 'A Service for the Sixties' and everything that followed, was a skilled worker… There was a downside to not opening Pandora's box, that is: 'What is the trade union about, what is it there for?' And if you know that your members are being compared to a group of people who don't actually reflect their earnings, then I think you are damned if you don't try.

The claim, the campaign and the ballot

It is an article of faith that support for the pay claim was universal, evidenced by unanimous conference votes and the huge majority for strike action. The interviews confirm firefighters' belief in the justness of their claim, yet some admitted they did have questions. There was a reluctance to abandon the pay formula, despite its weakness. Les Skarratts, North West Executive Council member, recalled:

> We were at Bridlington to be told what our pay claim in detail was going to be. The Merseyside Brigade Committee didn't support the claim. The reason was that we were happy with a pay formula that provided regular pay uplifts – which were not satisfactory at the time – but we had a mechanism that provided a yearly outcome rather than what would be annual collective bargaining. I think we were asked to second the pay claim and we politely turned that down, but we voted the right way every single time, we didn't rock the boat, we didn't argue against such a claim, but we felt it wasn't the best strategic move at the time.

Others questioned the specific figure, although not the claim's validity. Roddy Robertson, Scottish regional chair, remembered:

> It was April 2002 and I was in the hall at the STUC [Scottish Trades Union Congress] in Perth when we got a message that the pay claim was £30,000. I went to have a cigarette and met one of our officials from the Highlands. I said, 'Have you heard it's £30,000?' and he said, 'Roddy, do you realise that's 40 per cent?' to which I said, 'No, I didn't.' There was a strong mandate. Full-time firefighters believed they were worth £30,000 at that time and so did I. Absolutely. They wanted recognition for all the things they were doing: line rescue, water rescue, rescue from heights, sewer rescues, chemicals, nuclear, biological, you name it. Retained firefighters were extremely poorly paid.

Jim Barbour was witness to and participant in the decision:

> There was this EC meeting where we took the decision. I said, 'Look, guys, I don't see any paperwork.' Mick Harper, who was president, and Andy, the general secretary, arrived. Andy described that he... had come up with the position that we

should go for 30k. Now I'm a wee bit of a mathematician. I was working out what percentage that was, based on a firefighter's wage. I says, 'This is a 40-per-cent pay rise we are going for.' And we checked the figures again. Andy was still going through his reasoning for this approach and, of course, on the face of it, it was a massively attractive thing for firefighters. And someone[54] queried, 'Andy, do you realise this is a 40 per cent pay rise?' And Mick Harper very quickly closed him down and says, 'Don't talk nonsense.' Blah, blah, blah, they hadn't done the maths… It was Andy's figure, exclusively Andy's figure. None of us knew until that moment.

John Paul McDonald, Scottish region Executive Council member, confirmed that £30,000 was not discussed before it was announced and drew a contrast with the first national strike:

I had no idea when the figure was announced to a meeting of officials in London. A tiny circle around Andy came up with the figure, absolutely no senior officials knew. Their jaws dropped when the £30k figure was announced. If there hadn't been the national campaign, there wouldn't have been a demand for £30k, there might've been a demand for 25 or 26 grand, or 10 per cent or a 15 per cent increase. It was very much EC-led and driven by the general secretary, whereas in 1977-78 the thrust was from below.

Mike Fordham, a key figure in negotiating the pay claim, suggested a lack of preparedness:

Being self-critical – I'm not distancing myself from the leadership – but there was not a lot of groundwork done, certainly none with the government. I was amazed when I returned to work[55] that there had been virtually no political exchange. So when we hit with a £30k pay claim, backed by a strike ballot, it got a counter-reaction in a very, very violent way.

However much the pay claim might have been top-down in its formulation, and the campaign driven by national officers, it was enthusiastically embraced by firefighters and emergency control staff. Paul Embery, London Executive Council member, reflected:

> There was this immense feeling of confidence and excitement really about the road that we were about to embark on. I think we believed our own publicity a bit at the time. We looked around and saw all these other unions being attacked and decimated in some industries and felt, well, that hasn't happened to us, we're as strong as we ever were, the employers are frightened of us… And I think we were really confident to the point of being a little bit complacent. So when the leadership said, 'Right, we're going to stick in this pay claim for 40 per cent and this is what we want', I think there was a mood of 'Well, if that's what we want then we're going to get it and no one's going to stand in our way.'

Reservations regarding the timing of the claim should be set against the realisation that engagement with the employers over pay was not solely a matter of union choice. As Chapter 3 indicates, conflict was coming even though many did not fully grasp the significance of the imminent employers' offensive.

The strikes

An important theme in the interviews is the powerful commitment firefighters and control staff had to their job and their profound sense of responsibility for public safety. Going on strike was not taken lightly. Cerith Griffiths, regional secretary for Wales, voiced attitudes far from the tabloid stereotype of mindless militancy:

> I can remember the first night we walked out on strike, I'm sure it was a Friday evening. It was six o'clock, it had gone dark, the doors opened and we walked out with a big banner. It was a real strange feeling and it's got to be probably the same for any worker going on strike. To walk away from something that you are so used to doing when things go wrong for people, is very difficult. I know it was difficult for the vast majority of people I worked with, it wasn't something we were comfortable doing.

The testimonies vividly portray the vibrancy, creativity and humour of the picket lines and how, common to all strikes, they played an indispensable role in forging collectivity, demonstrating unity and providing a focus for public support and solidarity. Chris Downes, former West Midlands regional secretary, remembered how one picket line referenced John Prescott's epithet at the time, 'Two Jags' – after the two official Jaguar cars he was said to use:

> Down at Brierley Hill they had a big container. They opened the swing doors and inside there was an old battered suite, and the brazier was outside, so it was not quite home from home... And right next to the station there was a chip shop and the guy said, 'Lads, one of the blokes' dads put a couple of hundred quid on the counter and said, "Just keep feeding them."' The picket lines were good. We had two jags dropped off from a scrappy. We painted them hydrant yellow, put a big red 'Y... Because We're Worth It' on it for Prescott. We had a bar built in our little camp out the front, we had electric from the fire station, braziers with pallets everywhere. It definitely built the camaraderie.

Even those parts of the country not renowned for militancy witnessed extensive involvement. Tam McFarlane, Somerset brigade secretary at the time, reported:

> There was an explosion of activism, because the truth was firefighters were grossly underpaid. Don't forget, I'm talking about Somerset, which we hardly think of as a hotbed of political activism, but everywhere firefighters took over the stations for the period of industrial action. It was an incredible time. It woke us up to the whole importance of solidarity. I have absolutely no doubt we won massive support from the public.

Wide-scale public support for firefighters was an outstanding feature of the dispute. The FBU created a memorable logo, emblazoned on yellow stickers, flags, T-shirts, beer mats and baseball hats. The rallies and demonstrations were colourful, noisy and visually striking affairs. Each decorated fire station stood out as a fortress of defiance, a symbol of the fight for justice. A MORI poll showed 70-per-cent public support for the firefighters' claim,[56] which reflected in part the hard work of firefighters and emergency control room staff across the country. Denise Christie, then in the Lothian and Borders brigade, gave a vivid account of members' activities:

> I remember doing a lot of campaigning, out on the streets with petitions. In fact, you can still go into pubs in Leith and Edinburgh and they've got these yellow beer mats – 'Y... Because we're worth it'. We used to go into pubs and put the beer mats down with our buckets for collections.

Despite the FBU being up against the New Labour government, a small number of Labour MPs, including John McDonnell and Jeremy Corbyn, did provide support for the union. Then there was the backing of musicians and comedians, notably Mark Thomas and Mark Steel. Examples abound, such as Lemmy of Motörhead wearing a firefighters T-shirt at the Barrowlands in Glasgow. However, pride of place goes to a gig which has assumed legendary status in the annals of FBU and rock and roll history.[57] Joe Strummer played his last London show, a benefit for the FBU, a month before his death.[58] The gig was the result of the farsightedness and élan of activists. Linda Smith, former London treasurer, remembered:

> Me and Ghada [Razuki], my best friend, went to see Joe Strummer playing at Finsbury Park in 2001. We said, 'Look, at some point there's going to be a strike. When there is, let's put on a fundraiser.' Anyway, along comes the strike and Ghada said, 'I'm gonna phone them.' They agreed! So it was Joe Strummer and the Mescaleros and we hired Acton Town Hall, we roped in Acton red watch and others – Mark Steel and Simon Green, an ex-firefighter who did the projection. It coincided with the end of the first 48-hour strike, which finished at six o'clock that night. And it was absolutely sold out, mainly to Joe Strummer fans. It was an amazing night. I was staffing the FBU merchandise stall. People had gone to France and bought loads of beer and wine to sell. I was responsible for the money, I'd have about five grand in my pockets. Green watch had come from Acton on the fire engine. I'd give them the money, they'd take it back on the engine and put it in the safe. I got a break and went in and the crowds were going mad because Mick Jones from The Clash

had got up on stage and was playing. So we reformed The Clash that night! To this day, I remember standing there thinking we'd had a totally solid 48-hour strike, we'd managed to put this on, one of the best moments of my life. We made 10 grand that night and, as I say, reformed The Clash.

21-22 November 2002: a turning point

At this chronological point, two contrasting interpretations are suggested. On a positive reading, a highly effective campaign had provided a convincing case for £30k and had mobilised the membership, the ballot for industrial action had delivered an enormous majority and the first solid strike had garnered widespread public support. Accordingly, the FBU was in a favourable negotiating position, and able to apply further pressure, given members' preparedness to take eight-day strikes. On a negative reading, despite members' enthusiastic embrace of the campaign and the impressive strike mandate, the government had demonstrated its intractability, refusing to make concessions. A major dilemma confronted the FBU. Given an unwillingness or inability to take indefinite strike action, what could it do in the face of government intransigence?

The interviews confirm that, albeit with the benefit of hindsight, 21-22 November came to be seen as a watershed. President Ruth Winters recalled the talks that night between the union, employers and the TUC:

> These talks went back and forward all through the night, we never went to bed. We came to an agreement, a draft agreement, I think it was £26,500... and most of the other points of the pay claim. It said anything brought up by the Bain Report, we would have an independent panel that we could both put our views at, employers and union. So we took that back to the EC, they thought it would be a go-er and it would be enough to suspend the strike action the next morning. We went back to the EC about four or five in the morning, and at half-six in the morning, John Monks and Brendan Barber turned up and said it had been pulled.

Strathclyde chair Alex Miller was clear that the responsibility for what became a long, drawn-out conflict lay with the government, which had scuppered the possible settlement:

> The deal was more or less brokered on the Thursday night. At the last minute, before anything could be signed off, the Treasury got involved... Gordon Brown intervened and more or less said there would be no agreement. He wanted further modernisation and I think that's the first time we realised, suddenly, there was another agenda. The government had intervened with the employers and the government were pulling the strings.

The government's unyielding opposition was witnessed by Mike Fordham[59] and came from the heart of the administration:

> Unfortunately, Gordon Brown did get out of bed. We knew it was going badly wrong when journalists said to us, 'Brown's stomping around Whitehall, wanting to know who has authorised this, who has not authorised this', and it ain't happening. The Treasury blocked it on that Friday morning. Contrary to what we might say publicly, Prescott himself was never the problem, but he wasn't strong enough to deal with ministers and civil servants. The problem was Nick Raynsford, Prescott's minister of state, and the senior civil servant, Clive Norris.

Whether such a judgement is too generous to Prescott, the truth in this statement is that the die was very much cast.

Iraq, the powers of the state and halted momentum

The impending Iraq war brought enormous pressure. The leadership conveyed to members the media impact if they proceeded with strike action in the circumstances of war. Keith Handscomb recalled:

> On the eve of the recall conference in Brighton on 19 March 2003, the EC met to get the latest report. And a dodgy deal got delivered to the EC which took the decision to call off the strike even though conference is the supreme decision-making body. There was some progress on negotiations but nothing of

note, still no settlement. But we were also told what the front page story would be if strikes went ahead. Andy was matey with Piers Morgan and the *Mirror* had been supportive, but this time, because the Iraq war was just starting, they would not be supportive of us striking, in the national interest. And he said that the *Sun* had already got the story set up with a picture of firefighters in their sleeping bags at work, with soldiers in their body bags being flown home.

Roddy Robertson believed the strike was hugely influenced by the government's preoccupation with Iraq. His comment contains conjecture but captures the essence of the consequences of the government's stance:

After the turn of the year [Iraq] became the focus of everything the government was doing and we got in the way. My feeling is that Andy Gilchrist or somebody was taken into a darkened room and read the facts of life, or the facts of what they were about to do to us if we carried on and took strike action during military action in Iraq. I might be wrong, but that was the feeling I got.

Alan McLean, North East Executive Council member, expanded on the powers of the state and media arrayed against them:

I was always aware of the resources of a government, but never truly aware of the powers of the state and the newspapers and the turning of the wheels and phones bugged. We knew our phones were bugged. We don't know if it was by Murdoch, but we knew because things were being repeated to us. Twice I picked up the phone and there was a recording of my voice on an earlier call. So I knew something big was happening and I couldn't even begin to think of how Andy Gilchrist must've been able to face that. Plus the role of the media was to have a villain and Andy became the villain. He was the most hated man in Britain until the war with Saddam Hussein. So we think we had to settle because the country was going to go to war. I think that formed part of our thinking in the settlement.

A widely shared view was that if 21-22 November represented a decisive turning point which revealed government intransigence, then Iraq shifted the dispute to even more unfavourable terrain. In the words of Les Skarratts, 'the cannons were then turned on us'. Increased frustration at the stalled momentum and internal tension over tactics manifested itself in debate and division at conferences and through social media, specifically the 30k website.

30k website and Grassroots FBU

Kevin Brown, then Manchester brigade secretary, understood that the instantaneous nature of reporting represented a broader challenge for the union:

> The communications issue, I believe, played a significant part. As our officials were coming out of discussions in London they were immediately interviewed by all kinds of media, the BBC, ITV, Sky. And our members were getting instant information before the union could analyse what was on the table and respond in a thought-out, structured way. It was very difficult to deal with and I think, as a union, we were probably the first to have to cope with it. Younger members had this thirst for instant communication, but maybe some older officials, including myself, were not up to speed with what was required. I certainly wouldn't say we were making it up on the hoof, but we were responding to a developing situation and, as always, government departments have more resources than we have — spin doctors able to get out there, get into the national press. And it can be a lonely place when you are on a picket line and you're hearing the news you believe you should be receiving from your union and it's not coming from the union.

The FBU, which placed so much emphasis on reports and debates through the democratic structures of branch and brigade and utilised a steady flow of written communication, tried to fill the gap and be imaginative. Ruth Winters recalled: 'I think we were one of the first unions to use block text messaging in our dispute because that was a newish thing. So for picket lines we would block text to the national executive and ask them to text their officials.'

John McGhee remembered the origins of the 30k website:

> Yes, we created the website funnily enough. We started it because at the start of the pay campaign, bearing in mind social media was just really developing, we developed this website because we wanted to create a forum for members to be able to share stories and ideas and campaigns and things. And it got to a point where we couldn't really administer it, it grew arms and legs.

Other interviewees had different recollections – that the national union had certainly contributed financial support but had not directly initiated the website. Sean Starbuck, then Humberside brigade secretary, suggested that site was valuable when official channels were problematic:

> I think there was just a void in the information and it filled the void. Me and Ian Murray were particularly disappointed with the information we got from our EC member and we had to look elsewhere. There were some good, informed people posting on the 30k website and, yes, it was a good source of information. We had to sift through a lot of shit if I'm honest, but there were some good nuggets.

Gordon McQuade and others appreciated the site's benefits but explained how its character changed:

> I became aware of it around the start of the dispute and I was a contributor. The union controlled all the information coming out and going back. All of a sudden, you had a website where everybody could communicate and find out what was going on and pass opinions. The hierarchy clearly did not like this site. Well, at the start they did, they liked firefighters talking to each other. All of a sudden, people were making friends with people in Wales, Northern Ireland, Essex, London. But then the site sort of changed. Once the dispute started going down the tubes people began venting off.

Interviewees also focused on the website's negative effects. Alan McLean recounted:

It became a free-for-all for anybody who had an opinion. I knew a number of managers who were on that website giving opinions on the leadership, on the way the dispute was being run. A few people in head office were prominent on the website. I didn't like the anonymity. I don't believe that anything we say on behalf of this union should ever be anonymously posted on a website. Everybody should know who we are when we're speaking about the union and I found it quite frustrating that a number of officials were undermining processes, either by being insomniacs or just by being that way inclined. A lot were well-meaning people who had different opinions, but it genuinely did affect the dispute and the democracy of our union. Management who went on that site had a handle on what members were thinking. I remember my old chief and his deputy, and them telling me what was on the site the night before. So they were monitoring the site very, very closely and I think that had a part to play in the way that some officials were perceived and the way some of our national officials perceived some of the membership, and that was very unfortunate.

Kenny Ross from Strathclyde also expressed the view, held particularly by officials and officers, that 30K disrupted established information flows and compromised decision-making processes:

What it tended to do was bypass the recognised structures and that caused difficulty, particularly if you were an official trying to coordinate things and keep things disciplined. There was a big problem with leaks. I felt sorry for Gilchrist because he was in there dealing with the negotiations and members rightly wanted to know what is going on, but sometimes things are delicate and you can only tell them so much. But things were getting leaked and it was all over social media before you got a chance to consider, assess and discuss. What is released has to be time-barred to make sure our leverage in bargaining isn't compromised. I was at the rostrum at a recall conference and there was a programme on BBC2 at the time called *True Spies* about how the MI5 had infiltrated the NUM [National Union of Mineworkers]. I said, 'Do you know what? MI5 and Special Branch don't need to infiltrate the FBU. All they need to do is go online and read what you lot are putting up.' Rather than enhancing communication, and in some ways it does, it's been more of a hindrance – it bypasses structures.

Others believed the website widened the emerging divisions arising from dissatisfaction with the settlement and the leadership's perceived tactical failings. Jim Quinn, then Northern Ireland regional chair, reflected:

My view was it started out as a reasonable tool but it was of an age. It did have a big impact, it did win a lot of people but it broke a few people. Social media became a monster to handle. One important thing was that we did end up with a very split workforce in some areas and I think it was precipitated by sites where people were misrepresenting what was going on. And a little knowledge is a dangerous thing sometimes. What happened was, particularly after the agreement, through 30k all sorts of things were thrown in and a lot of personal vendettas and ambitions were played out in that arena. It was the first time the FBU had a dissenting voice having such a widespread influence and probably disproportionate as well... It certainly left us far more split when we came out of it.

Some complained that the website became not just a medium for unwarranted criticism of the leadership but, worse, for personal invective. John McGhee saw that 'it became a tool of very angry people slagging off the leadership every time something happened. It was unjustifiable.' Ruth Winters believed the '30k website turned into a vile thing', because of unmoderated personal attacks, while others commented on the vitriol directed at her. Mike Fordham recalled:

There was a side to it that was absolutely vile in the personal attacks and a significant chunk of that was aimed at Ruth Winters. Some of the stuff against Ruth was absolutely diabolical from a union that was supposed to be progressive on equality. Why go for Ruth? They went for Ruth because she was a woman, because she was control staff.

However impassioned these criticisms, a balanced account must also acknowledge the rational kernel to many members' posts, for they were reflecting genuine concerns regarding the lack of progress in negotiations, and disappointment with the suspended strikes, the stop-start nature of the action and the prospect that the settlement would fall way below the claim and what the campaign had led them, rightly or wrongly, to believe was achievable.

Grassroots FBU evolved out of the 30k website, as Matt Wrack explained:

> Out of 30k we launched Grassroots FBU which, of all the various rank-and-file initiatives I've been involved with, was actually the most rank-and-file ever, with lots taking part without any political background. We launched a bulletin, had meetings and I remember we had a launch-type meeting in Euston. The problem with 30k was that there was no structure – people put on whatever they wanted. There were some over-the-top attacks on Gilchrist and others. Equally, [Gilchrist and other leaders] were launching back similar attacks at conferences. The idea was to have an organised rank-and-file group, we needed structures, we needed to organise people in different brigades if we were to move resolutions, etc. And they launched an investigation. There had never been a culture of expelling people or banning things. They named myself, Andy Dark, Gordon Fielden and Paul Embery for investigation. Under the rules the disciplinary official sits with the EC member for the region. They subsequently amended the rules in 2005, actually the year I took over. They brought evidence to Mick Shaw London EC member and Mick said, 'What rule have they broken?' And they couldn't come up with anything that made sense. And Mick, to his credit, refused to do it and became very isolated on the Executive. They then created this bizarre alternative rule saying that if the EC member does not investigate, then the general secretary may appoint someone else to investigate. I remember it all becoming a sort of inevitability that I'll either be expelled or might get elected to a senior position next year.

A number of interviewees, although highly critical of the 30k website, disagreed with the attempt to ban it and to proscribe Grassroots.

Evaluation of the tactics

Nowhere are differences in perception more evident than in the interviewees' discussion of the tactics of the dispute and the evaluation of its outcomes.

The seriousness of the leadership's determination to implement the programme of strikes has been questioned. Matt Wrack recalled:

> I think that the thing that took us aback was when they announced the whole series of strike dates. When Mick Shaw reported back to our regional committee, he said that you could hear the gasps from the press. It strikes me that they were not intending to take those strike dates. What I haven't got a clue about is whether there was some understanding of this, or [whether] they thought that the threat would bring about a settlement. The members had voted for discontinuous strikes, which they thought would be a series of one-day strikes, possibly escalating.

A common critical comment was that expectations were set at such a high level that they could not be realised. The members' mood was so positive and they were so convinced of the justice of their claim that critical oversight of the tactics might have been neglected. Paul Embery reflected:

> They, the leadership, probably thought that all they had to do was threaten a national fire strike... and the employers and the government would come to heel and give us, if not 40 per cent, then a significant pay increase. We wouldn't actually need to go on strike. The problem is that no one really legislated for what might happen if the government said, 'Stuff you! Under no circumstances are you getting anything like that, whoever you are, whether you are firefighters or not, whatever public esteem you're held in. We're not giving in.' And, when it became actually clear that was the government's stance on anything near the demand we'd tabled, I just think the leadership thought, 'Where do we go from here? This is not how it was supposed to happen',

and there didn't seem to be a Plan B... But I think it was pretty clear to certainly those of us active in the union that actually the leadership from very early on were looking for a way out, even before we'd taken any sort of strike action. No one really thought it through, that's the brutal truth of it.

The testimonies are contradictory in their assessments of whether extended, additional or even all-out strike action was sustainable at different junctures. For Steve Harman, strike action in whatever form was beset with difficulties, especially given the government's obduracy:

> I could borrow on my mortgage and I could have gone on all-out strike for a year. But I knew younger ones had [mortgages of] £100,000 and they'd be crippled and I knew they were really worried about that. And quite soon we were taking short periods of strike action and there were concerns. So strategy-wise it's really difficult to think how to do a strike. If the government is going to try and destroy you, well you're up against it, it's a big machine. But if you're taking short periods of strike, there's an end to the actions. So you take two days or take eight days but once you go on strike there tend to be no negotiations until the strike ends. So your strike is a statement of solidarity, but when you're out for eight days nothing happens, you are waiting for the eight days to be over. But if you go on all-out strike, it's all or nothing isn't it?

National officer Dave Green doubted whether further strike action was sustainable after the June 2003 agreement, given unevenness between brigades:

> There were certain regions whereby it was becoming abundantly clear they'd had enough and that is where you have to take responsibility as leaders. And certainly, the bulk of members in London weren't prepared to go back, a lot in the Mets weren't prepared to go back. Wholetime in Nottinghamshire didn't want to go back, but all the retained did. My view was you can't sustain a national dispute when half your members want to go back... It was an impossible situation.

Others, though, were convinced that FBU members would have been prepared to extend, even escalate, action. Former London Executive Council member Ian Leahair recalled and believed:

> It was a very close call to accept the deal. When you look around the country at who chose to accept the deal, a lot were from very small brigades that relied very heavily on retained. If it had been left to the big brigades – with the exception of Strathclyde, who really shifted the balance because if they had voted to reject the deal we would still have been on strike. I can only really speak for London, but members there would have gone out on strike a lot longer because we felt that the only way we were going to win the dispute was to take the government on. There were many who would have been happy to have gone out on eight days' consecutive strike action at that time of the final offer because it was an ideal opportunity for us to not only show our strength but to take the government on. I do think [the outcome] was avoidable. I think that we played to our weaknesses rather than our strengths. I think there was an opportunity there for the EC to turn round and say we're not going to recommend this deal to the members just because government were getting harder on us. I do think we should have carried on, we should have made a stronger case, even if that meant taking longer periods of strike action. People were bitter because they did not get the opportunity to test that.

Keith Handscomb had been involved in the 1997 Essex strike:

> All the way through the dispute, the mandate from Essex, because of what we went through, was 'Do not suspend'. The phrase was: 'We can walk and talk. Never suspend a strike for talks, only suspend a strike for a settlement.' We suspended the eight-day strike and we're in that downward spiral. That's when the membership support for Andy Gilchrist shifted. I'd say half the country actually thought he was doing the right thing because they didn't particularly want to strike – and why not have talks? – whereas the other half, who were up for it, were saying, 'This is bad tactics', and they hated and blamed him for that decision.

Censure of the leadership's tactics deepened over the following months, culminating in the angry response to the Executive Council's decision to suspend the Bridlington conference. Alan McLean gave critical insight into the tensions and divisions that emerged:

> As a region, we backed Andy Gilchrist. I thought and genuinely believe that the person who was general secretary and acting on behalf of the EC and acting on behalf of a democratic decision by conference was hit too hard and given the blame for something that really the EC should've taken more responsibility for. I think, with hindsight, we should never have done the dispute in that manner, but it's an exact science is hindsight. I thought that there would be an exit strategy and I got on the EC hoping to find out what the exit strategy was and there wasn't one, or if there was one, it eluded me.

Outcomes

The testimonies contain diverse, mixed and, even from the same individual, contradictory evaluations of the outcomes. Some were inclined to regard the settlement within the context of the impending managerial and government offensive on pay and modernisation and, thus, were more likely to emphasise the positive. Les Skarratts, North West Executive Council member, reflected:

> People should remember that our industry was going to change, the government had us in its sights. Look back to the 2001 White Paper and Mike O'Brien[60] was very clear what he was going to do to us. It spelt it out and the union had to react. So sometimes I feel saddened when people just say that the dispute was a disaster full stop and we gave everything away, when the government with its enormous majority had said, 'This is what we are going to do.'

Dave Green acknowledged that the agreement was really unpopular and generated genuine dissatisfaction. However, he also understood:

I think it's a completely wrong thing to do to look at the decision in isolation, without looking at what was happening politically with Iraq. And the pressure was really on the leadership. I mean I was an EC member and I was certainly feeling the pressure. You know, there were a couple of times when I nearly buckled. The pressure was mainly from the media and the employers were digging in. And the Labour Party were getting very aggressive. I mean there were some really horrendous things said.

Criticism of the outcome was far from universal. Roddy Robertson, for example, could see strengths:

To get retained firefighters on to the same hourly rate and to get the rises we got was fantastic. Control members were taken from 92 per cent to 95 per cent and so again a recognition and an increase. So there were a lot of victories at the end of it.

Lynda Rowan-O'Neill, emergency control rep from Northern Ireland, saw some achievement although they did not attain the full equality claim:

It could have been better. I'm saying that from control, but our pay increased to 95 per cent so we did get a part of it – we got a bigger percentage pay rise but we still weren't at 100 per cent of firefighters' pay. So for us it was better. It wasn't what we wanted but then again when you sit down and look at it, was what we set out to achieve realistic?

John McGhee acknowledged the widespread disappointment that the headline 30k was not achieved and the criticism that expectations were set too high. Nevertheless: 'I think we only had 16 days strike and ended up with a 16 per cent pay increase. Firefighters went from having I think 21 grand to £25,000, it was quite a considerable increase. It took longer than we hoped but we did get there.'

More typical, though, were negative assessments. Alan Chinn-Shaw from Essex commented:

It worked out at about 16.5 per cent over two years but in that we lost two public holidays, from 10 to 8, and changed our long-service entitlement. We used to get a long-service increment at 15 years that was pensionable, that was at the time a reasonable amount of money – around £909 a year after 15 years. We did feel with the resolution that came out that we had signed a bit of a blank cheque. And firefighters still aren't on the £30,000. Here we are some 14 years later and we're still not on the pay that we went out for.

Bob Walker, former Devon and Somerset brigade chair, shared this position stating, 'And I'm sure you've been told many, many times but we've still got firefighters that don't get £30,000. You know, still!' Phil Coates from Nottinghamshire was explicitly critical regarding the loss of the pay formula:

You know, we gave that away for nothing, for absolutely nothing. We gave away the pay formula which guaranteed us a pay rise. It didn't matter how much it was, we got a pay rise every year and we gave it away. It was an absolutely catastrophic mistake by this union to go out for £30,000, which we're still not on.

Joe McVeigh, former London region secretary, was critical of the settlement and its aftermath:

There were four pillars and we didn't really achieve any of them. On pay we got 16 per cent over just under three years, so nothing like the 40 per cent immediate claim. We got a new pay formula but for only two years. And, I think, if you speak to control and retained members they fell short. And yet the leadership said we'd achieved three and a half of the four pillars, which frankly was just complete nonsense and insulted people's intelligence. In fact the downsides were considerable, the fact that the Grey Book was hollowed out. The argument made by the people who supported the agreement – I'm talking about senior officials and some more senior regional officials – was that we could fight the government and the employers by having localised disputes and there would be so many that they would not be able to handle them. What a load of flannel! We argued, quite rightly as it turned out, that if you isolate an individual brigade they will marginalise them and will defeat them that way. And that's exactly what happened. We've reaped not the rewards, we've reaped the whirlwind.

Many reflected on the point of departure, namely pay increases beyond the pay formula. Jim Barbour commented with characteristic candour on the fundamental dilemmas facing the FBU:

Ken Cameron would have said this – don't take them on on pay yet, it's not the right time to be doing it. They should never have lifted up that stone because you didn't know what was underneath it. It's probably because we were so cocky in that we had a very strong union, never been touched. We opened the door to shift changes, cuts, the whole lot. Now maybe they would have come anyway, but the speed and the weight of them was appreciably higher than it would have been. We gave them the opportunity. I don't know, maybe a more modest request might have made things easier. But we were always told as well that they were looking for us as a scapegoat as a trade union. The Labour Party at that point in time wanted to make an example, because Blair in my view was pushing his programme. The temerity of going for a 40 per cent pay rise, it was just seen as 'Who are these guys?' And the pay formula had served a purpose, there's no doubt about it, but even in the mid-1990s and well before 2002, it wasn't an effective methodology. Now, whether what we did in 2002 was right, that's the big question. And I tell you that was a difficult time for any of us who went through that.

Election of Matt Wrack

Although the testimonies reveal mixed perceptions, dissatisfaction with the leadership of the dispute and discontent with its outcomes were evidenced by the results of elections to national positions, which saw incumbent leaders, or candidates who supported them, defeated by activists critical of the leadership. Already, by December 2003, Paul Woolstenholmes had been elected as national officer with 52 per cent of the vote in a three-way contest.

As indicated above, Matt Wrack was elected assistant general secretary in February 2005 and then in May defeated Andy Gilchrist to become general secretary, while in September Andy Dark was elected assistant general secretary.

The testimonies provide insight into the dynamics that led to Wrack's election as general secretary. Keith Handscomb identified the decisive moment as the March 2003 recall conference, when the Executive Council recommended the suspension of strikes:

> The conference went mad and Matt led the charge from the floor because he was the delegate from London, the biggest brigade in the country. Well, the destiny was set then. I don't think that Matt ever wanted to be general secretary but then you got the end of the dispute... well who else was going to stand against Andy Gilchrist? Half wanted to keep him, half wanted him out. Matt was the obvious candidate.

Andy Dark reflected on the process by which Wrack and he were elected as general secretary and assistant general secretary:

> I don't think the thought was we would challenge for the leadership. Trying to be accurate, it was more a case of dissatisfaction and unhappiness. No one else was going to do it, so we will. We weren't our first choices! So, for example, the first national election that came up was a national officer, but we didn't stand for that job. We waited to see if anyone else wanted to because we were quite clear, you can't have London dominating the union. And a fella called Paul Woolstenholmes from East Anglia region and a fella from Manchester got it. I can genuinely say that it wasn't based on ego, but then the assistant general secretary election came up and Matt was successful. Then Andy came up for his five-yearly term and Matt won that. Mike Fordham retired three months after conference, which left a vacancy, and I stood and won. It was not 'We must plot the downfall'; there was none of that. We had policy differences, but we supported Andy for the leadership when he stood. But when Matt stood and when I stood, I knew that we would win.

Conclusion

The 2002-04 firefighters' dispute was a protracted period of industrial conflict. Its dynamics cannot be simply read off from number of strike days (16) taken, small in comparison to the 11 weeks of continuous strike action in 1977-78. While the first strike had a bottom-up, rank-and-file-led character and that of 2002-04 was initially driven by the national leadership, it was no less intense a struggle than its predecessor and its consequences were equally momentous. If the 1977-78 strike changed the terrain of industrial relations for the better, in that the union secured a pay formula that benefited its members for more than a decade, then the outcome of 2002-04 stood in marked contrast. It was not merely the loss of a pay formula, nor the failure to come close to achieving the 30K claim, that was most debilitating. Of key import were the consequences of opening Pandora's box: a settlement which paved the way for modernisation, implemented at brigade level, which potentially diminished the union's ability to repel the managerial offensive. The next chapter outlines the FBU's response to this offensive and documents the union's resilience in the prevailing, more unfavourable conditions under a national leadership that had recently been elected on a wave of member discontent at the conduct and outcome of this key dispute.

Control staff demonstrate during the Essex dispute, 2015

Firefighters' march, South Yorkshire dispute, 2009

5

Always in dispute: defending local services, national shift patterns and emergency control

Ever since the 2002-03 strike it felt like we were always in dispute, there was always something; and then they came for something else and then they came for something else and then they came for something else. And it felt relentless, relentless.

Sian Griffiths, former National Women's Committee member, London

In paying tribute to his predecessor, Matt Wrack emphasised that he and Andy Gilchrist agreed that it was 'imperative for the union to unite to face the challenges ahead', namely the attack on pensions, the plan for regionalisation of control centres. They highlighted the importance of campaigning against cuts and for a national standard for fire and rescue emergency response planning.[1] Wrack pledged to rebuild the confidence of members in their ability to fight back against attacks on the service, and to strengthen membership. Importantly he stated that one of his priorities was to put the finances of the union on a sound footing.[2] For FBU president, Ian Murray:

Following the national pay dispute and a new leadership being elected, the priority was to try to reunify and rebuild trust in the national union. Members had come through a long and bitter dispute. There was deep resentment from those who believed the deal wasn't good enough. The outcome and bitter divisions had built mistrust in the Executive Council and head office officials and so the first task the new leadership faced was to try to rebuild that trust in the national union across the whole of the membership. That took a lot of hard work and a number of years to attain but ultimately was achieved by the general secretary,

Matt Wrack, and president, Alan McLean, around 2010. It came just in time, as the union was under attack again from UK-wide cuts being implemented from the coalition's austerity agenda, not to mention the attack on the public sector pensions, which led to our next national strike. That would never have been achievable with a membership that didn't once again trust the leadership.

The removal of national standards of fire cover[3] and their replacement by local Integrated Risk Management Plans (IRMPs) after the 2002-04 dispute led to increased fragmentation of the service. Alongside the abolition of the Central Fire Brigades Advisory Council (CFBAC) and the Scottish CFBAC, these changes produced, in the view of the union, a 'postcode lottery' of variable levels of service, including equipment, training and planning for emergency response.[4] In terms of industrial relations, according to Ian Fitzgerald,[5] IRMPs signalled the death of corporatism; that is, the joint regulation of the national fire service based on structured relationships between employers, management and the FBU. In future, local fire authorities would be able to introduce flexibility in fire cover, at the expense of national terms and conditions and national duty systems. The restructuring of the management of the service produced attempts to introduce a myriad of shift systems, including 12-hour shifts, annualised hours and, most controversially, close proximity crewing. For the FBU, these new duty systems were designed to reduce firefighter numbers and were reliant on daily personnel movements, additional shift working, rest-day recall and overtime to cover staffing shortfalls. They would mean longer hours, undermining the work-life balance of firefighters and control staff, while threatening the tight-knit teamwork crucial to emergency work, the watch culture and historical industrial cohesion. At the 2010 conference the union recommitted itself to fighting for national standards of emergency response, launching the campaign 'It's About Time'.

Matt Wrack described the years between 2005 and 2010 as 'the most difficult ever faced by our union', with more industrial disputes than at any time in its history.[6] He urged a return to grassroots organisation. This chapter focuses firstly on these many local battles against fire authority attempts to use IRMPs to deliver cuts to jobs and services and to downgrade fire cover. They took place in a new context: the government's removal of military cover in the event of industrial action. Secondly, at national level, the chapter records the battle over FiReControl, the government's doomed initiative to secure the regionalisation of emergency control. Thirdly, the chapter documents action taken to prevent unacceptable changes to shift systems. Finally, it looks at task reallocation among the emergency services and the possible tension around firefighters' adaptation to wider roles. These roles range from co-responding and emergency medical duties for firefighters, plus multi-agency emergency response involving not only marauding terrorism and firearms incidents and environmental challenges (floods), but also youth and community engagement, and inspection and enforcement. Union contestation after 2004 cannot be interwoven readily into a straightforward chronological account and so, to aid explanation, the chapter is structured thematically rather than chronologically. However, it is important to acknowledge the intensity of the challenges confronting the FBU at national and local levels, including the battle over pensions (Chapter 6). As the words of Sian Griffiths quoted at the beginning of this chapter convey, union officers and members experienced these attacks and threats as relentless and part of a generalised, multi-faceted offensive.

Defending local services

Between 2005 and 2007 strike action was taken in four different brigades – with a successful strike ballot in a fifth – following attempts by employers to implement cuts in fire cover, reductions in jobs and, in four of the five, new shift patterns.[7] Suffolk FBU was the first to strike against cuts arising out of the new, local IRMP regime. In June 2005, after years of sustained wholetime and retained brigade understaffing, the authority sought to cut 12 wholetime firefighter posts at Bury St Edmunds, which provided the 24/7 crewing for one of the county's two turntable ladders, meaning, at best, significantly delayed response times. In a ballot 68 per cent voted in favour of strike action, leading to 22 short, discontinuous strikes over an eight-week period, which produced a negotiated settlement involving a reduced wholetime establishment (from 256 to 253), rather than the proposed reduction of 12 posts.

The authority promised to maintain the agreed levels of wholetime staffing, to recruit to the full retained establishment and to fully involve the FBU in future Suffolk IRMP processes, using evidence-based methodologies, including the Critical Attendance Standard (CAST) strategy (Chapter 8).

In June 2005 a ballot in Somerset produced an overwhelming majority in favour of action short of a strike, consisting of a refusal to participate in 'New Dimension'[8] training, until the issue of insurance cover for firefighters attending terrorist incidents was resolved. Management very quickly agreed to a joint FBU-management working party on the issue. In May 2006 FBU members in Hertfordshire returned an 85 per cent vote in favour of taking discontinuous strike action in response to budget cuts driven by the IRMP. These included a reduction of more than 50 wholetime firefighter posts, 10 community fire safety posts and 24 retained firefighter posts, the closure of two fire stations staffed by retained firefighters, the removal of one wholetime pump at night, the axing of one of the county's three aerial appliances, a change to the start and finish times of the day and night shifts across all the wholetime fire stations and the reduction of a seven-day fire station to only five days a week. The proposals were particularly unacceptable, given the inadequacies in personnel numbers, equipment, emergency cover and strategic planning, which had been highlighted by the deaths of two Hertfordshire firefighters at Stevenage in February 2005,[9] and by the explosions at the Buncefield fuel depot in December 2005.[10] The planned losses were of firefighter posts and equipment at stations which were the first to respond to the incidents.

A key issue in the Hertfordshire dispute was the Department for Communities and Local Government decision in 2003 that the Army would not provide cover during industrial disputes and that local authorities would be responsible for contingency planning. Matt Wrack recalled that the Labour fire minister, Jim Fitzpatrick, had called him in to confirm that military cover would no longer be provided and that authorities were required to identify and fund replacement labour. This significantly changed the dynamics of subsequent strikes. This strike would be the first where the Army would not provide back-up and Tony Smith, Hertfordshire vice-chair, stated: 'If Whitehall is experimenting to see what happens if there is no military cover, then that is inexcusable. The legal responsibility for providing emergency cover rests with the council.'[11] Three eight-hour strikes and unity between wholetime and retained members secured a settlement with significant improvements, including a guarantee of no cuts to frontline crews, appliances or fire stations for three years, a recruitment drive and continuation of the 2-2-3 shift system. Nevertheless, Bovingdon and Radlett fire stations were closed, despite a temporary reprieve for the latter.

In March 2006, despite robust representation from local officials, Cleveland Fire Authority resolved to implement a 'Safety Improvement Plan' which included the removal of 66 frontline posts, the downgrading of fire stations and the axing of specialist rescue equipment. A ballot in July delivered a 74 per cent vote for industrial action. The threatened strike mitigated the worst of the cuts.[12] Later in 2006 a ballot was held in response to Staffordshire Fire and Rescue Service proposals to downgrade stations and remove appliances. The dispute was lifted prior to the completed ballot process, when the authority gave assurances of no reduction in retained establishments and no redundancies.

Local skirmishes over cuts continued. In autumn 2009, *Firefighter* suggested that 8,000 members – around one in five firefighters in England – had taken local industrial action at any one time since August that year.[13] In 2009 Essex entered a dispute, over the introduction of an IRMP to cover the period to 2012 involving cuts to 44 frontline jobs and the introduction of jump-crewing of aerial appliances. In July Essex FBU members returned a 78 per cent vote in favour of industrial action short of a strike, which resulted in bans on voluntary overtime, acting-up and new secondary contracts (taking on additional duties under a second contract of employment). The chief fire officer (CFO) and senior management team adopted an aggressive approach from the outset and resorted to union-busting tactics and intimidation to break the resistance and solidarity of union members. The spring of 2012 saw management propose a further round of frontline cuts, with highly controversial proposals to employ new firefighters on conditions outside the Grey Book. After a further consultation with members in June 2012, Essex FBU members voted 71 per cent in favour of adding strike action and 999-calls-only action to their action short of strike. A complex series of strike action and action short of a strike ensued, including strike periods called specifically for RDS members at times when the employer had locked out striking wholetime firefighters, so that they could not return to their stations to complete the remainder of their shift after the cessation of the lawful strike period.

Once again, the issue of contingency in industrial disputes emerged and the dispute saw the first use of resilience contracts to cover industrial action. Negotiations ensued while strikes and action short of a strike continued, resulting in a detailed dispute resolution document. The agreement included written assurances from the CFO to maintain the wholetime complement across Essex up to March 2015. Importantly, the document confirmed the

The Spartacus Letters

During the 2009-12 Essex dispute an FBU member from Basildon wrote to local councillors asking questions about the pay levels of senior managers and criticising frontline cuts to the 999 service. Despite the fact that he had raised these concerns in confidence, the letter was forwarded to fire chiefs and resulted in his suspension. In response, the councillor received 41 identical letters from firefighters in Basildon, which became known by management as the *Spartacus Letters*, as Riccardo La Torre, Eastern regional secretary, reported:

> I think quite a few letters went in to councillors, fire authority members. One went into the chair of the fire authority from a Basildon member. He handed it straight to the chief and it was deemed gross misconduct, because he basically said that these cuts are going to cause deaths 'that'll be on your head'. He was suspended straight away. And we had another member suspended for a similar letter and then sacked at the first hearing down the road in Grays. Within a matter of 48 hours, purely through coincidence of course, everyone's individual choice, every single member of that branch, plus other branches, sent the exact same letter to the exact same person. Now they've got 42 people they've got to deal with. And the outcome of it was everyone got disciplined – 42 people got written warnings. It was a persecution of an organised union

service's full commitment to the Grey Book, with all new recruits to be employed under its conditions and all future contractual variations or changes in terms and conditions or duty systems to be negotiated in accordance with Grey Book provisions.

London experienced a series of disputes from 2009 to 2011, particularly over shifts, as discussed below, but also in August-September 2009 over cuts to allowances and access to continual professional development (CPD) payments of £1,000. Following resolution of the dispute over shifts in 2010, in November 2011, London members voted by more than nine to one in favour of industrial action short of a strike against further attacks on conditions of service. Issues included the introduction of stringent sickness criteria, attacks on middle managers' leave and pay, the introduction of all-day standbys, restrictive changes to the policy

branch and they sent in the disciplinary officer. Every day for about two weeks, people were lined up just waiting to go in. 'Did you write the letter yourself?' 'Yes.'

The 42 Basildon firefighters and officers were charged with using defamatory and disrespectful language deemed detrimental to the service. The disciplinary cases concluded with 37 receiving written warnings and four having final written warnings hanging over their heads for 18 months. National officer Paul Woolstenholmes concluded:

This whole affair has been a disgraceful abuse of authority and confidentiality, and strikes at the heart of the fundamental democratic principles in our country. If firefighters are gagged from raising matters of concern with local MPs and councillors then how on earth can the public rely on their elected politicians being sufficiently informed to hold the running of our public services to account?[14]

FBU members were particularly aggrieved by the fact that the IRMP had removed fire standards from the remit of national government and made IRMPs subject to local decisions and consultation. In seeking to engage in the consultation process union members were effectively censored.

on mutual exchanges and the authority's decision to renege on its commitment to incorporate CPD into core pay. In addition, the London Fire and Emergency Planning Authority wanted new contracts on promotion, which would compel members to undertake duties outside the Grey Book, and the introduction of secondary contracts requiring non-contractual work for less than National Joint Council (NJC) rates of pay. Firefighters refusing to move from nationally agreed terms and conditions were threatened with demotion. The dispute also covered the continuing freeze on London weighting allowance and plans to privatise the brigade's control and training functions. The ensuing industrial action was supported overwhelmingly from 25 November 2011 until it was suspended, following a proposed settlement, on 14 June 2012. It achieved an increase in London weighting, the incorporation of CPD payments into core pay, acceptable changes to sickness policy, abandonment of all-day standbys, and further discussions on changes to middle managers' conditions, changes to the policy on mutual exchanges and the question of secondary contracts.

Resistance to local cuts continued. At the end of 2016, members in North Yorkshire voted overwhelmingly for industrial action short of a strike over the introduction of tactical response vehicles with reduced crewing and unsafe changes to standard operating procedures at incidents, which imposed additional duties on firefighters. However, in September 2017, the fire authority responded to union concerns about public safety, announcing that four firefighters would crew each tactical response vehicle instead of three, possibly saving up to 20 firefighter posts.[15] *Firefighter* also reported successful campaigns in Cheshire, Surrey, Warwickshire and North Wales, fending off fire station closures, the removal and downgrading of appliances and cuts to firefighter posts.[16]

The fight over FiReControl

In 2004, the government declared its plan to introduce regional control centres (RCCs), known as the 'FiReControl project', and this became a major preoccupation, nationally and locally, for the FBU. The government's plan for regionalising emergency control rooms threatened the loss of up to 900 jobs.[17] England's 46 standalone fire and rescue control rooms would be replaced by a national network of nine purpose-built RCCs. From the outset concerns were raised about the feasibility of centralising control work and the reliance on unproven technology. The FBU led a campaign against the scheme and its implied job losses, highlighting the insufficient scrutiny of costs and contracts and predicting that the plan was doomed to failure. The union commissioned three reports by the Institute of Public Finance.[18] These endorsed the union's view of the matter.

In early 2008, the Scottish government halted plans to reduce the number of emergency control rooms when these plans were deemed unworkable.[19] Nevertheless, in South West England, 123 fire control staff were handed preliminary redundancy notices, with no notice or consultation, as part of proposals to shut all seven control rooms and replace them with an RCC in Somerset. Of the seven fire authorities, only one, Avon, guaranteed no job losses. Kelly Vincent of Avon control told *Firefighter*:

> We all love our jobs, we've done a lot of training, we're good at it and we don't want to leave the service, but it's not going to work as a regional control. At the moment we have trained, dedicated staff. We have numerous people who live all around the county so we know the area. We get a lot of holidaymakers in the region and they don't know where they are half the time and we're able to question them with landmarks and different things. In the regional control [centre] there are so many duplicates of different areas, places with the same name in different counties, that it's not easy to know where [people] are. But it is easy to mobilise an appliance to an incorrect location. I'd hate to see lives lost as a result of it.[20]

The announcement of redundancies among control staff in the South West region sparked a debate in all fire and rescue service workplaces on the implications of regionalisation. In its communications on the matter, the FBU emphasised that the government appeared not to want a highly skilled, well-paid workforce in RCCs. Evidence from government guidance to contractors suggested that the FBU would not be recognised, that there would be reduced pay rates for any redeployed staff, that control staff would be subject to new, indepth security checks and that fixed-term contracts would effectively mean casual labour.[21] John Drake, South West regional secretary, perceived that regionalisation would 'be the first true privatisation in the UK fire and rescue service', 'leading to the hiving off of the local authority-controlled companies currently running RCCs to the private sector'.[22] An emergency resolution at the 2008 annual conference stated that FiReControl would not result in the savings claimed, but would reduce call-handling capacity and resilience, adversely affect the safe and efficient mobilisation and control of fire appliances, personnel and equipment, mean the loss of jobs and leave much work currently completed by control room staff to be carried out by individual brigades. Conference resolved that in the event of the government enforcing the scheme, the minimum FBU aims should be to ensure there were no compulsory redundancies, and to secure Grey Book conditions and FBU recognition for all staff required to work in RCCs. All means available should be pursued, including industrial action, to meet these aims. Wrack urged conference to defend control jobs: 'Get back to your branches and start building that fight.' Union officers visited control members around the country, talking about the battle to defend jobs, and (as Chapter 2 records) the campaign against regionalisation increased the profile of control members in the union.

Eventually, FiReControl was cancelled by the Coalition government in 2010 because of the predicted failings of the contractor to fulfil the scheme's requirements. At a cost of at least £469 million, the Committee of Public Accounts described it as 'one of the worst cases of project failure that the committee has seen in many years'.[23] The committee concluded that lack of consultation with local fire and rescue services contributed significantly to the failure. The FBU added that ministers had ignored the voices of control staff and their reps. The government had commissioned the construction of RCCs under the Private Finance Initiative (Chapter 1) and ten years on, four of the nine buildings remained unused. The unoccupied building in Taunton, intended as the South West RCC, subsequently cost more than £16 million in charges, almost double the £8.9 million it cost to build. South West Executive Council member Tam McFarlane, posting on the FBU blog, observed:

Every day as firefighters make their way to work, they are forced to pass a useless empty shell of a building that the government continues to pour millions of pounds into. All of this while frontline firefighter posts are being axed, life-saving equipment is being reduced, and firefighters have been robbed of their pensions.[24]

Despite the abandonment of the plan for RCCs, restructuring continued. Between 2010 and 2017, 15 control rooms closed. Although stand-alone control rooms with networked collaboration were still preferred, 17 authorities consolidated their control rooms into seven joint fire control centres through locally determined agreements and partnerships. The Scottish Fire and Rescue Service – the outcome of the merger of eight local fire and rescue services – amalgamated eight control rooms into three, covering north, east and west Scotland. In England three fire and rescue services co-located their control rooms, sharing facilities and infrastructure, but retaining their own staff and operating systems.

The threat of outsourcing and privatisation persisted. In 2012 London Fire Brigade awarded a 10-year contract to Capita to take over its publicly funded control centre, with the prospect of 120 staff being transferred. However, with the departure of the Conservative chair of the London Fire and Emergency Planning Authority, Brian Coleman, it was decided that outsourcing represented too great a financial risk and a contract was awarded for a replacement mobilising system, rather than a fully managed outsourced service.

In 2011, Cumbria County Council proposed to cut its fire and rescue service command and control centre and move the work to Cheshire, described as 'a bolt from the blue' by the 12 staff involved.[25] A further move to a regional control room in Warrington, serving four North West fire and rescue services, was envisaged, and was perceived by the FBU as an attempted regional revival of the national FiReControl project, until Merseyside pulled out. However, despite the FBU's campaign, emergency controls in Cumbria, Cheshire, Greater Manchester and Lancashire were replaced in 2014 by the North West regional fire control. Meanwhile, Buckinghamshire control members were told their work was being outsourced to Cambridgeshire with the loss of

20 posts; the decision was communicated to staff by letters delivered to their homes by taxi. In 2015 Buckinghamshire, Oxfordshire and Berkshire control rooms were replaced by the Thames Valley Joint Fire Control.

These developments have been accompanied by a litany of system faults and failings in mobilising systems, causing disruptions to emergency 999 call-handling. Control staff have experienced understaffing, increased workloads and stress, causing mid-career resignations and retirement. All this has been exacerbated by changes to shift patterns.[26]

In 2016, 84 per cent of members in South Yorkshire voted for industrial action short of a strike over plans to cut a quarter of control operator posts and against changes to firefighters' leave arrangements caused by the imposition of a localised availability system.[27] Pete Smith, Yorkshire and Humberside regional secretary, insisted:

> Emergency control staff are the very first people you'll speak to when you're in an emergency. Firefighters rely on them to get all the vital information to perform a rescue as fast and efficiently as possible. They are an invaluable component of the lifesaving service firefighters provide. The public in South Yorkshire will be put at greater risk if these posts are cut.

Action began in February, when the union refused to undertake detached duties and to co-operate with the electronic system underpinning localised availability. The action secured significant gains, including a review and the maintenance of the status quo.

In July 2017, Steve Howley, North Yorkshire brigade secretary, stated that budget cuts were placing the service's control room at crisis point and were putting lives at risk. The number of emergency control operators had been reduced from 22 to 15, untrained staff were fielding emergency calls from the public and emergency calls were being diverted to Cornwall in peak periods, causing response delays. Operators were frequently forced to work up to 90 hours a week to cover staff shortages.[28]

The battle over shifts

The 1977 strike embedded not only the pay formula, but also a reduction in the working week to 42 hours, based upon a nationally agreed 2-2-3 shift system, which meant that staff worked 48 hours over an eight-day cycle. The system involved working two day shifts of nine hours and two night shifts of 15 hours. The rest of the day following the end of the second night shift was a rota day (or day off) followed by the next three rota days as preparation for the next 48-hour period. The 15-hour night shift had included a stand-down period for firefighters and rest facilities for emergency control members (midnight to 7am) during which they remained on duty at work to respond to 999 calls.

One outcome of the 2002-04 dispute was the removal of the 'constant crewing' provision in the Grey Book, which ensured similar numbers of staff on night shifts to those on day shifts. In 2006 *Firefighter* reported that since 2003 authorities had begun to experiment with shift and duty systems and to cut night time fire cover,[29] involving substantial threats to work-life balance and disruption to the watch system. In 2003 an FBU survey found almost unanimous opposition by control staff (97 per cent) to Bain's suggestion that the 2-2-4 pattern was not family-friendly; they strongly supported the maintenance of the existing system. Following Bain, fire authorities, such as the West Midlands, had promoted changes to shift patterns on the basis of equality, which had produced some division on gender lines, with women in control blamed by some for alteration in firefighters' shift patterns.[30] This response occurred despite the fact that the FBU National Women's Committee had opposed changes to shift patterns (see Chapter 7).

Yet, as elsewhere in the service, cost cutting has been the main driver of changes in control shift patterns. For Wrack, 'The simple truth is that the best service to the public is provided by 24-hour cover. If there is no attempt to reduce the level of fire cover, then the requirement to change shifts and duty systems disappears.' The move has been towards locally imposed 12-hour shifts, detrimental to national terms and conditions (for example, 7am-7pm or 7pm-7am) over two days and two nights, followed by four days off. For former Executive Council member Keith Handscomb, changes to shift patterns go beyond cost savings:

The employers still use it as a weapon to try and disband watches, because what they want to do is get rid of the industrial strength, they want people working different times, different contracts, divide and rule. And they're slowly bringing it in bit by bit. They don't want every watch to be working a nationally set watch system or duty system that applies across the country. They don't want a set duty system to be the same at every station – they want a variety of duty systems at different stations. They want people to volunteer to work on different shifts and be more flexible with their times. They like simple 12-hour shifts because it makes it easy to swap people around, night and day. There are already some brigades where they forcibly move people off of one watch to another on the grounds you're contracted to work for the brigade not at a particular place of work and so they move people on a rota to stop them building up too strong allegiances with each other.

The West Midlands was one of the first authorities to attempt to impose what proved to be unworkable shift systems. A ballot for strike action against their proposed implementation in October 2005 delivered a 77-per-cent vote in favour. Three discontinuous strike days secured reassurances on shift changes, including protections of existing leave, compensation for additional travel costs when rostered to different stations and an enhanced hourly rate for late duty finish. In 2006, North Yorkshire Fire and Rescue Service sought to impose a move from a 10-hour day and 14-hour night shift pattern to 12-hour day and night shifts, while reducing the midnight to 7am stand-down period to just four hours. The employer argued that the changes would increase diversity in recruitment. The NJC national disputes machinery proposed that a 12-hour shift period be piloted after a transitional year on 11/13-hour shifts (an 11-hour day followed by a 13-hour night), and an independent review, which evaluated recruitment diversity, should follow the pilot, with the authority responsible for childcare costs incurred by staff during the pilot.

In 2008 South Yorkshire Fire and Rescue Service resolved to introduce a 12-hour shift system from 1 April 2009 without collective agreement. Following union objections, the implementation date was delayed. However, South Yorkshire Fire and

Rescue Service management wrote to all affected employees in February 2009 informing them that, with effect from 4 May 2009, the longstanding shift system would change to 12 hours, with start and finish times of 8am and 8pm. A ballot result overwhelmingly in favour of industrial action short of a strike prevented the imposition of new shifts. The issue progressed to the NJC's Resolution Advisory Panel, which concluded without an acceptable recommendation by the independent chair. In June 2009 management initiated a process to dismiss and re-engage 744 firefighters on new contracts, the first time mass sackings had been attempted in the fire and rescue service.[31] Nicky Brown, subsequently brigade chair, recalled how the dispute generated her own union activism:

> The chief organised a big forum and they basically sat down station members and said, 'Right, when you go on to 12-hour shifts…'. Nobody really was saying anything, so – and I don't know where it came from – a little voice in the background says, 'So you think the fight's over do you?' Apparently I was quite aggressive towards him. I think that was the starting point for me. After I'd been hauled into the office a few times, they realised what my true colours were. I became a rep shortly after. Anybody that wasn't fully on board certainly came on board as soon as they threatened to dismiss and reengage us all – that was the big thing.

In September 2009 members voted 80 per cent for discontinuous strike action, and on 28 September 2009, to coincide with the next South Yorkshire Fire and Rescue Service meeting, the FBU organised a mass rally in Barnsley town centre supported by 4,000 firefighters from across the UK. Pete Smith, regional secretary, remembered the response to the ballot result:

> I was with a firefighter who was really nervous – he'd not been part of a trade union – and I remember the result coming through on a text or an email and the euphoria. Even the lad that wasn't a traditional trade union member was thrilled to bits that we'd got this result and we were finally going to respond to management in the way, the only way sometimes, that they understood.

John Gilliver, former brigade secretary, clarified:

> I think the thing is, it sometimes can sound a bit odd when people start talking about the euphoria of going on strike and getting results, but someone who's been bullied and punched and kicked and told what to do and they've got the thumb and everything pressing down on them all the time – so the reason why it's euphoria is because you felt like you just walked into the light and the punches have stopped. We fought back and people actually stood up and turned around and faced the aggressors.

South Yorkshire members commenced their first 24-hour strike on 19 October 2009 and their second four days later. Four further strikes took place up until 4 November, when action was suspended following agreement to seek third-party assistance, which secured a compromise on 11/13 shifts. Gilliver explained:

> We were starting at 9/15. That was our start point, because that was the best shift system and that came out of the 1977 strike. If you want 24-hour emergency fire cover, which also gives decent welfare to its workers, then that is the best shift system. And we didn't want to give up. However, because of things that were going off and the compromises we kept the 11/13. As part of the resolution, not only did we secure a shift system that kept nearly everything intact for us really in one respect, even though we'd altered the hours, but we also got that secured for five years. So they couldn't make any shift changes for five years.

In the dispute's aftermath, Ian Murray described how the dispute had forced the brigade committee to address union organisation in order to ensure a majority in the second ballot.[32] The brigade secretary, Neil Carbutt, confirmed that after the 2002-04 dispute firefighters had been 'wounded':

> We were licking our wounds for years because it was a bitter and brutal dispute. When you're getting slated in the media, like we did, and by the Labour Party, as we did, and firefighters were licking their wounds, and to go on strike again after that,

we had to really get our act together, but we'd come to the point of 'Look, if we don't stand up for this...'

The response included constructing a matrix for South Yorkshire branches and colour-coding them on a traffic light system to ensure all watches at wholetime stations had been visited by officials and to reflect feedback from members. The brigade committee also targeted RDS branches, as the authority had assumed they would provide cover in any industrial action, and they would, therefore, be pivotal to effective strikes. Murray reported that '[t]his was hugely successfully and resulted in five out of six RDS branches immediately backing action'. After the ballot, organisation continued, with weekly campaign meetings open to all members. All branches had representatives and since the majority were officially elected, this initiative reinvigorated the brigade committee. Graham Wilkinson, former regional treasurer, remembered:

We had over 100 people attending and we were just passing out information, letting them know where we were with management, what was going on. It allowed the information to pass a lot quicker on to stations, which got everybody on board. It didn't take us long to realise we had the backing of the membership. And from that we ended up going back to a divisional structure with a fairly new brigade committee, because people had become part of this and really got into it and realised they wanted to get active and we ended up with a really strong brigade committee.

The threat of mass sackings re-emerged in 2010, this time in London. After entering formal negotiations over new working patterns, the London Fire and Emergency Planning Authority threatened to impose changes to terms and conditions by the dismissal and re-engagement of the 5,500 strong workforce. Ian Leahair, former London Executive Council member, recalled:

In 2010, the then chief officer decided he wanted to change the shifts and he wanted to change the shifts to equalise days and nights into 12 hours. He made all kinds of quasi business arguments for doing so, some even weirder health and safety arguments. But the real reason was if the day shift and the night shift were of equal length, you can operate fire stations flexibly. So you can afford to shut some of them at night and some of the others in the day, depending on the nature of the environment around them. So you might want to have suburban stations that are open at night time but not open in the day time. Stations in the City of London open in day time but not at night. You can very easily make people's contract flexible, make your workforce more flexible, with all the downsides that workers get out of that by equalising the shifts. So it was opposed. I suppose this is eventual fallout from 2002, the ability for brigades to locally bargain other shifts. It was opposed to the extent that the chief officer threatened to sack all of us and issued a 90-day notice under section 188. He was going to sack every single firefighter and bring us all back on a new contract unless it was settled. And there was only one thing you could do – 'Let's go on strike', which is what we did.

Members faced being forced onto new contracts on promotion, transfer or recruitment. A ballot delivered action short of a strike, which incurred stoppages of pay for some members, and, in the face of employer intransigence, a second ballot produced a 79 per cent vote for strike action. The dispute became embittered, with managers threatening disciplinary action against members wearing anti-bullying stickers. Several activists were suspended. Eight-hour strike action took place on 23 October and 1 November 2010.

The government's decision not to provide military cover during strike action had led to the emergence of Project Fireguard in 2008. Managed by the Chief Fire Officers Association, it aimed to deliver 'business continuity' in the fire and rescue service, but for the FBU, '[i]n simple terms it is a plan for organising strikebreaking within the Service'.[33] Even more provocatively, the project recommended Group 4 Security Services (UK) plc provide these services, with set-up costs estimated at £9.8 million and annual running costs £9.2 million. Wrack visited Denmark and persuaded Group 4 parent company, Falck, not to bid for the contract. The FBU also wrote to retired members urging them not to sign up for any resilience or contingency contracts. However the use of private strikebreaking firm, AssetCo, to bus in emergency fire crew into fire stations to break the London dispute, inflamed events and led to mass picketing of fire stations, secondary action rarely seen in the UK since the miners' strike of 2004-05. Equally notable was the overt support of the union leadership for such action and the attendance of the general secretary, president and assistant general secretary on mass picket lines. Two FBU members and a police officer were injured by vehicles driven by strikebreakers at Southwark. Ian Leahair was one of those injured:

> We used to travel to Southwark fire station quite regularly to meet those fire engines when they came back, and we asked those people to not cross picket lines. And the chief saw that as some sort of disorderly mob and obviously when you're in that situation and you're a firefighter who's losing pay and seeing someone take your pay, and not just take your pay but actually get a really good bung on the top, because they were getting paid quite generously for the hours they was doing. They weren't doing the job that we do, they were just standing there squirting a bit of water on something and quite often they didn't attend a lot of jobs because they didn't have the appliances. So it was obvious to whoever was there that firefighters were not going to take kindly to that, and they vented that anger in several ways and again – I make no excuses for it – they used foul language. They were frustrated and angered and they called these people who wanted to cross picket lines all forms of names. But when you're in that situation and having been threatened that your contract is going be ripped up, I defy most people to sit there and go 'OK, thank you. Carry on and do my job for me.'

The London Fire and Emergency Planning Authority pursued an interim injunction against the FBU, alleging breaches of legislation on picketing. Further strike action had been called for 5, 6 and 7 November 2010. The judge made no finding either way on the authority's allegations. He accepted the union's undertaking to abide by the laws governing picketing in relation to any further industrial action during the dispute. The strikes forced management to suspend temporarily the threat of mass dismissals and the matter was referred to the Resolution Advisory Panel. A consultative ballot in December 2010 agreed the outcome, which involved a 10.5-hour day shift and a 13.5-hour night shift – more acceptable working patterns than the original proposals.

In Essex, in 2015 a dispute over shift patterns led to strike action initiated by female control staff and supported by firefighters. From January to September 2015, members in Essex Fire and Rescue Service took 30 days of strike action[34] against fire authority attempts to impose reductions in staffing and fire cover, particularly with regard to night working. The wider context was an evaluation of the service involving the relocation of the control centre and the introduction of a new, computerised system of call allocation and distribution. The new centre had no rest facilities, signalling a threat to the rest arrangements that allowed workers to function the following day. The key trigger was the imposition of a 12-hour shift system on 44 emergency control staff and wholesale changes to operational and supervisory staffing levels. These changes threatened to eliminate their carefully constructed work-life balance and, in a press release, the Essex FBU emphasised the 'physical and emotional stresses on members' family and work lives'.[35] The 12-hour shifts led to some in control being forced to leave full-time employment and others having to reduce their working hours and face pay reductions. Emma Turnidge, a control room rep, discussed the impact of the proposed shift changes:

All the members said they preferred to keep the nine-hour days – the shorter days and the longer nights. Whether that be a nine-hour or a ten-hour day, they didn't want to do 12-hour days and nights, they were adamant about that. A lot of control staff have partners within the service, have children, and the implications that they were proposing were – for me personally – unreasonable because I don't have childcare at seven in the morning. And my child has already spent a night or two away from me a week because of my night shifts. It's unreasonable [to expect staff to do that] just to sustain a job. So that was me personally, but then there's an awful lot [of staff] within control with young families. I had to go to job-share because my partner is in the job, he's a firefighter doing the same shifts.

The changeover times were horrendous so I had to either go job-share or do flexible work. So I couldn't really afford to go job-share but I needed to, but after nine months I had to go back full-time, which was a big struggle for me. I love the job, don't get me wrong, and I never thought of going job-share, because I just love the job, but there are four people now on job-share. The big issue for control was that the days are too long, people going home so tired.

Joy Bingham, another rep, concurred:

I don't see my children for two days, two full days, because I leave at half-five, six in the morning, get home at eight and they're in bed by then. I put in for flexible working because I couldn't possibly start at seven, because of childcare, so I started at 9.30; I reduced hours. So there were girls I was working with, Karen for instance, luckily her mum lives round the corner, but her kids go to her mum's two days a week so they have to stay overnight. She says, 'Otherwise I have to get them up at five and then wake my parents up to say, "Can you take the kids because I need to get to work?"' So it's unreasonable but they're struggling through at the moment – but the amount of people that have had to take flexible working, or job share…

Riccardo La Torre, Eastern regional secretary, saw the employer picking on the 'least unionised, smallest membership – women members – to actually break the nut'. For him management had cynically selected the control staff for the imposition, as a Trojan horse for spreading 12-hour shifts to all Essex firefighters. Women were thus 'on the frontline' of resisting changes that had implications for firefighters locally and for brigades nationally.[36]

With the new system due to go live in December 2014, a strike ballot of all Essex FBU members was called on four issues, including staffing levels, terms and conditions, fire cover and the formal issue of 'an unworkable work-life/home-life balance' for control staff. The ballot spanned three weeks from 31 October, with brigade officials organising 67 member meetings. They noted the historic difficulties in mobilising control staff, surrounded in their workspace by senior management and isolated from firefighters. Across the service – control room staff *and* firefighters – 64 per cent voted in favour of action. The union employed the tactic of calling out different sections of the membership at different times, while the minimum notification required by law was given for each period of strike action (rather than as a block), creating a 'staggered surprise' effect. In January 2015 all members took strike action for three days, followed by two days in March that coincided with control staff members taking ten straight days of strike action. The union then called out retained firefighters and station-based watch managers, with control members taking six further days in August, sometimes alongside these colleagues. Emma and Joy recalled the solidarity provided by firefighters when control members picketed the fire brigade headquarters, blocking the A12. Emma became a rep during the dispute and described her politicisation, recalling the historic fight for equal pay by women machinists at Ford in Dagenham, Essex, which resonated with her, perhaps because of its popularisation through the film *Made in Dagenham*:

> I think management have realised that I'm not a walkover, and I didn't know anything about politics or anything – but I love it, I do love it, the whole thing. It's been mentioned to me a lot by different firefighters and also our regional secretary, Riccardo. He said, 'You don't know how many people have said to me how much they look up to you now and how the wheels have changed because of the fact that you're all strong women.' It was all in the papers wasn't it, all these 'Dagenham girls of control' and you think 'Wow!' We're only standing up for what we believe in and because we [women] are the majority – aren't we? – and a couple of men or one man in tow at the minute, we just thought it was what we should do. That's all we were doing and the firefighters really appreciated that.

Negotiations began in spring 2014 and the dispute was finally settled in May 2017 with the withdrawal of the 12-hour shifts in favour of a 10-hour day, 14-hour night pattern and the restoration of rest periods and rest facilities. Additionally, it was agreed to reinstate 48 firefighter jobs, increasing staffing on watches, and there was an assurance of no unilateral change to duty systems. The strikes thus secured major concessions.

Determination to reconfigure shift patterns was unabated. In 2016 the Greater Manchester Fire and Rescue Service threatened to sack the entire 1,250 Greater Manchester firefighter workforce and re-employ only those who agreed to new 12-hour shifts. Greater Manchester firefighters were at the time working two 10.5-hour shifts a week plus two 13.5-hour night shifts, alongside some 'rostered' reserve shifts. The employer also sought to cut one-fifth of the workforce – 250 jobs. Matt Wrack and president Alan McLean visited Manchester and the general secretary urged a packed roomful of firefighters to 'fight back, not beg'. Once again the FBU drew attention to the damage such shifts cause to work-life balance. There was extensive local and national media coverage, with publicity generated at FBU stands at the TUC and Labour Party conferences. A petition of 20,000 called on the Greater Manchester Fire and Rescue Service to abandon its plans and resulted in withdrawal of the threat of dismissal. Manchester brigade secretary, Gary Keary, summed up members' response:

We were absolutely staggered that GMFRS [Greater Manchester Fire and Rescue Service] would jeopardise workforce relations in this aggressive way. To start the process for dismissing firefighters to then simply re-engage them on an un-negotiated contract is appalling, and a serious breach of agreed mechanisms for industrial relations in the UK fire and rescue service. We did everything we could to avoid a bitter and damaging dispute and, thankfully, in the end GMFRS saw sense and withdrew their threat. We are continuing negotiations to try to find a way forward.[37]

Close proximity crewing: LLAR-LLAR land

In 2006, Merseyside experienced, what was at the time, the longest strike in the fire and rescue service outside the 1977 national strike, reflecting an issue of real national significance.[38] Industrial action was triggered by the first attempt to introduce 'day crewing plus' at five stations considered 'low level of activity and risk' (LLAR). Under Merseyside Fire and Rescue Authority's plan, firefighters at these stations would work 96-hour shifts over

Kerry Baigent employment tribunal victory

In 2014 Kerry Baigent was told that after 20 years she would be transferred from Cambridge fire station to Ely and to a different duty system. Cambridgeshire Fire and Rescue Service claimed that the mobility clause written into every firefighter's contract gave them the power to instruct firefighters to work at any station. Baigent would have had to move from a 2-2-3 duty system to a five-day schedule – working 8am to 6pm. This would have not only disrupted Baigent's work-life balance and commute, but also her trade union duties as the FBU's brigade organiser in Cambridgeshire and secretary of the national women's committee. The FBU supported Baigent in taking the Fire and Rescue Service to an employment tribunal on the basis of constructive dismissal.[39] At the tribunal it emerged that the employer had taken into account other employees' personal circumstances, but not Baigent's, with the service unable to explain the decision to transfer her to Ely. It was described as 'an irrational and perverse exercise' by the tribunal.[40] It found that managers had used an inaccurate skill-set record for Baigent in their selection process, meaning she should never have even been shortlisted for the compulsory transfer. The tribunal case established the significant principle that firefighters have to be consulted prior to any proposed relocation.

four days – four consecutive 24-hour shifts, consisting of 12-hour day shifts and 12-hour nights on call. The on-call time had to be spent at or in close proximity to the station. *Firefighter* reported that such shifts had not been seen since the Second World War, prior to which firefighters had lived on stations. Under close proximity crewing, a variant of day crewing plus, firefighters may stay on premises near the fire station, so that they are not technically 'workplaces', and in some cases dormitories or pods are purpose-built. Day crewing plus requires secondary contracts for overtime working, involving pay not only below Grey Book rates, but lower than normal basic pay. Forty-eight of the 96 hours would be paid at one-fifth of the NJC rate, effectively less than the minimum wage.[41] National officer Sean Starbuck commented:

> Some people call it day crew plus, some people call it close

proximity crewing. In Merseyside they call it LLAR-LLAR – they affectionately call it 'Live Like A Refugee'. Then there's the 24-hour shifts. There's a lot of different duty systems being bandied about and our officials have got to get their heads around them all and deal with them and a majority of the duty systems are just a mask for cuts to the fire service.

Alongside day crewing plus, Merseyside Fire and Rescue Authority attempted to cut 120 operational firefighter posts (1 in 10 of the workforce) and 15 emergency fire control posts, and to axe four fire engines at night time, in addition to the 68 posts lost in the previous year. Plans included a control shift system that for the first time included variable staffing – staff on flexible contracts to cover for reductions in personnel during periods of higher demand. For the FBU, the CFO and the authority had a clear union-busting agenda. A ballot for discontinuous strike action achieved a 71 per cent yes vote, and four days of strike action were called to commence on 31 August 2006, soon followed by a further four days. It quickly became clear that the dispute would be protracted and bitter and after a brief return to work, 26 days of almost continuous strike action followed. A march and rally on 15 September was attended by thousands of FBU members and senior trade union figures, including general secretaries Bob Crow (RMT), Billy Hayes (CWU) and Tony Woodley (TGWU) alongside Matt Wrack. After the continuous strike action the FBU and the employers reached a basis for resolution, with the union prepared to suspend further industrial action, although the FBU reported orchestrated harassment of those taking action. The settlement included a recruitment process, minimum staffing levels of five and four on two-pump stations, a staffing level of five on a one-pump station, plus protection for control staff. A definition of the term LLAR was agreed, which specified the difference between the part-time working and overtime working, with work additional to 42 hours tied into NJC role maps and paid accordingly. The agreement also resulted in a collective agreement on retained resilience. The settlement established a review into industrial relations within Merseyside and a return to work agreement.

The issue of day crewing plus emerged again in 2009, when Lincolnshire Fire and Rescue Service proposed to sack 112 wholetime firefighters and re-employ those who agreed to work on a new 12- hour shift system by February 2010. The plans would have affected firefighters at the county's two 24-hour stations (Lincoln North and South), who were working nine-hour day and 15-hour night shifts, as well as those employed at day-crewed stations. Firefighters would be required to be on duty for up to 108 hours without a break, with day crews at four stations working outside Grey Book terms. Firefighters designated as day crew would have to live close to stations to respond to alerts outside of the agreed working week of 42 hours. Chris Hides, Lincolnshire FBU brigade chair, reported that there was no meaningful consultation and that 'the shift system is not family-friendly and is discriminatory against females'. Following negotiations, agreement was reached on 11-hour day and 13-hour night shifts.

Attempts to introduce close proximity crewing persisted and, in 2015, the FBU won an employment tribunal case where the imposition of close proximity crewing was declared unlawful. The union brought a case against South Yorkshire Fire and Rescue Service after 24 FBU members were forced to transfer stations when they refused to sign up to changes in shift patterns. The employer's action breached the Working Time Regulations 1998 (WTR), but the close proximity crewing system required individual employees to opt out of the WTR. The new pattern additionally meant firefighters would not have the minimum 11-hour rest period in any 24 hours required by the WTR. Despite no FBU agreement, South Yorkshire Fire and Rescue Service required firefighters to 'volunteer' to work under close proximity crewing, with refusal leading to compulsory displacement. The employment tribunal judge found the transfer to a new shift pattern to be unlawful and that, when the firefighters who did not wish to work under close proximity crewing were forced to move to another station, they suffered a detriment for which they should be compensated.[42]

The employment tribunal ruling stated that CPC duty systems were operated in other authorities in conjunction with self-rostered crewing, where firefighters have flexibility in the distribution of their shifts. Despite the legal ruling reps reported, in the context of a pay freeze, that it could be difficult to prevent individual firefighters opting out of the WTR to take on CPC or day crewing plus shifts. Steve Harman, former Lancashire brigade secretary, observed:

> Day crewing plus became a big problem. They get rid of half the staff so they've saved from 28, they've saved 14 jobs and gone down to 14. And those 14 get a third extra wage and they do an 84-hour week. It's not three days on, three days off; they do 42 positive hours and 42 stand-down. They build these flats next to the station, this accommodation with bedrooms. They pay a peppercorn rent – they're sort of social housing around the station – although a lot has been sold off now. It's like a Travelodge: there's a room with a bed and a settee and a lounge area and then there's a communal kitchen. They're all en suite. It was massively over-subscribed and so we had a big problem. We got some concessions and made it as reasonable as we could, but we knew it was going to come in at these limited number of stations. This is before the Tories got in. The authority was just skint, really desperate, the budget was so low they were really struggling. It's at the 11 stations now. Firefighters like the money and they do like the flexibility because they can plan their shifts. When you're on red watch, you're on red watch and that's it, and you know whether you're working a wet Tuesday in four years' time. Whereas on this shift, they can say they've got a wedding coming up, and they just book that off and [agree] between friends, 'Can you cover that shift, and you do that and I'll do this?' And it gives them some flexibility. I just said it has to be voluntary. There's a dilemma. You're representing your members, aren't you? You can only guide them so much, but if you try to dictate too much they'll either tell you from within the structure of the union or they'll leave the union.

Similar issues emerged when in 2016 Cambridgeshire Fire Authority offered firefighters financial inducements to opt out of the WTR and move onto day crew plus contracts. Brigade secretary, Cameron Matthews, reported:

> They're trying to buy people out every day – look at Cambridgeshire. Firefighters who have been on a pay freeze or [had a pay rise of] 1 per cent, which in real terms is a cut, are now

being offered a 20 per cent enhancement to go on an unlawful shift system, and you've got firefighters thinking, 'Well, that's 20 per cent, I need that' and it's trying to buy people out of the Grey Book left, right and centre.

Emergency medical response: extending the role of firefighters

While open to negotiations about expanding the role of firefighters, the FBU has resisted efforts to impose additional responsibilities without the necessary safeguards of national standards and agreement over pay and conditions. One challenge has been authorities' attempts to introduce emergency medical response (EMR), also known as 'co-responding', and described as one of the most controversial issues facing the FBU. For the union, co-responding initially represented changes to national contracts of employment without negotiation.[43] The first FBU response to co-responding came in 2004 in the London Borough of Tower Hamlets, where members voted 122-21 to take industrial action short of a strike over plans by the London Fire Brigade to compel firefighters to attend ambulance calls. The FBU highlighted serious concerns regarding the ability to provide a speedy response to major medical emergencies. Firefighters, unlike paramedics, were not trained to make medical diagnoses, nor could they administer drugs. Firefighters attending an ambulance call would be unable to attend concurrent fire calls, and attending medical calls lay outside the national agreement. The London Executive Council member at the time, Mick Shaw, said:

> This dispute is not about firefighters refusing to use defibrillators. It is about firefighters not wanting to be ordered to attend a range of medical emergencies for which they will not be adequately trained, at the expense of providing a proper fire service. The ambulance service also needs to explain why it cannot deliver a speedy response to the most urgent medical emergencies. If it cannot perform the basics of what it is set up to do then that needs to be addressed by the health service.[44]

Members were instructed not to attend training for co-responder duties, to refuse to handle equipment for that purpose, and not to respond to calls that were part of the proposed co-responding scheme. Consequently, the pilot scheme could not be implemented.

In 2005 firefighters at Retford in Nottinghamshire and Grantham in Lincolnshire took industrial action over proposals to introduce compulsory co-responding schemes that would have forced them to answer 999 medical emergencies on behalf of the ambulance service without additional payment. Retford branch at first refused to undertake EMR duties, believing it to be outside their role map and contractual obligations. They were then balloted to take action short of strike action and voted 81 per cent in favour. Refusal to undertake EMR duties from October 2005 led to the fire authority withholding 10 per cent of members' pay, arguing that they were not completely fulfilling their contract of employment. A hardship fund enabled action to be sustained until October 2006, when a legal ruling supported the union case and pay was reinstated. Nottinghamshire and Lincolnshire fire authorities claimed that the right to assign additional duties such as co-responding had been agreed in the 2002-04 dispute settlement and sought a legal declaration on the contractual status of co-responding. The High Court ruled that co-responding was not a contractual requirement nor did it lie within the role map of a firefighter under the Grey Book and it could only be introduced on a voluntary basis. The employers' appeal against that decision was unanimously rejected by the Court of Appeal in February 2007. Wrack welcomed the ruling:

> It's clear these two counties jumped the gun and tried to impose co-responding without national discussions, with no proper procedures and with no UK-wide standards. Rather than being the solution, co-responding as it currently operates is part of the problem. We believe it is being used to mask, and will potentially worsen, performance problems in the ambulance service.[45]

Following strategic discussions on wider areas of firefighters' work, the FBU agreed at 2015 conference to participate in 20 UK EMR trials in collaboration with the ambulance service, to respond to some categories of suspected cardiac arrest. In total, 38 trials had been approved by the end of 2016, although the initial 20 to have been concluded by June 2016 were extended to February 2017. Key objectives were securing additional funding for the fire and rescue services, protecting it from further government cuts, forestalling station closures and job cuts, and securing improvements in pay. Conference determined to monitor trials closely and review participation. An Executive Council resolution at the 2016 conference noted the lack of government engagement and that, while EMR promoted public safety, it did so in the context of fire and rescue service cuts. A London resolution proposed that there should be no agreement on additional responsibilities in the absence of extra pay. Cleveland moved an emergency resolution calling for trials to be halted to allow full evaluation. Debate included concerns that firefighters were being used to cover cuts in ambulance personnel and social care, although trials were seen to be saving lives. Wrack argued for continuing with the trials, stressing that the role of firefighters had evolved over the years to include preventative work, inspections and road traffic accidents and that the FBU had always led on the development of the service and profession. The case for additional funding had to be made.[46]

While conference supported continuation of the trials, a one-day recall conference in 2017 discussed the lack of additional pay on offer, and also experiences of inadequate training and stress arising from incidents. Firefighters had attended more than 30,000 co-responding incidents during the trials, including 4,000 cardiac arrests and, in the context of ambulance service cuts, were first on the scene in two-thirds of cases.[47] The union also convened a workshop of FBU members in the (voluntary) marauding terrorism and firearms teams as part of continued discussions to seek acceptable arrangements for a negotiated response to incidents of this type through the NJC. For the FBU, both marauding terrorism and firearms and EMR work are examples of activity lying outside existing contractual role maps and should be determined with agreement, appropriate standards, procedures, training and additional pay. Pay had once again become fundamental in a period where firefighters, like other public sector workers, had faced 'the longest period of pay restraint in living history'[48] and the gap between their pay and that of CFOs had widened.[49] If firefighters' pay had kept pace with inflation since 2010, they would be earning £2,000 a year more[50] – a fact that underpinned the 2017 pay claim. Consultation with members in September 2017 led to the rejection of a 2 per cent pay offer that came with a host of strings, including the continuation of EMR trials and other, new work in the fire and rescue service. As a consequence FBU participation in the EMR trials was withdrawn on 18 September 2017, amidst the failure of a number of fire and rescue services to address the operational, safety, training and welfare concerns raised by firefighters participating in the trials.[51]

Conclusion

As the FBU centenary approached, local disputes with fire authorities showed no sign of abating. Since the 2002-04 dispute over pay, the industrial relations climate had changed and successive governments had pursued the modernisation and reform of public services and restructuring of the employment relationship. With power transferred to local fire authorities facing severe budgetary constraints, FBU members have experienced a relentless onslaught on national terms and conditions and on the standards of the service they deliver. This structural shift has changed the role of local officials, who have shown exceptional resilience, despite fall-out from the pay dispute. Tom Redman and Ed Snape's study of a northern fire brigade suggested that deteriorating industrial relations stemming from funding cuts, demands for greater efficiency and New Public Management techniques, actually increased union commitment and participation and encouraged activists to raise awareness of the need to defend terms and conditions, leading to union renewal.[52] This conclusion appears to be borne out by Tam McFarlane:

Actually the attacks on the fire service, I believe, have strengthened the union and made us up our game. I think we're a better union now than when I first started. We're more effective, we're better trained, we are far faster on our feet dealing with stuff and the experience we are gaining through these fights we can translate into the battles of the future. So perversely, I think the attack on us has worked in the opposite way the employers intended, because I think we've got a fitter, stronger, better union.

Scottish FBU rally on pensions, Kirkcaldy, 2013

FBU members lobby the employers on pensions, 2013

DECENT PENSIONS FOR FIREFIGHTERS
NO TO
MASS DISMISSALS
FIRE BRIGADES UNION
HANDS OFF
OUR PENSIONS

6

Work longer, pay more, get less: the battle over firefighter pensions

Summarising the pensions' campaign isn't easy. I'll never say we won but I think we got concessions that we wouldn't have got without campaigning hard. I think what members need to do is look at the initial position they offered us and look at where we ended up and realise where they'd have ended up if they didn't have the FBU fighting. We did get improvements – nowhere near as much as we wanted and we never got near to a position where we could agree on anything, but we did get concessions. Probably the biggest concession was in Northern Ireland, where we achieved the normal pension age of 55 for firefighters going forward. It's still not over and we have committed to using all avenues available to us. We have used our political and industrial options to date and now we are in the phase of using a legal challenge.

Sean Starbuck, FBU national officer for pensions

The Firefighters' Pension Scheme (FPS) was established in 1948 and essentially survived until 2006. The opening paragraphs of the Scheme commentary acknowledge that '[i]t is a generous scheme, because of the very nature of the job and the fitness levels which must be maintained throughout the career'.[1] Over 90 per cent of eligible firefighters were members, despite the fact that the ultimate benefits were offset by employee contribution rates of 11 per cent, among the highest in the public sector. In 1993 the government signalled its intention to review firefighter pensions.[2] Subsequently, as this chapter illustrates, the defence of members' pensions has been a significant part of the FBU's history, albeit in the context of wider government attacks on public sector provision, including attacks on the pensions of emergency control members who belonged to the Local Government Pension Scheme (LGPS). On his election Matt Wrack stated that building a united front with other public sector unions on pensions was at the top of his agenda.[3] From the start, the FBU had emphasised the need to build a united front with other public sector unions. Joint one-day strike action on pensions was achieved during both waves of attack, in 2006 and 2011, but given the specificities of individual pension schemes and the internal dynamics of different unions, sustaining the united front proved problematic.

This chapter begins with the first major attack on firefighter pensions, in 2005, culminating in the imposition in 2006 (one year later in Northern Ireland) of the New Firefighters' Pension Scheme (NFPS), which established two-tier pensions with a new 'normal pension age' of 60 (increased from 55) for new entrants. The chapter then documents the FBU's legal victory in winning access for retained firefighters to the pension scheme. It goes on to consider further attacks on firefighter pensions, including a notable case in 2007, when three London firefighters had their pensions withdrawn following retirement on the grounds of ill health. The implications were huge and the FBU campaigned both industrially and politically before the decision was overturned. The chapter concludes with the end of public sector final salary schemes, heralded by the Hutton Report in 2010 and instigated by the new Tory-Liberal Democrat Coalition government. Hutton proposed that normal pension ages be raised to mirror the state pension age (eventually 68) and that the government should 'consider' upping the normal pension age for *all* firefighters to 60. These changes would also affect emergency control members of the LGPS – some of whom now faced working an additional 10 years before receiving a full pension. The government offensive sparked a substantial vote for industrial action in 2013, leading to the longest dispute in the FBU's history and a campaign that generated and politicised a new layer of younger activists. The union pursued a combined industrial, political and legal strategy to defend, even advance, member's pension rights. Legal redress was sought not only to ensure that retained firefighters enjoyed the same rights as wholetime personnel, but also to challenge age, gender and race discrimination.

Two-tier pensions

In 1990 the FBU annual conference pledged to recall conference and recommend industrial action if the government proposed to increase pension contributions. Every annual conference between 1994 and 1998 passed resolutions in favour of strikes to oppose proposed changes to the pension scheme. The Fire Service Pensions Review consultation of 1998 suggested that the FPS was overly generous and that ill-health and injury retirement terms were excessive. In 1999 conference again secured pledges of industrial action, particularly against reductions in benefits for new entrants. Subsequent conferences in 2000, 2001, 2002, 2004 and 2005 reaffirmed this position.

In 2005, as part of the government's broader attack on public sector pensions, firm proposals were made for less advantageous pensions for those entering the fire and rescue service from 6 April 2006. They included imposing a new normal pension age of 60 for all new entrants, with severe actuarial reductions of over 40 per cent for those who wanted to retire from the age of 55, which was the normal retirement age in the existing scheme, although it was possible to retire at 50 after 25 years' pensionable service. Reductions in employee and employer contribution rates were reflected in diminished benefits. The government proposed making it more difficult to secure an ill-health or injury pension, by introducing lower and upper tiers with different levels of permanent disability criteria. The union opposed the government's proposal that firefighters should be redeployed into non-operational roles when they could no longer maintain operational fitness, on the grounds that it was unworkable. The government continued to deny membership of the FPS to control and retained members. In response to these proposed changes to the FPS and to the LGPS for emergency control staff, the Executive Council agreed to recommend a strike ballot to its recall conference in Southport in February 2006. At this point, following year-long talks with government and employers, eight unions, representing 1.5 million public service workers, had agreed to ballot for strike action over planned cuts to their schemes.[4]

FBU annual conference was recalled twice, in February and March 2006, in Southport to discuss pensions, by which time discussions on wider public sector provision within the TUC and between unions had resulted in a 'ringfencing' arrangement, which protected existing pension scheme members – a substantial concession. In particular, the government agreed to preserve the retirement age for firefighters who had entered the service before 6 April 2006, and withdrew proposals for a minimum pension age of 65, but held firm on the retirement age of 60 for new entrants, to which the union remained opposed. Following consultation at brigade meetings, the second Southport conference decided not to proceed with a ballot for strike action,[5] on the grounds that significant concessions on the proposed imposition of detrimental changes to the FPS had been secured. The conference welcomed proposals to permit retained firefighters to be granted occupational pension rights, thereby giving them a pension for the first time, although the union was already awaiting a decision from the House of Lords granting retained firefighters access to the existing FPS. The government had withdrawn the suggestion that retained firefighters joining the new scheme would lose the link to wholetime earnings in the event of ill health and injury. Changes to a new injury scheme would be subject to consultation, but the government would not move on proposals that would make it harder to access an ill-health pension. Conference also noted the withdrawal of proposals that existing allowances, such as flexi-duty allowances and London weighting, should not be considered pensionable for new entrants. A further concession enabled cohabiting partners, including those of the same sex, to access pensions, a long-standing FBU campaign.[6] Discussions were also to take place on allowing control staff entry to the FPS. Finally, pensionable allowances, such as London Weighting and flexi-duty allowance, would be retained under existing and new pension schemes.[7] Given its recovery from the arduous pay dispute of 2002-04 and the context of local attacks on the service, the FBU was understandably cautious about engaging so soon in another national dispute with the government, but it continued to contest the scheme, arguing that it was seriously flawed.

On 28 March 2006, over one million local government workers took national strike action against changes to the LGPS, which would affect emergency control members. FBU members and officials demonstrated their support by attending local pickets and demonstrations. The issue under dispute was the abolition of the Rule of 85, the means by which certain members of the scheme were able to retire at the age of 60, subject to them having 25 years' pensionable service. If this rule were abolished, some members would have to work an additional five years. The strike action brought further talks between the employers and the government. The outcome was an agreement that 50 per cent of the savings accruing from the abolition of the Rule of 85 should be made available for protection arrangements for existing scheme members, with further negotiations on such protection and the development of a 'new-look' LGPS. The FBU made some progress in securing discussions on admitting control members into the NFPS, but the process stalled when the government actuary considered the proposed cost excessive[8] and control members subsequently remained in the LGPS. April 2006 saw the imposition of the NFPS for new entrants to the service. The FBU pledged to continue to campaign on several issues, including the mechanism for ill-health retirement, and it would continue to oppose the introduction of a normal pension age of 60 for new recruits.

RDS pensions: House of Lords legal victory

The introduction of a two-tier pension scheme coincided with the FBU legal victory in the House of Lords regarding the pension and other rights of members working the retained duty system (RDS). An initial test case was taken to an employment tribunal by 12 retained members, six each from Kent and Berkshire, but was lost. Following this setback the FBU appealed through ascending legal levels and, in a decision given on 1 March 2006, the Law Lords upheld the appeal.[9] The case centred on the exclusion of RDS firefighters from the FPS and their inferior treatment under the sick pay scheme. The Law Lords ruled that retained and wholetime firefighters were employed on the same 'type of contract' and that the employment tribunal, which had originally rejected the FBU members' case, had overly focused on the differences rather than the similarities between wholetime and RDS duty contracts. This decision had implications for part-time workers in general, who could now use the new Part-Time Workers Regulations[10] to compare their work with that of full-time colleagues. However, the union insisted that retained firefighters should have access to the full FPS, not the new lesser scheme, and won concessions wherein retained firefighters could join a similar pension scheme to that of wholetime firefighters, a modified scheme which allowed them to retire at 55 instead of 60. Access to a workplace pension was described as 'a huge victory for all retained members' by Tam Mitchell, the Executive Council member representing the National Retained Committee.

Defence of ill-health pensions

A number of skirmishes occurred over ill-health pensions, including, in 2001, a dispute over whether fire authorities, in this case West Yorkshire, had the discretion to remove firefighters' rights to an ill-health pension, should they be permanently disabled.[11] The union went to the High Court and a subsequent appeal ruled against such discretion, so that this material attack on the FPS was repelled. Guidance issued by the government in 2006 aimed to restrict access to ill-health pensions and thus increased the potential for sackings on the grounds of capability. The outcome was curtailment of ill-health retirement and denial of ill-health pensions, on the basis that firefighters could perform other jobs although, if no such alternative jobs were available, they could be left without a job or a pension. The Justice for Firefighter Pensions campaign was launched in 2007 after three London wholetime firefighters, Martin Marrion, Andrew Scott and Neil Burke, had their ill-health pensions removed, and a retained firefighter, Mark Padgett from Nottingham, faced the loss of his ill-health pension. The FBU went for judicial review of these decisions on behalf of retired members. Political pressure forced an adjournment debate in Parliament in January 2008, during which the fire minister, Parmjit Dhanda, stated:

> It was never the Government's intention for an injured firefighter not to receive an appropriate award or to be left with no job or recompense. It is really important to have that on the record so that fire and rescue services are aware of that when they take these decisions.[12]

Lobbying resulted in new draft guidance for independent qualified medical practitioners that stated that in deciding on the case for ill-health retirement, authorities must consider whether a 'realistic prospect' of 'suitable employment' exists and whether its absence would be material to whether an award was made. The guidance specified that reference should be made to actual rather than hypothetical jobs. In May the judicial review had ruled against the union and the union decided to appeal against the decision, with the draft guidance used temporarily, pending the outcome. Meanwhile, in Scotland, a revised agreement on ill-health retirement was reached by the FBU and the Scottish government, which resulted in a higher level of protection.[13]

In early 2009 the Court of Appeal ruled in favour of the three London firefighters, 'a tremendous victory' for the FBU, which meant that firefighters who, through ill health, were permanently incapable of doing any part of their role would receive an ill-health pension or be redeployed to restricted duties. The pensions of the London firefighters, which had been withdrawn by the Pension Appeal Board, were restored following the legal action.[14] The onus was placed on the fire and rescue service to make reasonable adjustment to enable and encourage firefighters to stay in work within the role rather than take early retirement. In addition, any element of job redesign or adjustment would have to be consistent with the RDS, a change the union wanted in order to protect retained firefighters. The issue of access to ill-health pensions would re-emerge with the increase in the pension age to 60 for all firefighters, raising the prospect of dismissals on the grounds of capability.

The Hutton Report: the end of public sector final salary pensions

A major attack on firefighter pensions came in the wake of the 2010 election. The Conservative-led Coalition government commissioned the Independent Public Service Pensions Commission (chaired by former Labour minister John Hutton) to undertake a review of public sector pension provision. The report, which was published in March 2011, covered all three firefighter pension schemes. It assumed that increases in employee contributions would use the Consumer Prices Index (CPI) instead of Retail Price Index (RPI) as the measure for uprating. It proposed that all existing public service pension scheme members be moved into new schemes adhering to a common framework but tailored for different groups of workers. The common framework entailed final salary pension schemes being replaced by Career Average Re-valued Schemes (CARE)[15] and the normal pension age being aligned with the state pension age, increased where necessary to 65 and including any future age uplifting. The only exception would be uniformed services (including firefighters), where the normal pension age would be lower and government should 'consider' setting it at 60. Tiered contribution rates would be introduced to reflect the different characteristics of higher earners. A fixed 'cost ceiling' in each scheme would limit the risk to employers and a default mechanism would be put in place to adjust scheme benefits or employee contribution rates to keep costs below the ceiling. The report also proposed that all accrued benefits would be protected.

The FBU responded by arguing that there was no evidence that firefighters were able to safely perform all parts of their role after the age of 55. A union-commissioned report concluded that there was 'no substantial case for major structural changes to public sector pension schemes in general or in the Fire Service in particular'. Indeed, changes could create 'major dangers to schemes, which are a crucial part of occupational pension saving in the United Kingdom'.[16] The union opposed increased pension contributions, and a YouGov survey of FBU members in May 2011 found that 27 per cent would consider opting out of the scheme if the government's proposals were implemented. An initial report, *Protecting Good Quality Occupational Pensions in the FRS*, submitted in October 2011, suggested that higher contributions would increase opt-outs, thereby eradicating anticipated savings. This document used the government's own evidence that every 1 per cent who opted out cost the scheme £3.5 million.[17] For Sean Starbuck, the national officer with responsibility for pensions:

> The Hutton Review was just a vehicle for slashing the value of public service pensions. It was about them trying to justify why they could attack pension schemes and make members work longer, pay more, get less. We submitted quite a lot of information to the Hutton Review and attended all of the face-to-face meetings, but one of the problems was, halfway through, even before his review was published, they'd already decided that they were going to increase firefighter contributions by at

least three per cent. We knew that, as usual, we would be the only ones who would campaign for firefighter pensions and we started in earnest. The first part of the campaign focused on why it was unaffordable and we showed, using our experts, who were actuaries as well, that it was a false economy to increase contributions for firefighters because if they opted out then basically the scheme lost more than it was actually going to save through any changes. We put together a financial argument clearly showing why the increases to employee contributions were flawed. In addition to this, we built an argument around normal pension age which evidenced that the majority of firefighters would not be able to maintain their operational fitness until they're 60 and showed why this made the scheme unworkable and unfair.

On 30 June hundreds of thousands of civil servants, teachers and lecturers represented by the Public and Commercial Services union (PCS), the National Union of Teachers (NUT), the Association of Teachers and Lecturers (ATL) and the University and College Lecturers Union (UCU) struck in defence of their pensions. One month later, the TUC public services liaison group (PSLG) agreed to progress scheme-specific talks, despite the FBU and NUT arguing that this was a premature move as key points of principle were unresolved. However, scheme-specific consultation took place with unions with a view to implementation by 2015. In September 2011, the FBU lodged a detailed trade dispute opposing government proposals on pensions, including arguments that the scheme would be unaffordable and that the pension age of 55 should remain for firefighters. The union used actuaries to challenge certain assumptions used by the government in setting the initial cost ceiling, which led to the FBU working to a different timetable from the one other unions worked to. Unlike other unions, it did not proceed to ballot in autumn 2011 because talks around cost ceilings were going on. On 30 November 2011, two million public sector workers in four pension schemes – health, education, civil service and local government – took strike action against pension reform.

Discussions between the FBU and the government led to the cost ceiling for the firefighter scheme being raised. Subsequently, the government agreed to reviews of the normal pension age and of the impact of higher contributions on opt-outs. The FBU conference decided to participate in the two reviews but also resolved that industrial action remained a possibility. In March 2012, as a result of the evidence submitted, the proposed increases in firefighter contributions for 2012-13 were reduced by approximately 50 per cent, making them the lowest employee contribution increases of any of the six unfunded public sector schemes.[18] In May 2012, the government produced a proposed final agreement, which, despite concessions, remained unacceptable to the FBU. The government stated that final agreements had been reached with other unions and that legislation would proceed. In September 2012, the Public Service Pensions Bill was published. It included references to firefighters and thus pre-empted the outcomes of the reviews: the normal pension age would be 60, increased contributions (14.2 per cent for FPS and 10.4 per cent for NFPS) would be introduced from April 2013, but there would be a review of opt-outs in the first year. The FBU promoted an amendment to the Bill on the new pension age, submitted at the report stage in the House of Lords. Despite lobbying efforts the amendment fell, although it did open avenues to politicians from Northern Ireland, who were working to different timescales.

Following pressure from the FBU, the government commissioned Dr Tony Williams, Medical Director of occupational health consultancy Working Fit, to consider the health and fitness implications of the revised retirement age. The report, *Normal Pension Age for Firefighters – A review for the Firefighters' Pension Committee*,[19] was published in January 2013. It concluded that the only way that the new pension age could be achieved was by changes to entry requirements, improved monitoring of fitness and health and better fitness training. The report broadly supported many FBU concerns, concluding that many existing firefighters would be unable to work until they were 60. For the FBU the implication was that employers would be prepared to dismiss firefighters, including through capability processes, and it did not believe there were sufficient redeployment opportunities in operational roles for those who could not maintain their fitness. Professor Andrew Watterson, head of the Occupational and Environmental Health Group at the University of Stirling, provided professional opinion that corroborated the FBU's concerns. While the Scottish minister for Community Safety and Legal Affairs, Roseanna Cunningham, pointed out to the Westminster government that the Williams Report did not appear to unequivocally support changes to the pension age, the Westminster government did not respond to the findings.

Meanwhile, the consultation document on the LGPS (covering control staff) was published in January 2013. The proposals, agreed with the other unions, were unacceptable to the FBU, particularly the introduction of a normal pension age of (up to) 68 and the revaluation and accrual rates of the new Career Average Revalued Earnings (CARE) scheme. However, UNISON, GMB and Unite members, alongside other unions with LGPS members, voted in favour. The FBU, following extensive consultation with its members in the control section, were the exception in voting against the proposals.

Despite FBU lobbying, the Public Sector Pensions Act became law in spring 2013, with secondary legislation then required to activate each separate public sector scheme. In terms of the fire and rescue service, in June, the government – facing industrial action – made a new offer with an actuarial reduction of 21.8 per cent,[20] less than half of the original proposal of 47 per cent. However, firefighters still faced a significantly reduced pension if they were unable to work up to the age of 60, and this remained unacceptable to the FBU. A ballot of FBU members – excepting emergency control members in the LGPS – in England, Scotland and Wales took place in July and August 2013, producing a 78 per cent vote for discontinuous strike action.

In Northern Ireland members were not balloted for strike action, owing to a different legislative timeline. Here the FBU submitted a detailed, evidence-based case that argued that a firefighters' pension scheme must reflect the nature of the occupation.[21] In October 2013, national and regional officers presented evidence on Northern Ireland's draft Public Service Pensions Bill at the Northern Ireland Assembly's Finance and Personnel Committee, with Matt Wrack emphasising that 'our case is essentially around the argument that if it's an occupational scheme it must be based around the occupation'.[22] Constructive dialogue with the Department of Health, Social Services and Public Safety led to changes proposing a normal pension age of 55 in Northern Ireland. FBU members subsequently voted by 93 per cent to lift the trade dispute, with the Executive Council concluding that the normal pension age of 55 'is currently unique in the proposals for pension age anywhere in the public sector in the UK'.[23]

Separate negotiations in Scotland and Wales proved more productive than those in England. In September 2013, the Scottish government formally proposed a Scottish 2015 FPS with improved transitional protection and a guarantee that firefighters would not be sacked simply for failing fitness tests. Protection arrangements would be based on length of service and age, with a fairer actuarial reduction at the age of 55 instead of the more punitive 21.8 per cent imposed in England. The Scottish government gave assurances that it would match any further improvements proposed in England. FBU members in Scotland were asked not if the proposals were acceptable, but if they were sufficient to prevent strike action, with 55 per cent voting in favour.[24] While the proposal was not acceptable, it was nevertheless sufficiently more advantageous than the one put forward in England to allow strike action to be suspended, even though members were subsequently involved in action short of a strike.[25] Despite these improved proposals in Northern Ireland and Scotland, the union reiterated its determination to continue the fight over the issue of transitional protection, which remained unacceptable across the UK. Nevertheless the suspension of strike action in Scotland caused some concern in the union, both north and south of the border, as it was seen to undermine the effectiveness of UK-wide action.

During 2013 and 2014, 50 separate periods of strike action took place in England ranging from one-hour action to a one-day strike in December 2014 and a four-day strike in October-November 2014. This amounted to a total of 11 days over 37 separate days across a 14-month period, alongside action short of a strike.[26] Ongoing discussions with the Welsh Assembly led to agreement to consult on an improved actuarial reduction for firefighters aged 55. Consultation was due to end in January 2015, meaning that FBU members in Wales did not participate in the four-day strike in October-November 2014 nor in the one-day strike in December 2014, despite their involvement in all previous national action. In early 2015 the Welsh government proposed a fairer actuarial reduction, so that Welsh firefighters would have their pension reduced by 9 per cent at 55 (rather than 21.8 per cent in England).

The December 24-hour strike coincided with a march of 3,000 firefighters through Aylesbury calling for Executive Council member Ricky Matthews to be reinstated following his dismissal by Buckinghamshire Fire and Rescue Authority for participating in lawful strike action between 31 October and 4 November. The authority claimed that the FBU had made an administrative error when giving the service the required seven days' strike notice, although it did not challenge the union legally in court. Buckinghamshire, alongside Essex and Surrey, refused to accept 'partial performance' of duties implied by strike action, and locked out FBU members. Ricky Matthews highlighted his local situation:

> The majority of the strikes were short, two-hour periods. It's because they suited firefighters; couple of hours off, stand outside the front of the fire station. You can deal with a couple of hours' lost pay – you make a point, you're outside the front of the fire station, people know what's going on, it grabs the news, it's not a big deal. Buckinghamshire, after a few months of that, they said, 'No, if you go out on strike at any time during your shift, we don't want you for the rest of the shift.' Every two-hour strike anywhere else in the UK, you're getting docked two hours' pay. In Bucks, they were losing either 9 hours or 15 hours pay. And for every strike period the authority was making money because they were paying fewer firefighters. It was perverse. They were deliberately reducing the amount of fire cover available to the residents of Buckinghamshire and Milton Keynes and profiting from it because they'd reduced the budget for the year.

National Officer Sean Starbuck described the national industrial strategy:

> We suspected that they were going to cover our strikes with scabs or agency-type workers with very little training. We called these 'boil in the bag firefighters' because they got a couple of days' very basic training before they got shoved on a pump without much of a clue. We also knew that it was costing them a lot of money to keep these scabs and agency workers ready

to go. We knew the government would not pay because we had seen the exchange of correspondence between FRAs [fire and rescue authorities] and government, where their request for additional money was turned down. FRAs had been economical with the truth, at best saying they had contingency resources arranged, so they were told they had to pay for them out of their own reserves. They obviously expected us to take shift-long strike action which they [the FRAs] would pay for by not paying our members, so we decided, what we'll try and do is make it as hard for them as possible, but not to hit our people as hard financially. We were calling an odd couple of hour strikes, knowing that they'd have to get people and appliances to their strategic spots to prepare for it. We'd be on strike for a couple of hours but they'd have to pay for strike cover for the full day. We'd already got intelligence to say they were getting £150 a shift. So we thought, '£150 a shift, I wonder what they're going to pay them for an hour?' So they'd turn up, get the £150 and all of a sudden the resilience bill[27] for fire authorities was massive. And our members were saying, 'We can carry on doing this because we're only losing an hour here and an hour there.' So the tactics were about not hurting us and being as disruptive as we could to them and mixing it up, doing it in the middle of the night, doing it at tea time, doing it at whatever time. So that's what we tried to do, but we purposely tried not to anger the public as well. We avoided key days such as Bonfire night and Christmas and we were out there trying to get a public message that we were forced into this. We did really well with the media. We were that confident in our arguments, and the government's responses were so poor that we were giving live interviews and getting a standard recorded statement back because nobody from government wanted to take us on on live TV or radio.

A successful pensions and cuts march was held in London in October 2013, and in March 2014 around 200 FBU members lobbied MPs in Westminster, with a similar action in Scotland. A further lobby was held in December 2014 when, following effective pressure from FBU members, the Labour Party triggered a parliamentary debate over an Early Day Motion in the name of the Labour leader Ed Miliband. The motion challenged the new firefighter pension regulations, but the vote was lost. During the debate the fire minister, Penny Mordaunt, declared that any firefighter unable to maintain operational fitness after the age of 55 would either be redeployed in role or offered an unreduced pension. This guarantee was repeated by the secretary of state Eric Pickles the following day to the Communities and Local Government Committee and helped ensure the passage of the Pensions Act. The guarantee responded to the FBU's concern that firefighters who could not work safely beyond age 55 would face dismissal or significant reductions in their pension. In particular, the union resisted the proposal that firefighters could be sacked on capability grounds if they failed to maintain operational fitness through ageing or injury, with employers increasingly reluctant to fund ill-health retirement. However, in England and Wales, fire service employers responded that the government guarantee could not be implemented, on diverse grounds, including legal ones, despite the Scottish government guaranteeing an unreduced pension for firefighters failing fitness tests through no fault of their own.

The government claim that all firefighters would be fit enough to work until the age of 60 was challenged throughout the pension campaign. The FBU raised concerns that this claim was based on a fitness level of 35 VO_2 max (maximum rate of oxygen consumption measured during incremental exercise) which was lower than the current required safe recommended minimum. Supporting evidence from academics included a report by Dr James Bilzon of Bath University, *Occupational Fitness Standards for Operational UK Fire and Rescue Service Personnel,* which demonstrated that firefighters with a minimum occupational fitness standard below 42.3 VO_2 max would not necessarily be able to safely, and effectively fulfil essential roles. The previous safe recommended level was 42 and the report found the lower maximum standard of 35 potentially unsafe for most firefighters.[28] Some considered that the increase in pension age to 60 had greater implications for women. Scottish regional secretary Denise Christie, observed:

They have increased the pension age from 55 to 60. Now that has a huge impact on women having the capacity to reach that. There's evidence to say that it's much more difficult for women to be fit enough to be a firefighter at the age of 60 than it is for men because of things like osteoporosis, the menopause, brittle bones.

Kevin Brown, North West region Executive Council member, discussed the issue of firefighters working until 60:

I think it's choice. I believe that if firefighters can maintain their fitness I have no issues whatsoever in the removal of the compulsion to retire. In fact under the old FPS there was a compulsion to retire at 55. So I've no issues whatsoever with people working as long as they wish to work, as long as they can pass the safety checks needed. I think it's a significant punishment now for those retiring before the normal pension age of 60, a huge reduction. They lose out massively and that's where people feel cheated, having paid into a pension scheme for so long.

FBU members in England took strike action over pensions for 24 hours on 25 February 2015, accompanied by a mass rally in Parliament Square and near Downing Street. Andy Noble, Executive Council member for the North East region, recalled, 'We had in excess of 4,000 firefighters in Parliament Square, and Westminster was brought to a complete standstill. It was completely impromptu! There had been rumours it was going to happen, it wasn't necessarily planned – it was 'impromptu' for legal reasons.'

The demonstrators wore masks of Penny Mordaunt with a Pinocchio nose, following the revelation that her 'guarantee' to Parliament – that firefighters who could not work to 60 would not be denied a full pension – was hollow. Eastern region Executive Council member Jamie Wyatt also reflected upon the apparently spontaneous nature of the protest:

We had a rally in the Methodist Hall and then a whole load of us, a thousand, I suppose, decided to have an amble down to Westminster. And all of a sudden, someone went, 'We'll sit down then.' So right outside the front – where the front gates are, where the police are – we just sat there and the police stood there. They didn't know what to do. When you're going up there every Wednesday, you get to know the police officers in there, they're all right. They are quite often saying to us, 'Go on boys, give them a kicking', because their pensions were getting a kicking as well. And our copper turned to us and said, 'We don't know what to do.' He said, 'There was so many of you sitting down, there was only a couple of us.' He said, 'We just don't know what to do about this.' We got cold and bored so everyone went, 'Right, we'll go and do something outside Downing Street.' So we wandered off up the road, sat outside Downing Street. And we thought the coppers were nice. It's almost become a civil disobedience thing the trade unions have rediscovered, because I'm sure we must have done it years ago, but I can't remember for the first 30 years of my trade union activism anyone doing it.

In fact, as Matt Wrack clarified, this action was not spontaneous, but the march and sit-down protest had been planned in advance, despite lawyers advising that there could be arrests. Trevor French, South West regional secretary, also attended the lobby:

I remember being at Methodist Hall and Matt said, 'We're going out', and all of a sudden there was this huge surge and I thought, 'What's going to happen here?' And it was literally onto the roads and we, the wave of the march, blocked the entrance to Parliament. Seeing the police's eyes – and don't forget these are the guys with machine guns – you could see the nervousness in their eyes. And to see Matt at the top and then the president up there as well. And something did organically happen and then firefighters started lying down, blocking, and that was a real sense of injustice developing into a bit of action. Which was a case of: politicians are refusing to listen to us, they're refusing to let us in, but I tell you what, no one's getting in. And to see Parliament effectively picketed, is something to see.

Gary Spindler, chair of Avon brigade, recalled:

My memory is walking along with Avon colleagues and they were talking to some London brothers and sisters and then I noticed, one of them, or two of them actually, had black carrier bags, literally like refuse sacks, on their back and we're coming up outside the Methodist Hall, on the steps. 'What's in the bag?' And with that, out of the bag came a full-on brazier, out of the other bag came a full-on bag of wood. And with that, we set up a pitch outside the Methodist Hall and it was absolutely brilliant – we lit the fire.

The braziers were an 'iconic' feature of the pension dispute, including during the summer, as recalled by Eastern regional secretary, Riccardo La Torre:

It was the middle of July. We couldn't use a fire, but we had a brazier and this new union-buster, the head of HR, called me in to say there's no need for a brazier. Well, they'd already kicked us off their property and the conversation was: 'You have us on your property where we admit you do have a bit of control about what we do. Now you've kicked us off, you don't have a say in it.' That got out and on the very next picket line, nearly every single picket line had a brazier! It's July and there's a brazier. 'You can't have a brazier', so on the next picket line there was two braziers. I mean, in July, who needs two braziers? But there's going to be two braziers because they said you can't have one – so we'll have two.

The South West Executive Council member, Tam McFarlane, described how the pensions' dispute felt qualitatively different from previous industrial action, and was member-led:

The carnival atmosphere that was prevalent in the pay campaign was replaced with a real sense of anger and that was a far more bitter dispute – the pensions campaign. The reason we have so many young activists now coming through and now taking positions is because the real target of the pensions campaign was the younger firefighters. Whereas in the pay campaign we were asking for a pay rise and putting our case forward, this was firefighters having their pensions robbed from them. Firefighters felt very strongly it wasn't just them under attack, it was families as well. So it was a bitter dispute, there was a real – I don't know the best way to describe it – a real 'f*** you' atmosphere and it was membership-driven. I sat on the [E]xecutive [Council]; I'm telling you it was membership-driven. Demands for strikes over the Christmas period, demands for strike over the midnight period into the New Year and demands for strike in really innovative ways. So two-hour strikes over shift periods to cause maximum disruption. And that came from the workplace. So it was about maximum disruption. It was a very bitter dispute that we're still fighting and the anger in that dispute is palpable even today in fire stations. And it was primarily younger firefighters, who, the more they were finding out what was happening to their pensions, the angrier and angrier they were getting. And I think it's basically regenerated the Fire Brigades Union.

The Cambridgeshire brigade secretary, Cameron Matthews, agreed that the pensions dispute generated activism and activists:

Pensions, I think, definitely in Cambridgeshire, helped generate more activists and more organisation that started to take on a more political aspect. So we had a discussion: 'The last thing we want to do is go out on strike, so what can we do beforehand?' So we had a discussion about going to Parliament on a regular basis and said when we go there, we want to be as visible as possible, we want to make sure there's a maximum amount of politicians there, so we started going to each Prime Minister's Question Time. Every Wednesday, during Question Time, there were MPs going in, you knew they were coming out. We're turning up, between 5 and 10 firefighters in tunics [fire gear], making ourselves visible and actually grabbing MPs and saying, 'Look, this is what's happening, our pension campaign. It's unfair, unjust', and having it out with them, and it led to the point we got Eric Pickles and had a massive discussion with him. He started saying, 'I'd much rather have your pension than mine.' We offered to exchange, which he refused, but then he ended up running away, so we were chasing him down central lobby, all the way, and he had to run off and hide. But he didn't know how to deal with it because we were there week in, week out. They didn't know what to do and that action generated a lot of confidence in our members.

The Firefighters' Pension Scheme was imposed on 1 April 2015 across the UK. Firefighters not covered by protection were transferred into the new scheme, with the Coalition government reneging on agreements made in 2006 about protection for those in the 1992 FPS. For the FBU, although the scheme's proposals, in particular over contributions and actuarial rates had been improved and some concerns addressed in Wales, Northern Ireland and Scotland, the dispute was far from over. The imposition of the scheme caused anger among FBU members, as Ian Leahair, former London Executive Council member, describes:

> Firefighters across London are resentful of the way that the pension dispute has been played out. They feel robbed and I don't blame them. Somebody who was setting their life up around 30 years' service or 55, whichever was sooner, they'd planned their mortgage to be paid off at the same time, planned their retirement, now to be told, 'Well, actually, you can't do that. You've now got to work an additional five years till you're 60 or you've got to do 40 years' service'; it's huge, it's huge. It became very bitter, very nasty. I've heard some heartache stories of people who missed out on their protection by a couple of days and have now got to do an extra 10 or 5 years. Don't get me wrong, we're not an isolated sector, but I do think the whole ethos of pension changes was dealt with badly.

Assistant general secretary Andy Dark considered the new scheme unworkable and predicted it would create future difficulties:

> An artificial retirement age was being introduced which isn't applicable or appropriate for our workforce, whether current or future. Is the fact that members pay such a huge amount, and now an increased amount, for contributions for that pension fair? It was an inevitable dispute because it wasn't simply about what money firefighters get and at what age they get it, it was whether or not they would actually remain in employment in order to reach pension age and achieve a pension. And that still remains the case and it undoubtedly is, whatever might happen in the immediate [future] or short term. It's got every potential and likelihood that it's going to become an issue in 10

years or so, when people aren't getting the pensions they were expecting to get. We had strike action over a long period; it was always going to be a difficult battle because, essentially, it was a clear government agenda. It was an all public sector battle by the Coalition government.

With some scepticism the union joined a Working Group on firefighter fitness run jointly by the Department for Communities and Local Government and the NJC. In 2016 the Home Office and NJC published approved Firefighter Fitness Best Practice, an outstanding issue from the imposition of pension changes and the increase in normal pension age. The guidance sets out a supportive rather than punitive approach to occupational fitness. Importantly, it established a mechanism for taking firefighters off the run on fitness grounds for their own safety and necessary steps to return them to full duties.[29]

Although industrial action was suspended, the campaign for pensions would continue and the FBU warned members against opting out of the reformed scheme. Steve Harman, former North West regional official, commented:

> The pension is 14 per cent, and firefighters are not joining it. So they're joining the fire service and they're not joining the scheme – not in Lancashire – and some have left, some wholetime firefighters in Lancashire have opted out, which is frightening. They'll massively regret it because I've always said to them: 'No matter what the outcome of this dispute now, no matter how bad it appears, that pension, it's much, much better than any other pension in the country.' It's still better than the local government pension scheme or the civil servants' pension scheme.

Following four years of negotiations for improved transitional protection arrangements for firefighters, the FBU launched a legal challenge. The case contested changes to pensions introduced by the 2015 FPS, and transitional arrangements for both unprotected members of the FPS and unprotected members of the modified section of the NFPS, with both challenges based primarily on age discrimination. In the former, the challenge was backed by the claims of 14,500 members and in the latter, by 6,000 members of the 1992 FPS and the RDS modified scheme. The union registered the details of members whose pensions were not fully protected, information that was then used to identify those who faced a disproportionate attack on their pension. The FBU argued that the members affected suffered discrimination on the basis of their age, but that the injured parties in this group were also more likely to be women and/or have an ethnic minority background, because female and ethnic minority firefighters were relative newcomers to the service. Consequently, the union initiated two further legal challenges, on the grounds of gender and race discrimination. Fifty claims were made against different fire authorities and for each one a partner/dual claim was made against the secretary of state in England, ministers in Wales, ministers in Scotland or the Department of Health, Social Services and Public Safety in Northern Ireland. The FBU argued that the transitional provisions, which permitted older firefighters to remain in the previous, and significantly better, 1992 FPS, discriminated on the grounds of age. Younger firefighters who were members of the 1992 Scheme had just as good a case as their older colleagues for retaining the former, better pension arrangements. All had an age discrimination claim and an equal pay claim. Women also had a gender discrimination claim and black and ethnic minority members had a race discrimination claim. Five employment tribunal test cases were brought by the FBU on behalf of members who were forced to transfer to the inferior 2015 FPS. The FBU argued that firefighters younger than 45 on 1 April 2012 were unfairly penalised because they were forced into an inferior scheme while older firefighters remained in the original scheme. When an employment tribunal declared that the 2015 FPS[30] did not discriminate against firefighters on the grounds of age, the FBU appealed. On 29 January 2018 the Employment Appeal Tribunal partially overturned the original judgment and found in favour of the union's case, referring the issue of proportionality back to the employment tribunal. The employment tribunal had ruled in favour of the claimants in a similar but separate case involving more than 200 judges, and the government had appealed against the decision, with the prospect of the cases being reviewed together if the FBU was granted an appeal. Khaled Haider, London branch secretary, supported the union's legal strategy:

> At the moment my guys – because it affects a lot of the younger guys – are happy that we're using the law to beat them [the government] rather than lose money by going out the door and standing outside the fire station. The shift in strategy is good because we can't always win through industrial muscle but sometimes we have to use the law to best effect. The union is using some new techniques rather than just the same old technique of 'right, out the doors, let's go, bang the drum'.

Former North West Executive Council member Kevin Brown also discussed the FBU's combined legal and industrial approach:

> I think by and large the FBU strategy has been solid. It was based rightly in different areas. We had the industrial, which I think was of necessity, but we've also had the political and legal strategy all being run at the same time, maybe at a different pace, and not forgetting, of course, that we were part of the wider reforms of the public sector pensions – these so-called gold-plated schemes.

A further outcome of the legal strategy was the successful challenge in 2015 on behalf of those aged 18-20 who had joined the 1992 FPS, on the basis that a 30-year accrual cap meant they had paid two years' contributions without equivalent benefit.[31] The union estimated that around 2,500 firefighters in England alone received some kind of compensation following legal action. A second legal victory came when a court ruled that firefighters and police officers who had retired between December 2001 and August 2006 were not awarded the correct lump sum payment.[32] The FBU provided support and legal assistance to more than 5,000 retired members. *Firefighter* reported that more than £19,000 had been donated to the union's campaign fund by retired firefighters and police officers who had benefited from recent FBU legal victories.[33]

Conclusion

In spite of changes to firefighter pension schemes, the FBU continues to emphasise the importance of members joining. For Matt Wrack:

> Despite the valid criticisms of the scheme, which does not reflect the physical role undertaken by firefighters, it is better for people to be part of it rather than not. It is better for people to have an occupational pension than not to have one. If you opt out of the scheme, you are essentially signing up for a pay cut, as the government will not contribute anything toward your workplace pension.[34]

The union effectively mitigated aspects of the attack on pensions, but did not shy away from conceding the damage caused to members. The Executive Council acknowledged that 'unity, solidarity and determination' have sustained the union throughout a prolonged pensions dispute and, in particular, those whose pensions are protected have stood by those facing pensions robbery. However, for the FBU the pension issue remains 'unfinished business'.[35]

FBU B & EMM school, Wortley Hall, 2012

FBU women campaigning for suitable PPE: Jenny Impey, Denise Christie, Mandy Cregin and Sam Rye, 2010

7

Leading the way: equality and diversity in the fire and rescue service and the union

The FBU were the first people that took up the case and I think to a large extent succeeded in making an environment where people from under-represented groups could actually have successful careers. They always led the way when it came to ideology of equality and had a political understanding of what equality means. And that is so important because whilst management may be able to produce policies, it's important that everything is based on understanding why equality is important. And it's not because the law says you must do it; the FBU are the people that understand the real reasons for equality. And only equality based on that will be long lasting.

Linda Smith, former London region treasurer and former chair, Women's Advisory Committee

Since the 1980s equality and diversity have been the focus of significant attention in the fire and rescue service. The FBU has played a leading role, not only in pressing fire service employers for action, but, crucially, in providing a voice for minority members and promoting cultural change within the union. This chapter traces the early role of women in the fire service during the Second World War, and then looks at their experiences as wholetime firefighters from the 1980s. It highlights the discrimination, harassment and bullying faced by women, black and ethnic minority (B&EM) members and lesbian, gay, bisexual and transgender (LGBT) firefighters during the 1980s and 1990s. The development of the union's role as a powerful force for pressing employers to advance equality and diversity is examined in the second half of this chapter.

Progress within the fire and rescue service, though, could not have been made without changes in the union. The chapter charts the development of the self-organisation of women, B&EM and LGBT members in the union, which was embraced by general secretary Ken Cameron. This legacy was remembered by general secretary Matt Wrack on Cameron's death:

> It was Ken who pioneered the discussion in our union and our service on the issues of equality and diversity. In the 1980s this meant some very difficult discussions with politicians, and sometimes firefighters, about the need for our service to better reflect the communities we serve. Ken was willing to take that issue up and to pioneer policies aimed at challenging discrimination, bullying and harassment.[1]

The union's internal structures for minority members emerged from informal meetings of women, B&EM and LGBT members during the late 1980s and early 1990s, and developed into structures for the representation of minority members that were widely admired across the UK union movement. Labour historian Mary Davis, who was a tutor at the union's Women's Schools for around 20 years, recalled:

> The fact that the FBU, which was a male-dominated union, the fact that that union in particular took a very progressive stand in relation to recognising inequality had a very big impact in the trade union movement as a whole. The FBU was quite highly regarded anyway... it had a very progressive leadership. It did have a big impact and I can think of other unions that hadn't previously taken up the equality issue, which followed on. The FBU created a climate.

The union took on the challenge of 'putting its own house in order', tackling bullying and harassment among its membership through policies like Fairness at Work, which included changes to education programmes and rules on representation. However, as in wider society, the politics and strategies for advancing equality were frequently contested, with identities based on race, ethnicity, sexuality and gender sometimes seen as counterposed to the class basis of union solidarity. The chapter evaluates these tensions within the FBU. Furthermore, action on equality and diversity is subject to varying priorities at a broader political level. Government policy, notably the introduction of equality targets in 1999 by the Labour government and their abandonment by the Conservative-led Coalition government in 2010, has both supported and frustrated the work of the FBU in advancing equality and diversity for its members.

The history of women in the fire service

Firefighting has traditionally been a masculine occupation, with a history of recruitment from the navy and consequent adoption of many naval traditions. There were small numbers of women in private brigades, such as the one attached to Girton College, Cambridge (then a women's college), before the Second World War,[2] but it was as members of the Auxiliary Fire Service (AFS) during the war that women played a role in larger numbers. By March 1943 the number of wholetime women in the National Fire Service (the renamed AFS) reached 32,200, while the number of women part-timers peaked at 54,600 in 1944.[3]

While women mostly worked as telephone operators, and in clerical and canteen work and driving, their role as active firefighters during the war has been underestimated, according to Terry Segars, who has recorded many stories of women active on pumps during bombing raids. One such woman was Joyce Hicks, who was a driver of trailer-pump appliances and who drove a small band of men from Barnes to the London Docks to fight one of the worst blazes of the Blitz in the autumn of 1940, demonstrating considerable bravery as the fire spread into the East End.[4] Yet there was opposition to women pump operators from both the Home Office and the FBU on the grounds of women's supposed lack of stamina and fitness, with general secretary John Horner calling for 'a stringent medical test' before women could operate pumps.[5] Twenty-five firewomen lost their lives during the war, and the courage of 21-year-old Gillian Tanner was recognised by the George Medal for bravery for delivering petrol to fire pumps around Bermondsey while the docks were being bombed in 1940.[6]

At the start of the war (and before the start of national pay bargaining), women received only two-thirds of men's pay, and after nationalisation in 1941, women's pay was still less than men's.[7] While the majority of women occupied different roles to men, many were doing the same jobs, for example, in control rooms, as despatch riders or in small numbers as pump operators, but they still received lower rates of pay. A claim for equal pay was first made at a special FBU Women's National Conference in London in 1943 and was included in the union's pay claim for that year, but it was rejected by the Home Office in the absence of a general acceptance of the principle of equal pay for equal work at the time.[8]

Women's membership of the FBU increased significantly during the war, rising to 8,200 by 1943, but had declined dramatically to around 500 by 1948,[9] reflecting the drop in the number of women in the fire service with the return of peacetime. Segars noted that even during the period of greater membership, women did not play a prominent role in the union, although three women's organisers were taken on between 1941 and 1943, with two seats allocated to women on the union's Executive Council.

After the war women's presence in the fire service was largely confined to control rooms, but in 1976 Mary Joy Langdon became the first operational female firefighter when she joined the retained service at Battle in East Sussex.[10] In 1982 the first female wholetime firefighters were recruited, notably when Sue Batten joined the London Fire Brigade in September.[11] In London, the Greater London Council's equal opportunities policies prompted efforts to recruit women and B&EM firefighters, with other women following Batten in the 1980s. Sian Griffiths (a founding member of London Women's Advisory Committee) was among a group of six women who passed recruit training in 1985 (although another five did not succeed). She recalled, 'I think most people thought that we probably weren't going to be there very long and that it was just a bit of a fad and nothing had to really change.'

However, she proved them wrong, retiring in 2015 after 30 years, having reached the role of watch manager. Other women remember being made unwelcome in the fire service in the early days. Yannick Dubois, chair of the LGBT Committee, joined as a retained firefighter in Amersham in 1990, but two years later, when her station was upgraded to day crewing, she went to training school to become a wholetime firefighter. On her first day she encountered a hostile sub-officer, who, she says, told her: '"We don't want women in the fire service. I'm going to get rid of you." That was my first day. I thought, "Now I think I'm going to stay".'

In 2016 Sally Harper and Katie Holloway became the first mother and daughter wholetime serving firefighters, a signal event marking the progress of women. Harper joined the London Fire Brigade in 1988 and was joined by her daughter 28 years later, when Holloway started at the same station that Harper had first joined.[12] In 2017 the London Fire Brigade appointed its first female commissioner, when Dany Cotton took over the top position in January.

In the early days women lacked basic facilities on fire stations, such as toilets, showers and separate sleeping accommodation, and were forced to endure ill-fitting uniforms and personal protective equipment. Furthermore, there were no maternity policies. Many women entering the fire service in the 1980s left because of the poor treatment and conditions, with Griffiths commenting on the low retention rate of women between 1985 and 1999 in the London Fire Brigade. The number of female operational firefighters increased very slowly, from two in 1982 to 38 across England and Wales in 1987 (or 0.1 per cent of the total number),[13] rising to 436 (0.9 per cent) by 1998.[14] More detailed figures for England show that the proportion of women employed as operational firefighters rose from 1.7 per cent in 2002 (1.3 per cent of wholetime and 2.5 per cent of retained firefighters) to 5 per cent in 2016 (5.2 per cent wholetime and 4.5 per cent retained firefighters) in England.[15] In Scotland the figures are similar, with women representing 5 per cent of wholetime firefighters and 6 per cent of retained in 2016.[16] In Wales, the latest gender breakdown available is for 2011, when women represented 4 per cent of wholetime firefighters and 3 per cent of retained.[17]

Women have always outnumbered men in control jobs, accounting for 68 per cent of wholetime control staff in England and Wales in 1987, and 90 per cent in Scotland.[18] Gender segregation has prevailed; in England women accounted for 79 per cent of control positions in 2002, and 76 per cent by 2016, and 84 per cent in Scotland.[19] In Wales control staff were 82 per cent female in 2011.[20]

The history of black and ethnic minorities in the fire service

Britain's first black firefighter is believed to be George Roberts, who joined the national fire service in the Second World War, was posted to New Cross fire station in London, and was later promoted to section leader. He was awarded the British Empire medal in recognition of his firefighting activities and his role in co-founding the fire service's well-attended discussion and education groups, intended to promote political and cultural debate.[21]

The first full-time post-war black firefighter in London, and possibly the country, is thought to be Frank Bailey, who joined the West Ham Fire Brigade in 1955. He recalled that he applied to join the fire service after being told by an FBU delegate at the TUC that there were no black firefighters in England:

> I asked, why not? I knew that black men worked in mining, on the railways and in factories. He said that the authorities were not hiring black men because they were not strong enough physically or well enough educated to do the job of a firefighter. I immediately recognised racism and I said I'm going to apply to be a firefighter and see if they find me unfit. I joined in 1955.[22]

Bailey became the FBU branch rep in his workplace and counted the then FBU general secretary, John Horner, as a friend. However he was consistently passed over for promotion and left the fire service in 1965 for social work. He remained active in unions and politics and, as 'an avowed communist, he consistently championed equality and the rights of working people, particularly black people',[23] often attending FBU B&EMM Schools as an honorary member until his death in 2016.[24] Bailey features in a film on the history of B&EM members of the fire service, *Rise to the Challenge*, made in 2004.[25]

In the 1990s B&EM firefighters faced systematic discrimination. Micky Nicholas, who joined Stratford fire station in January 1990, said that treatment of black firefighters was 'pretty shocking' at that time: 'Black people who had joined the fire service hadn't really stayed because of their treatment… language, ill treatment. Under the term banter – banter never stopped. Your complaints went nowhere, if you had the courage to complain.'

By 1981 there were six black firefighters in the London Fire Brigade, a number that reached 192 (or almost 3 per cent) by 1989.[26] When the Home Office first began publishing statistics in 1993 on the ethnicity of fire and rescue staff in England and Wales, black and Asian staff accounted for less than 1 per cent.[27] More detailed figures on staff by ethnicity and role have been published from 2011, when 3.5 per cent of firefighters were from B&EM backgrounds in England, rising to 3.8 per cent by 2016.[28] Representation has varied widely across the country, depending on the composition of the local population, but local communities continue to be under-represented in terms of their ethnicity. For example in Greater London in 2016 12.9 per cent of firefighters were from B&EM backgrounds (compared to around 40 per cent of the local population), in the West Midlands the figure was 8.1 per cent (compared to around 30 per cent of the local population) and in Greater Manchester it was only 3.1 per cent (compared to around 16 per cent of the local population).[29] In Wales the proportion of ethnic minority firefighters was only 1 per cent in 2011 (20 wholetime staff and 10 retained).[30] Similarly in Scotland in 2016 fewer than 1 per cent of wholetime and retained firefighters belonged to an ethnic minority, representing no increase over time.[31]

The history of LGBT employees in the fire service

Little is known about the early history of LGBT members in the fire service and the FBU, primarily because of fears about the disclosure of non-heterosexual sexuality in a male-dominated work environment. Research has shown the difficulties of being openly lesbian or gay in the watch culture of the fire service, which requires 'fitting in' with masculine customs and norms of behaviour.[32] In 1999 the Home Office Thematic Review of Equality and Fairness in the Fire Service noted that sexuality was 'an absolute taboo to most members of the service', adding that 'the fact that many of those we spoke to were unaware of any gay or lesbian members among the workforce indicates the fear that exists in respect of declaring sexuality within the service.'[33]

Despite taboos around discussing sexuality, many women reported that there was an assumption that they were lesbians. Yannick Dubois explained:

When I first joined they said, 'You're either a slut or a lesbian; that's why you want to be surrounded by men all the time or doing a man's job.' I thought, 'Well, maybe I'll have more friends if I say I'm a slut'. But that's how they see women, they already think you're a lesbian anyway. You want to do a man's job. It's not really surprising and it's less threatening for them. It doesn't mean that all lesbians have had a good time. It took me six years to come out.

Thus, although some lesbians say that once they are open to colleagues about their sexuality it can defuse sexual tension, there is also a risk of harassment on the basis of their sexuality.[34] For gay men, a number of stereotypes must be overcome, as Pat Carberry, national secretary of the LGBT section, found when coming out to colleagues on a retained station in Bedfordshire:

Once I made the decision to come out, I was a crew manager and I had my own watch, and I remember sitting them down and saying: 'Hypothetically, how would you feel if a gay guy came on a watch?' I had – well – not very good responses. 'Oh, I wouldn't like that. Good God, the dormitory at night, they would be trying to get into bed with me.' 'I wouldn't want to be going into the shower, they'd be trying to look at my bits.' One of them turned around and said, 'Oh yeah, you say that but that will never happen. Gay guys are only interested in serving drinks on planes and cutting hair and flower arranging.' So, yeah, maybe today is not the day to tell them! So I left it for about a week and a half, [then] once again [we] sat round the same table, having a cup of tea and I says: 'That situation hypothetically about a gay guy joining the watch; [there's] something I've got to tell you: it's not a hypothetical situation, it's a reality, and I'm gay.' 'What! Hold on a sec. How come it's taken you this long to tell us? It's not as though any of us would have had a problem with it.' 'What! Last week you said this, you said that.' 'Yeah, but you know what we mean! We didn't mean it that way.' But you said it! And yeah, they were great, really supportive.

Since 2011 the government has published annual 'experimental' statistics on the numbers of LGBT firefighters in England, which range from 3 per cent to 3.5 per cent for wholetime firefighters, 1.3 per cent to 1.7 per cent for retained firefighters, and 2.5 per cent to 2.9 per cent for fire control and support staff. However these figures should be treated with considerable caution, as the proportions in the 'not stated' and 'not collected' categories are very high, reflecting the fact that firstly many brigades do not ask for such information, and secondly that there are high levels of non-disclosure when people are asked about their sexual orientation.[35]

Transgender issues have recently gained a higher profile in society and in the fire service, and in 2016 trans firefighter Nic Brennan told his story to *Firefighter*. Born female, Nic joined Cheshire Fire and Rescue Service in 2001, but recalls that 'ticking the female gender box felt so wrong'. After more than seven years in the fire service, Nic had a 'light bulb moment' and began the transition from female to male, although he did not tell colleagues initially:

> Like everyone who has gone on this journey I found it difficult, but I couldn't have wished for better treatment from my workmates. I was initially hesitant to come out for fear of not being understood. I thought being transgender would be seen as too much of a problem and I wouldn't be accepted at all. I worried that I'd be dismissed or harassed out of the job I loved if people knew. I couldn't have been more wrong.[36]

Following his transition, Nic moved to a new station where he has always been known as a man, but is open with colleagues about his past, who he describes as 'some of the best workmates possible'.

The development of FBU equality policy and structures

The development of the FBU's internal equality policies and structures took place in parallel with its work in pressing the fire and rescue service for change, described in the second part of this chapter. This section first traces the growth of the union's equal opportunities and Fairness at Work policies from the 1990s, and then describes the formation and development of the structures to represent women, B&EM and LGBT members.

As the harassment and bullying experienced by many female, B&EM and LGBT members became evident, it was clear that action was needed within the union, as well as from employers. FBU research officer at the time, Philippa Clark, remembers Ken Cameron's commitment to putting the union's own house in order:

> Ken was absolutely convinced of it, this has got to change. The stories were just awful, awful from the black members – razor blades in fire boots, shit in fire boots, and those were the extremes, obviously, but there was other stuff. And Ken took it on. At that time, 1996 I think it was, Andy Gilchrist became national officer, and he had responsibility for equality, and he was very good on it… but within the union there was hostility, there was silence. … What Ken saw was a huge amount of talent that wasn't coming through the union structures, 'They were articulate people; why aren't they coming through, why haven't we got these people as officials? Something's wrong.' So for him and Ronnie Scott, the president, and for Andy it was a political issue, totally and utterly… We can't claim to be socialists if we're excluding people, and you may say we're not, but the effect of how we're working is that we are, and that's got to change. … And we couldn't tackle the service if we hadn't tackled the union, and he was absolutely clear about that… We've got to make sure our house is in order.

Equality and Fairness at Work policies

The Executive Council had formed an Equal Opportunities Committee in 1986 and launched its first equal opportunities policy booklet in 1987, intended to support negotiations with employers on issues such as recruitment, promotion, training and monitoring and to educate members to overcome prejudice and discrimination.[37] But it was during the 1990s that the union's equality policies and structures for representation of minority members developed significantly. The 1992 conference heard from women members about the sexual harassment they were experiencing and passed a motion strengthening the union's equal opportunities policy so that members who breached it would be subjected to disciplinary procedures. Fife delegate Linda Shanahan (who became the union's first female brigade secretary) said at the time that the policy had 'not been properly policed or updated', adding, 'Our complacency and lack of action has meant that the profile of that policy has diminished.' Ken Cameron committed the union to a major review of equal opportunities policy, urging all members to 'question both our own attitudes and those of comrades and colleagues' even though it may make them 'the butt of ridicule'.[38] However by the 1995 conference, and following the Tanya Clayton case (see page 244), women members were still complaining about a lack of union progress on tackling verbal and physical abuse towards women and called for a dedicated equal opportunities officer in the union to support officials.[39] In 1996 fairness at work became the responsibility of national officer Andy Gilchrist.

The union's equal opportunities work developed into its Fairness at Work strategy, endorsed by conference in 1996. It contained recommendations for issues to raise with management, for changes within the union and on education and training. Cameron stressed that it was not about 'protecting or progressing one group of members at the expense of others... It is about stopping the bullying of any member', consciously adopting the term 'Fairness at Work' to emphasise its relevance to everyone. Conference backed a rule change saying that 'it shall be the duty of every member to treat others with dignity and respect and to challenge offensive behaviour of any kind'.[40] Linda Smith contrasted the FBU's approach to educating members with the management approach:

> You don't win hearts and minds by producing a brigade order. You have to sit down with people that are sceptical or don't understand and explain why women, black people, gay [men] and lesbians are entitled to a job in the fire service and are good at their jobs in the fire service and it actually benefits everybody. And there were so many managers that didn't get that. They thought they did... but the FBU believed it and they enacted it. They put their money where their mouth is.

A new position, Fairness at Work rep, was added to the FBU committee structures at brigade and regional level in 1997 (a rep was in place in most brigades by 1999, engaging people in discussions on the issue),[41] alongside the Fairness at Work sub-committees, to assist in improving the working environment for all members working in the UK fire and rescue service.

In 1996 the All Different, All Equal (ADAE) policy was introduced, whereby members who were alleged to have carried out acts of harassment or discrimination were not automatically entitled to union representation.[42] This policy on representation, included in the ADAE document, has always divided opinion in the union, highlighting the difficulties for a trade union of both taking a strong stand against the bullying and harassment of minorities, and providing a right to representation. The former national officer responsible for equalities, John McGhee, explained the importance of the support for those experiencing harassment that the policy established:

> The fundamental thing was that we would believe someone who came to us and said, 'I'm being bullied and I'm being harassed...' So we put in place a process that said, 'Right, so you come along and say "I'm being bullied",' and our position was that you get our support instantly. The person you're accusing – and we did this because we knew that women and black members weren't coming to us, they never had confidence because the shop steward or the branch rep was usually the pal of the person that was being accused. So the process was that we would then carry out an investigation into the person who was being accused and determine whether we thought they had some kind of arguable defence. And if we felt they had an arguable defence then we would give them representation. And if we didn't, we wouldn't.

However, there was also a view that all union members initially deserved representation, and the policy was later changed to provide representation for the accused member until the regional committee had determined whether they had an arguable defence. Some believe that the policy is still unfair in denying representation before the case has been heard by the employer and that some cases may be better dealt with by informal discussions with members. Lucy Masoud, responsible for ADAE cases for London region, commented:

> We had a case not so long ago where it was a member's

word against another member. And we didn't give them representation and he went to the hearing and he got no case to answer. So how does that look to our membership, that someone is in essence innocent and we didn't give them representation?

Although the ADAE policy originated to address cases of racist, sexist and homophobic bullying, figures on calls to a union helpline in 1998 found that of the calls about bullying, 95 per cent were from male members, indicating that bullying was also a significant issue for heterosexual white men; 20 per cent wanted contact with the LGBT network and 12 per cent of calls arose from issues related to harassment based on race.[43]

The union reviewed the ADAE policy in 2015 and made some changes to ensure that investigations were conducted in a timely manner, but its purpose remains to show members that bullying, harassment or victimisation will not be tolerated in the union.[44]

Former director of education Trevor Cave points out that the ADAE course is 'one of the longest-standing courses we've been running', believing that equality education has always had a high priority within the union and has been effective in changing the culture around how equality issues are tackled: 'I think officials, our reps understand... what to look for, how to challenge, how to deal with things informally, which is a much more sophisticated [approach] – so the approach has changed.'

Equality sections and structures

The union's equality sections – the B&EMM section, the LGBT section and the women's section – developed from informal meetings among minority members who began to organise themselves from the late 1980s and 1990s, supported by the union head office. This 'self-organisation' occurred at a time when the feminist, anti-racist and lesbian and gay liberation movements were shaping wider political activism and influencing debates in the labour movement as to how to empower previously marginalised groups. Unions encouraged various forms of self-organisation, to give voice to previously under-represented groups, and promoted structural changes such as reserved seats on national executive committees. Such interventions represented a shift from 'liberal' notions of equality, which ensure equal or the same treatment for all, to 'radical' strategies, which introduce positive actions to counter previous discrimination or under-representation within mainstream structures.[45] In the union movement debates have taken place about whether separate organisation by women or other groups is a divisive strategy that weakens class-based solidarity or whether it is a necessary means to empower excluded groups so that they may play a full part within their unions.[46] This tension is encapsulated in John McGhee's recollection of how his initial resistance to separate sections was overcome:

> I think a big part of the opposition from officials like me at the time – I was probably a divisional secretary – was this idea that having sections in our union was a bit of an insult to me because I thought, well, I was a socialist and I certainly wasn't sexist or racist or homophobic. And if someone came to me I would absolutely deal with it and I became involved in politics through anti-racist activity and Anti-Nazi League type stuff in the very early 80s, probably even late 70s. So I felt, well, are you suggesting I wouldn't look after black members or women members or LGBT members? There was a lot of work done within the union to educate people and make us realise what was happening for women and black members that we weren't dealing with. And I think I was one of the ones who then saw, right OK I get this, so this wasn't a question necessarily of my ability as a shop steward, it was about [the fact that] we had created a culture where women were never going to come to me anyway because they saw white men as being part of the problem. And they had had too many experiences of where they weren't being listened to, where the issues weren't being dealt with.

In the late 1980s women firefighters in London began to meet informally. Sian Griffiths describes how she gathered women together: 'If I knew where there was a woman firefighter I would ring her up and say "Hello, my name is Sian" and introduce myself because there were so few of us. And I was so excited to try and get women together.'

In 1989 the inaugural meeting of the Women's Advisory Committee took place in London, supported by key male officials including Executive Council member Gordon Vassell. Early Women's Advisory Committee members included Ghada Razuki and Linda Smith, the latter recalled some of the issues discussed:

> We talked about uniform and when I first joined we slept in the same dormitories as the men. There wasn't a shower for women, even though there was a shower for officers and a shower for firefighters. So there were practical considerations, but the real importance of it was that women were having a bad time. Women that were being bullied, that were being harassed, and that was the real importance... giving the support to the women that were having a bad time.

The first Women's School was held in 1992 at Wortley Hall, Sheffield, attended by 24 women – a mixture of control staff and firefighters, as well as by national officials, who were shocked at the problems women were facing and at the fact that these had not been raised through the union structures.[47] Further Women's Schools took place in 1995 and 1996, and by 1997 it was recognised that a national structure was needed to support women members across the country. A national women's meeting, held in April 1997, elected a steering group comprising four women control members and three firefighters. This group worked to set up the structures and elections for the National Women's Advisory Committee in 1998,[48] and in March 1998 the first FBU National Women's Conference was held at Wortley Hall.

However, many women and men were initially opposed to separate organising for women. Denise Christie described how she went to the Women's School, expecting it to be 'the worst weekend ever':

> But I suppose I'd better just see what it's like and... I was really taken aback at, I suppose, how political it was, how organised it was, how supportive it was; how I felt that the issues that I was experiencing, that I was hiding, were experienced by other women. It was a safe space. It felt like a weight off my shoulders, I felt I can kind of be myself here. And I went from somebody who was against it to somebody that was really passionate – I became their EC [Executive Council] member. And that was

only through the support I had from the Women's [Advisory] Committee, and Lothian and Borders officials. The feminist political education that I had, the organising and campaigning skills and tools that they gave me as an individual, I would say has made me a better trade unionist.

Ruth Winters recalls that she and other women on the FBU Control Staff National Committee – which she perceived had been treated effectively as the women's committee of the union up to that point – were also opposed to women's self-organised structures, but she too changed her mind once she had attended a meeting and heard the stories of isolated women firefighters, becoming convinced that a women's committee would be best placed to address issues for all women in the fire service.

In the 1990s, B&EM firefighters in London began to meet informally, with the first meeting called because of the growing realisation that many black firefighters were being subjected to racist language and abuse. Carl St Paul recalled the empathy shared by 15 black firefighters at the first meeting:

> Everybody realised that we'd all had a similar journey, we'd all had the comments, we'd all had the jokes, we'd all gone through what the fella at my station had gone through when he thought that he was the only one that was going through it. And I told him, 'No, I've been through it as well.' So we all realised that we shared that common denominator of having to put up with the culture.

The group met regularly to provide mutual support, but St Paul remembers that he did not initially welcome the union's attempts to organise B&EM members more formally. However, his mind was changed at the first FBU meeting for B&EM members at Wortley Hall in November 1995, attended by 43 members:

> I was shocked to see all these black firefighters, from Scotland to the Isle of Wight, to Gloucester, with the various accents. And it was – I could only describe it as – wonderful, it was absolutely glorious. The meeting got off to a raucous beginning because the anger that we had been feeling in London was multiplied

from outside of London. At least in London I could be at my station in North Kensington as the only black firefighter for a while until somebody else came on the green watch, but at least somebody else came. But these people in the provinces were the only black firefighter – not on a station, not in an area, but in a brigade, in a whole brigade, the only one in the whole brigade. And it was then that we realised, my God, we thought we were having it bad; these poor people, have no one to talk to.

Despite the presence of Executive Council members at the first meeting, and their intentions to tackle the issues raised, many felt that by the second national meeting in November 1996, attended by 54 B&EM members, 'precious little had really changed' in the past year.[49] Micky Nicholas recalled that Ken Cameron and national officers 'got a fair bit of stick' because it was felt that union reps were complicit in the ill treatment of black members:

Some of the people causing a lot of distress and, dare I say, a bad time, were actually union reps and were people on stations, who were branch reps. They were all part of – I'm not saying necessarily they were the leaders of it – but they were part of the problem.

The meeting elected a steering committee, with Carl St Paul as secretary and Wayne McCollin as chair, to form a B&EMM Advisory Committee offering support, advice and training to B&EM members and advice on the union's equality work. Support for this committee was agreed at the Executive Council meeting in December 1996.[50] Roger McKenzie was an external tutor at the B&EMM School that established the B&EMM structures and he recalled that the FBU was one of only a very small number of unions that enabled structures to be developed by the black members themselves, rather than handing them down from above, which he felt was a brave and important step by the union:

It's one of the proudest things that I've been involved in in the trade union movement. I think Kenny Cameron and his colleagues at the time were just exceptional in their determination to root out racism from the fire service, but it would have been easy to have just left it at that, but they wanted to find ways of encouraging wider participation of black members within the organisation and I think that dual approach, along with the rest of their Fairness at Work stuff, which was borne out of real hardships, people facing real harassment in stations up and down the country... I think that the determination of the FBU to deal with that and the things that they put in place – it was one of the beacons to the rest of the trade union movement.

The B&EMM section has been predominantly male, although both Micky Nicholas and Carl St Paul highlighted the important contribution of West Midlands firefighter Samantha Samuels, who was the first female B&EMM rep, becoming B&EMM section chair from 2005 to 2007, then secretary until 2011. Conscious of the under-representation of B&EM women, the 2008 B&EMM School took the theme of 'Women in colour', with an all-female line up of speakers.[51] The 2016 FBU conference heard that there were still fewer than 100 operational black women and fewer than 20 black women junior or middle managers in the fire and rescue service. The B&EMM National Committee was considering the possibility of a reserved seat on its committee for a woman.[52]

The FBU Lesbian and Gay Support Group was announced in *Firefighter* in May 1996 as a confidential group providing support to lesbian and gay members. In 1997 the secretary, Terry Richardson, explained in *Firefighter* why the group was needed, highlighting the many areas in which lesbians and gay men still did not have equal rights under the law, and the fact that there 'appears to be a percentage of FBU members that refuse to accept lesbian and gay firefighters', a stance that he said was often based on ill-informed stereotypes.[53] In November 1999 the FBU Gay and Lesbian Committee held its inaugural meeting, with Pat Carberry elected as national chair and Stewart Brown as secretary.[54]

While the 1998 FBU conference had agreed to establish formal groups for women, B&EM members and lesbian and gay members, more far-reaching structural changes were proposed at the 2001 FBU conference, including an Executive Council seat for women members and for the B&EMM section, to mirror the way control, retained and officer members were represented. Vicky Knight remembered:

The proudest day of my fire service life was probably seconding that motion at our conference. The most nerve-wracking [day], but it was a time of massive political change or massive political potential for the FBU, not just within our own structures because women were so under-represented, but within the TUC as well. We became a leader in the TUC because we did such progressive stuff in relation to minority groups within that kind of forum and it was just a really exciting time. So that passed overwhelmingly at conference.

In January 2002 Vicky Knight was elected as the first Executive Council member for women and in March 2002 Micky Nicholas was elected as the first B&EMM Executive Council member. In 2005 Stewart Brown was elected as the first LGBT Executive Council member.[55]

Participation in equality sections can provide a route into union activism for a wider range of members. John McGhee found that the number of women holding union positions at brigade level almost doubled from approximately 5.8 per cent in 1992 to 10.3 per cent in 2010. Women were twice as likely to take up a union position as their male counterparts.[56] Denise Christie explains: 'You find that in the FBU a lot of women that become activists and officials have come because they came to the union for help for maternity, grievance, bullying and harassment, whatever it is, and thought, "Oh right, OK – now I want to give something back".'

This was affirmed by a delegate to the 2016 conference, Caroline Sturgess, who had attended the previous year's Women's School when suffering severe bullying and harassment at work, having for years distanced herself from the women's section 'for fear of segregation or being different and not being one of the lads':

I attended Women's School and I can honestly say it saved my career. I was shocked to hear that many of the delegates had experienced the issues that I had. Whilst this is shocking, it gave me a safe place to talk and to rebuild my confidence... Women's school has given me the confidence and skills, and knowledge to undertake not [just] one branch position but three.'[57]

The three equality sections mobilised members to achieve progress on equality and diversity in the fire service, and also in supporting wider labour movement and international campaigns (see Chapter 9). Crucially, though, they played a key role in FBU activism, industrial disputes and campaigns. Former women's section secretary Kerry Baigent explained:

> I was a trade unionist first – that's absolutely what I did. Everything I ever did in my workplace for women was all about improving the lives of all working people, including women. And any strike that was on, we were part of it. We were always at the rallies, we were always at the forefront of every campaign, industrially, the union had. And I was really proud of that work. It was really important that our members were really, really strong, like you would see more women on a rally in proportion to the numbers of women in the job than men. It was all really impressive.

For Baigent and others, the commitment to equality on the basis of gender, race or sexuality was integral to their trade unionism. However, since the creation of sectional representation at regional and Executive Council levels, there had always been discussion about the impact of the equality sections on the internal democracy of the union, in particular concerns about multiple voting – in that a woman member, for example, would have a say via both her regional and women's representatives – as well as questions about the relative size of the constituencies voting for sectional seats, in comparison to seats for the regional reps. Further concerns arose in the context of financial pressures facing the union. As part of savings in the growing budget allocated to union release, section secretaries had had their full-time paid release removed in 2011, a decision which Baigent believed significantly reduced her effectiveness in supporting women members across the service.

In 2012 the union held a special conference to debate an Executive Council paper on reorganisation, which sought to address the organisational challenges and financial savings that the union deemed necessary, and included recommendations regarding representation provided by the union's equality section committees. The Executive Council paper argued that the union structures were based on the workplace branch and brigade structure but that the equality section seats at regional and Executive Council levels gave additional votes to these groups, so that they voted on wider industrial issues that went beyond their remit under the union rules.

The Executive Council paper noted that, according to the rule book, the union's democratic structures were rooted in the representation of all members at their place of work, uniting them in workplace branches, with representation then provided through brigade committees and regional and national structures. The paper stated that the original aims of sectional representation were to enhance the existing workplace structure, to provide a network of support and to ensure the issues affecting under-represented groups would be properly considered by the union. The paper noted that the intention had never been for equality structures to bypass or replace the workplace branch and brigade committee structure nor for them to be a mechanism for discussing or determining industrial, political or other matters affecting all members. The paper argued that the system of reserved seats and additional voting had the potential to distort democratic structures. The question of voting structures was important for Wrack, who gave an example of a regional committee structure, all of whom had voting rights, with five brigades:

> You'd have one delegate from the officers, one delegate from control, one delegate from retained, one delegate from women, one delegate from B&EMM, one delegate from LGBT, so there's five representing the whole workforce and six representing sectional interests. No-one has ever made a robust defence of that structure to me, ever.

The Executive Council paper concluded that positions established to represent equality matters on the Executive Council had provided votes on wider industrial and political matters. It contained 14 recommendations, seven of which directly affected the equality structures. Controversially, it recommended the removal of the reserved seats on the Executive Council for women, B&EM and LGBT members. Instead the National Sectional Committees should provide advice and recommendations to the Executive Council.

Equality section reps attending brigade and regional committees would also lose voting rights and would attend in an advisory capacity. The Executive Council proposals prompted a passionately argued debate at the special conference. Supporting the Executive Council resolution, Phil Coates from Nottinghamshire insisted:

> Another big issue for Notts is democracy. Additional representation is divisive and unwelcome. Notts have brought a resolution about additional representation before to conference, but we've been pressured from all sides to withdraw those resolutions. We believe we were right then, we believe we are right now. ... For too long we have worried about being labelled racist, homophobic or sexist simply because we have a different outlook. I find that offensive, I'm sure a lot of you do. We need this discussion. We need democracy.

Karen Adams of Dorset expressed the view of many who felt that the union would be losing an important means of representation for minority groups when she argued that it was not always possible for the voices of minorities to be heard at branch meetings. She believed that continued representation at regional and Executive Council level was necessary:

> From personal experience [I can say] it takes a great deal of courage to draw attention to yourself and stand up and be heard by those who are unaffected by the issues that we, the minorities, face. If you support the isolation of our minority members, then vote for it... If you want to use it to stop being the progressive union that we are renowned for, then vote for it.

Conference voted by 71 per cent to 29 per cent to support the Executive Council recommendation to remove the Executive Council equality section seats and voting rights. The decision sharply divided opinion within the union and was felt very personally by many of those who had supported the changes, introduced 10 years earlier. While the conference decision was clearly supported by a large majority, some equality activists felt that the arguments justified on democratic grounds missed the point about providing representation for minorities within the union, as reflected by Pat Carberry: 'Democracy is about the wants of the many. But if you're a minority, you're kind of onto a loser from day one because the wants of the many, they don't see your interests being a priority.'

A further consequence of the decision, according to Micky Nicholas, who lost his Executive Council position as representative of B&EM members but chose to remain active in the B&EMM section of the union, was that it became more difficult to organise and motivate B&EM members to be active in the union:

> It had a massive effect on us in terms of organising and motivation because you had to motivate people, people who are keeping their heads above water, some of them sometimes with very challenging circumstances at work and you are asking them to do what? To go, and you're just an advisor, you're just advisory, so you can see something passionately wrong – and I'm not saying you would win the debate or the vote – but you can't even vote. And that's a massive thing.

Many activists within the equality sections did, however, remain committed to working within the self-organised structures that the union continued to support, or moved into mainstream union positions.

Advancing equality and diversity in the fire and rescue service

One of the FBU's first successes in bargaining for equality was the achievement of equal pay for female control staff with male control staff in January 1972, phased in from January 1970.[58] A resolution passed at the emergency control annual meeting in 1996, noting the prevailing 8 per cent disparity between control and firefighter pay, demanded action from the Executive Council on the equalisation of pay.[59] However it was only after the 2002-04 pay dispute that a comprehensive job evaluation assessment resulted in control operators gaining 95 per cent of firefighter pay (Chapter 4). The issue of gender segregation in emergency control had been confronted in 1979, when the union secured an industrial tribunal ruling that Lancashire Fire Authority was guilty of sex discrimination in its recruitment of emergency control officers, one of the 39 per cent of Emergency Controls in the UK that employed men or women only. Lancashire, along with Greater Manchester, employed only women in control rooms at the time, while Cumbria employed only men.[60] Control rooms have remained around 70-80 per cent female, as seen above.

The FBU first took action on racist and sexist initiation ceremonies in the fire service following a resolution to conference in 1985 based upon reports by a female firefighter at Soho of degrading and sexually abusive treatment, and ongoing incidents of serious sexual harassment. The conference passed an emergency resolution committing the union to fighting sexism and racism in the fire service.[61] The union supported members in a number of legal cases regarding sexism and racism, including the female member above, who was eventually discharged from the London Fire Brigade on medical grounds. The employer was taken to the High Court, resulting in a settlement of £25,000, then a record amount in a sexual harassment claim. The case was also significant in that the station officer was found guilty of neglect of duty in failing to protect the female firefighter, and the firefighters who had perpetrated the harassment were required to pay £2,100 between them, a penalty supported by the union.[62] In 1995, the union supported Tanya Clayton in her successful tribunal case against Hereford and Worcester Fire Brigade, which she had joined in 1989. The tribunal unanimously upheld her complaint of sex discrimination, which included verbal aggression, intimidation and subjection to dangerous and cruel drills. The tribunal said that 'the whole brigade should bear an individual and collective shame for the most appalling discrimination... and for the devastating effect that they have all had on the applicant's life.'[63] Despite this clear verdict, the brigade appealed, but in March 1996 the Employment Appeals Tribunal ruled in Clayton's favour, adding their condemnation of the brigade's decision to appeal.[64]

A race discrimination claim was supported by the FBU in 1997 when retained firefighter Warren Mann took Gloucestershire Fire Service to an industrial tribunal, which found that he had been subjected to racial discrimination and had been 'sent to Coventry' for raising his complaint. The tribunal criticised the brigade for the lack of equal opportunities training for retained firefighters and for inadequate procedures for tackling racial harassment.[65]

The FBU also used the negotiating machinery to raise equal opportunities matters, following the formation of the union's Equal Opportunities Committee in 1986, which drafted a model policy to be negotiated by brigade officials with their fire authorities.[66] A Central Fire Brigades Advisory Council (CFBAC) joint committee on equal opportunities was created in 1992. It met twice during its first year, considering issues such as the potentially discriminatory minimum height requirement and relaxing the minimum age for entry.[67] A 1994 Home Office research report showed slow progress on equal opportunities, and the FBU expressed its dissatisfaction with the fact that the majority of brigades had done very little to implement the recommendations of 1990 fire service circular *Equal Opportunities in the Fire Service.*[68]

During the 1990s, when employers across the public and private sectors were increasingly developing equal opportunities policies and actions, pressure grew on the white, male-dominated fire service, and in 1997 the Equal Opportunities Task Group was established, with representatives of the FBU, employers and fire service bodies. Its work included reviewing the Home Office equality statistics and working on the ongoing Thematic Inspections on equality in brigades.[69] A major jolt to the fire and rescue service came with the publication in September 1999 of *Equality and Fairness in the Fire Service: A thematic review by HM Fire Service Inspectorate*, which called the service 'institutionally sexist' and possibly 'institutionally racist', with homosexuality an 'absolute taboo'. It noted a 'macho', 'laddish' watch culture and a requirement to 'fit in'. Notably though, it identified that the service had shown a failure of leadership on equality at all levels, in contrast to the FBU:

> It was found that the most significant involvement by far was on the part of the Fire Brigades Union. At national level, a clear leadership role has emerged for this union. They have been particularly active in pursuit of equality issues over recent years and it is to their credit that most local officials have willingly accepted this emphasis. This leadership has resulted in extensive training for its officials to enable them to support policy objectives.[70]

In 1999 the home secretary, Jack Straw, announced equality targets for ethnic minorities of 7 per cent to be reached within 10 years across England and Wales, with variability to reflect local populations. These were followed by targets for women that stipulated that by 1 April 2002, 4 per cent of uniformed staff (excluding control) should be female; by 2004 it should be 9 per cent; and by 2009 15 per cent.[71] Also in that year, the Macpherson Report, commissioned following the murder of Stephen Lawrence, had labelled the police service institutionally racist, a term which national officer Andy Gilchrist said also applied to the fire service. An FBU motion to the TUC Black Workers' Conference condemned the 'sloping shoulders syndrome' of allowing people to take early retirement to avoid facing discipline charges of racism, calling it a 'conspiracy of silence'.[72]

The 'Thematic Review' was welcomed by Ken Cameron, as it strongly emphasised the employers' duty to tackle the bullying, discrimination and harassment reported to them, but he raised two aspects of concern. One was the 'attempts being made to undermine the FBU by suggesting that, in welcoming the Review, the leadership of the union accepts that all members are racist, homophobic and sexist. This is not only untrue and mischievous, it is potentially divisive.' A second concern was that employers would try to use the Review to instigate changes to watch and shift systems 'under the guise of equal opportunities thus trying again to make fundamental changes to our conditions of service contained in the Grey Book'.[73] Women in the FBU welcomed the findings of the Review, but Vicky Knight, National Women's Committee secretary at the time, similarly warned that it was being 'hijacked, used out of context and without consultation by some of the national employers'. She affirmed that the National Women's Committee, reflecting the views of most women firefighters, did not see the need for changes to the current shift system and wanted to see 'flexibility for us, not imposed on us' and called for childcare support and good paternity and maternity agreements.[74]

The FBU was able to use the positive political climate towards equality of the time to push for improvements on conditions such as maternity and paternity leave, as former women's section secretary Kerry Baigent explains:

When I first got involved, the Thematic Review had just taken place so the fire service was under a Blair government and there was a political will to address equality issues. This meant that we were able to make progress in brigades, because brigades were receptive to addressing equality. So we improved the maternity provisions for women across all fire services and in some cases we got nine months' full pay for women on maternity leave. The maternity policy we wrote – it's still very much a model because it wasn't just about money – it was about working lives. What they were doing with women was they were putting pregnant women in a cupboard somewhere, with tasks and duties that weren't relevant to them as a firefighter. We also upgraded the Grey Book. We didn't get everything we wanted but we got 12 weeks at half pay on top of the first six weeks at 90 per cent. Because that was topped up with SMP [statutory maternity pay] it was significantly more than the statutory minimum and we got two weeks of paternity pay.

The FBU's best practice document *Negotiating Maternity, Paternity and Adoption Rights* was endorsed by the fire minister, Parmjit Dhanda, in 2008, who found progress in many fire and rescue services 'disappointing', stating that the 'the guidance produced by the FBU will provide an effective tool in delivering improvement.'[75] Indeed local improvements negotiated by the FBU on the basis of the document included maternity leave of nine months on full pay at Staffordshire, 18 weeks in Kent, 11 weeks in London, and in 2009 the Isle of Wight agreed 39 weeks' full pay.[76] In Scotland, regional official Denise Christie succeeded in negotiating an improved national scheme, following reorganisation in 2013, that provided for 18 weeks' maternity and adoption leave at full pay. Baigent also highlighted the advances made for retained section women, including rights to paid time off when removed from full 'on-call' operational duties because they were pregnant, as well as maternity leave and pay. Informing retained firefighters of their rights was important: '[It] was very difficult for retained women to know they were entitled to that. It was our job to make sure that it was communicated and we tried really really hard to do that.'

While the Labour government may initially have provided a favourable environment in which to progress equality matters, many of the proposals for 'modernisation' of the fire service produced by Sir George Bain during the 2002-04 pay dispute (see Chapter 4) were seen in a less positive light. The Bain Report sought to link the advancement of equality and diversity to the introduction of more 'family-friendly' working patterns. However women firefighters hit back against attempts to 'use women' to argue for unpopular shift changes, as they had done following the 1999 Thematic Review, claiming that a large majority of women firefighters supported the existing 2-2-4 shift system.

Other key work by the National Women's Committee related to the provision of uniforms and personal protective equipment for women (see Chapter 8) and to workplace facilities, such as toilets and sleeping accommodation. Many such improvements benefited men too, such as the provision of vehicles with toilet and washing facilities at protracted incidents. The Committee's updated 'Minimum workplace facilities' best practice document was published in 2009 and resulted in 19 fire services around the UK providing improved fireground facilities for all members.[77]

Issues affecting older women became a focus for the National Women's Committee, as those who entered the service in the 1980s had significant concerns about the impact of the increase in the pension age to 60, as evidence suggests that women's fitness may decline at a greater rate with age than for most men (Chapter 6). A briefing on the menopause was circulated to all officials and branches in 2015 in order to develop workplace policies within brigades.[78] The menopause is one issue shared by female control staff and firefighters, as control section secretary Lynda Rowan O'Neill explained:

> It's good to keep control room members or control room reps involved with the women's committee, but I think that a lot of the issues that the operational women have are definitely different to what we would have. There's similarities; for example the menopause issues. They affect all of us because we all have the overheating and things like that. It wouldn't be the first time you'd have come into our control at night and maybe find somebody sitting in their bra with a fan and the next thing her coat was on! But for us that's uncomfortable, for the operational women it's dangerous.

The union was proactive in seeking to improve working conditions for B&EM members using the legal provisions established under the Race Relations Amendment Act 2000, which required public authorities to implement race equality schemes. The union worked with the Commission for Racial Equality (CRE, subsequently part of the Equality and Human Rights Commission) to force compliance among brigades which had not done so. These brigades received compliance letters from the CRE, requiring them to produce race plans and consult with the FBU B&EMM Committee. The B&EMM and CRE partnership was highlighted in the CRE's final report in 2007 as an example of best practice for the public sector.[79]

Recruitment of B&EM firefighters is one of the most successful areas of joint working with employers, according to Carl St Paul:

> In London in particular I think we were incredibly successful because they set up their own positive action team within London and the people that were instrumental in going out and doing the work were our members, our black members, FBU members working for management, going out to schools and to fairs in order to attract people to think about the fire service as a potential career. Through that work over the years, London has been amazingly successful. So I think in terms of what [the] B&EMM [section] has done, we can say quite clearly that we've been integral to the success of getting more black firefighters into the service, as well around the country.

The contribution of B&EMM section chair Lud Ramsey to the recruitment of a more diverse workforce in Scotland, including the creation of an outreach programme and a promotional film, was recognised when he was awarded the Scottish Trades Union Congress One Workplace Equality Award in 2012. Grahame Smith, general secretary of the Scottish Trades Union Congress, said that Ramsey had 'made an exceptional impact on challenging racism and promoting equality by working with his union and local community'.[80]

The FBU LGBT Committee campaigned at national level for workplace rights, for example by submitting evidence to the consultation on the Employment Equality (Sexual Orientation)

Regulations 2003, although it was disappointed over the exemptions on occupational pensions and survivors' benefits, which denied same-sex partners access where the employer specified that this benefit was restricted to married partners only within its scheme, as was originally the case with the Firefighters Pension Scheme.[81] This was partially addressed by changes to firefighter pensions involving the introduction of the contentious New Firefighters Pension Scheme in 2006, which extended rights to cohabiting partners, including same-sex partners (Chapter 6).

Working with brigades, the LGBT Committee sought to improve the work environment for LGBT employees, and welcomed the Avon Fire Authority's decision to hold the first UK conference on sexuality in the fire service in 2007, with FBU committee members involved in its planning. It was attended by over 200 delegates from 46 fire authorities.[82] A similar conference was hosted by East Sussex Fire and Rescue Service in 2010, with members of the LGBT Committee, particularly chair Yannick Dubois, being instrumental in its planning and delivery.[83]

The union promoted participation by brigades in the Stonewall Workplace Equality Index, a scheme which assesses employer progress in providing working environments that are safe and attractive to people who identify as LGBT, with steady growth in the number of fire services joining the index. In 2009 the union was joined by the fire minister, Sadiq Khan, in urging all brigades to sign up to the scheme.[84]

Representatives of the FBU equality sections, together with national officers, have been key contributors to the various fire service bodies responsible for equality and diversity. For example, when the Equal Opportunities Task Group was disbanded and replaced with the Equality Cultural Change Advisory Board, the new Board was chaired by general secretary Andy Gilchrist. The union also participated in the Department of Communities and Local Government (DCLG) Equality & Diversity Project Board, created in 2006, with the FBU equality sections and national officer John McGhee contributing to the DCLG's Equality and Diversity Strategy 2008-2011. At the launch of the strategy FBU LGBT Committee officials received an award for their leadership on LGBT issues. [85]

The 'Brick Wall'

The change of government in 2010 meant a significant loss of commitment to the fire service equality and diversity strategy. Within weeks of the formation of the coalition government, the fire minister, Bob Neill, dropped the national targets for women and B&EM staff in the service, leaving the application of targets to the discretion of local fire authorities, and removed the requirement to publish annual equality and diversity reports. LGBT Executive Council member Stewart Brown, who had been chair of the Equality and Diversity Stakeholders Group (EDSG), which involved unions, employers, and other fire service bodies, believed that progress on equality in the fire service 'hit a brick wall' under the Coalition government:

> Prior to that, we were doing some fantastic work with the Labour government; it wasn't always as productive as it could have been but at least there were focus groups... I was the chair of the EDSG for a year and some of the work that we were producing was phenomenal. We were bringing stuff forward to look at new ways of how fire services can work. And then all of a sudden we had the general election and then bang, that group doesn't exist any more. The equality and diversity framework that we had in place doesn't exist any more.

Conclusion

At its centenary the FBU had made huge strides to improve the working lives of female, B&EM and LGBT firefighters and it was much easier to be a woman, B&EM or LGBT member of the fire service. This did not mean that all problems of harassment or bullying had been eliminated, and the numbers of people from these groups employed in the fire and rescue service remained disproportionately low. The loss of 11,000 firefighter jobs across the UK between 2010 and 2017 and widespread recruitment freezes resulting from central government funding cuts of 30 per cent have placed limitations on progress. Following a period of lost momentum on equality and diversity issues within the fire service, there has been a revived concern to address them, with the work of the NJC on equality under chair Linda Dickens, the establishment of the Inclusive Fire Service Group in 2015, and a Memorandum of

Understanding agreed in January 2017 committing the fire service to take action to create a more inclusive workforce and culture, with the FBU as one of the signatories.[86]

The union's advances in terms of structures for representation of minority members were widely praised across the union movement, and were effective in empowering and generating activism among a diverse range of members. While the changes to equality structures represented a blow for many sectional activists, the union's support for self-organisation through the equality sections persists, including support for the B&EMM, LGBT and Women's National Schools. Denise Christie, who lost her position as Executive Council member for women but was then elected to a regional position, proclaimed that the fight for equality continues:

> I'm really passionate about the FBU. I'm such a passionate trade unionist that I thought, 'Do you know what? You change a goalpost, I'll just go back into mainstream', and I did when I was asked by the officials in Lothian and Borders. I've still got my feminist equality, progressive-left politics, except this time I've got a different hat on. And I'm now in a position where – do you know what? – I have got a vote and my politics are still the same to do that. So I'm in a position where I can now negotiate policies, so things like the maternity policy... I came into mainstream. It's given me a bigger responsibility, a bigger remit, a bigger negotiating platform to negotiate policies. So I'm still doing a lot of work that's benefiting the women members but just with a different hat on.

The FBU fights for improvements to breathing apparatus and PPE

Funeral cortège for two firefighters killed in the line of duty in Blaina, Gwent, 1996

8

Science, standards and self-organisation: FBU safety, health and environment work since 1945[1]

Safety and safety matters have been central throughout our history. We need to remember that firefighters don't go to work to be injured and don't go to work to die. We do not accept that there are accidents just waiting to happen. Accidents have causes, accidents have factors that need to be taken into account. They are better regarded as incidents which have to be investigated and lessons which have to be learned so the same mistakes are not repeated with the same terrible consequences... We will not forget our fallen comrades. We will honour them by learning the lessons, and we will honour them by fighting to ensure that the same mistakes are not made in the future.

Matt Wrack, general secretary[2]

Firefighters tackle hazards and manage risks as an essential part of their work, intervening to save life in a wide variety of situations, with tackling fires still a core part of the job – as underlined by the terrible Grenfell Tower fire, which occurred in June 2017 as this book was being written. Deaths at fires continue to devastate communities, as they did throughout the last century. In 1950, total fatal casualties from fires in the UK were over 500 annually. This rose to over 1,000 fire deaths in 1979. By 2016, fire deaths had been reduced to fewer than 400 in England, Scotland, Wales and Northern Ireland. Nevertheless, the UK has seen several fires that have resulted in multiple casualties, including at the James Watt warehouse (1968), Woolworths, Manchester (1979), Kings Cross (1987) and Lakanal House (2009).[3]

When the public are running away from danger, firefighters are often running towards it. But firefighters' activity is not reckless: it is planned, organised, trained for and carried out professionally, for the sake of those at risk and to protect their own safety. Yet firefighters have paid a grizzly price for their endeavours. Even on a narrow estimate involving incidents and training, since 1950 at least 300 firefighters have died in the line of duty, including over 100 deaths at fires across the UK.[4] These included multiple firefighter fatalities at the Cheapside whisky warehouse fire in 1960 and the Kilbernie Street Sher Bros warehouse fire (both in Glasgow); at the Dudgeons Wharf oil storage tank explosion and the Broad Street warehouse and Covent Garden market fires (all in London); at the Neatishead airbase fire and the Warwickshire warehouse fires; and at tower block fires in Hertfordshire and Hampshire. There have also been multiple firefighter fatalities in Hereford and Worcester, South Wales, London and East Sussex. In addition, thousands of firefighters suffer serious injuries in the course of their work, underlining the arduous nature of the job.[5]

The Fire Brigades Union has championed the safety, health and welfare of firefighters, both wholetime and retained, including officers, and of emergency control staff, throughout its history. This chapter suggests that the FBU continues to be the greatest guarantee firefighters have that they will return home safely after a shift, with self-organisation through the union central to preventing more deaths and injuries. The union has fought to protect public safety – demanding national standards of fire cover, the right resources and professional training to save life and serve their communities professionally.

This chapter details the union's involvement in the development of health and safety standards, first outlining its role in national consultative structures, and the way it used the emerging health and safety legislation to protect both its members and the public. Fire prevention and fire safety have also been key areas of campaigning for the union, together with demands for national standards of fire cover and sufficient resources to achieve them. The chapter then describes the union's efforts to minimise the physical hazards of the job and its significant role in achieving technical advances in breathing apparatus, personal and protective equipment and safety equipment and appliances. It also highlights the union's work to protect the health and welfare of members, increasingly addressing matters of fitness, risks of cancer and infection, and mental health, including post-traumatic stress disorder (PTSD). The later part of the chapter highlights how firefighters have dealt with environmental hazards, ranging from grassland fires to storms and, increasingly, floods. Finally, it sets out how the union's effectiveness in advancing health, safety and environmental issues is underpinned by its organisation of safety reps, committees and structures.

Legal and statutory framework

The FBU emerged from the Second World War well positioned to influence the direction of the post-war fire service. The establishment of the statutory body, the Central Fire Brigades Advisory Council (CFBAC), in 1947 (see Chapter 1) provided the FBU with a key means of intervention on fire service matters. Consisting of employers' associations, chief fire officers, civil servants and FBU representatives, the CFBAC's role was to advise the fire minister at the Home Office, and it was tasked with everything except pay and conditions, including standards of fire cover, training, uniforms, equipment and prevention.[6] As the early FBU historian Frederick Radford put it, the CFBAC was 'a new high-water mark in the tide of joint consultation'.[7]

Looking back on the CFBAC's legacy, Hertfordshire official Ron Couchman said that it had given the union 'a route to feed the views of firefighters directly into the body that draws up national standards', adding that the work of the CFBAC in setting national standards was 'the cornerstone of the British fire service'. However, the Conservative government diminished the powers of the CFBAC during the 1990s, before it was abolished by New Labour under the 2004 Fire and Rescue Services Act.[8]

The Health and Safety at Work Act 1974 and the Safety Representatives and Safety Committees Regulations 1977 provided further backing for firefighter safety. This legislation was, from the point of view of working people, the most significant achievement of Labour governments in the 1970s. FBU general secretary Terry Parry sat on the tripartite Health and Safety Commission as one of the trade union representatives, from its founding until his retirement in 1981. Parry also chaired the TUC's Social Insurance

Committee, which coordinated trade union safety work during that time. Parry led the TUC delegation to meet prime minister James Callaghan in December 1976, after the Labour government backtracked on its commitment to introduce legally sanctioned safety reps with wide powers for 'time off' during working hours to undertake union duties, and for inspection and training. The intervention succeeded and the regulations were introduced.[9]

The FBU was well prepared for the new legal framework, which augmented the health and safety work of the CFBAC. As Dave Matthews, FBU national officer for health and safety for most of the 1980s and 1990s, explained: 'Almost immediately every fire station (including retained) was covered by union appointed safety representatives who do inspections of stations and drill grounds, listen to members' views and carry out accident investigations.'[10]

The union had to face down the consensus of opinion among employers' associations and the chief officers' body (CACFOA) that the fire service should not be subject to the health and safety at work legislation regarding operations and training. The FBU fought battles, most notably in the (pre-merger) Dyfed brigade in Wales, to ensure that the new workplace law was implemented throughout the service. However, chief officers and others continued to seek exemptions. As late as 2010, the FBU had to fend off Lord Young's attempts on behalf of the Coalition government to exempt firefighters and police from health and safety law.[11]

The advent of the single European market in 1992 and the consequent legislation, including the Working Time Directive and management regulations, and the display screen equipment, manual handling, work equipment, workplace, and personal protective equipment laws, had significant implications for firefighters' health, safety and welfare. The union was represented on European and world bodies setting specifications for firefighters clothing and equipment. Assistant general secretary Mike Fordham worked with Public Services International and the European TUC to establish a European firefighters' network in 1992, which brings together union representatives from across the continent to improve conditions.[12]

Fire safety

Alongside important improvements to procedures and equipment, the FBU has been a strong advocate of fire prevention. This has involved a commitment to fire inspection and risk assessment, to better understand the situations firefighters could be sent to, which not only benefits the public in terms of rescue, but also protects firefighters from otherwise hidden hazards. The FBU has long been committed to reducing risks, in order to prevent incidents from ending in tragedy. This orientation was summed up in pithy fashion by brigade rep Ray Lee, when he stated: 'We have an aide memoire on Merseyside: it is called the 6P principle. It stands for "proper planning prevents piss-poor performance".'[13]

Firefighters in the immediate post-war period advocated prevention activity after a spate of terrible fires, including those at Covent Garden Market, Smithfield Market and the Cheapside whisky warehouse in Glasgow, all of which involved firefighter fatalities. One outcome was the Office, Shops and Railway Premises Act 1963, which introduced fire certification for around a million premises.[14] Harry Richardson from the Poole brigade argued in *Firefighter* magazine that 'fire prevention should be the main role of the fire service, that much more money, manpower and legislation should be devoted to fire prevention'. In the aftermath of Cheapside, the CFBAC established a prevention committee. In the 1960s the FBU published hard-hitting pamphlets, such as 'Without a chance' (1969), strongly backing the Holroyd Report on the fire service (see Chapter 1), which recommended that only those with 'operational firefighting experience' should be used for enforcing fire prevention legislation.[15]

The FBU influenced changes to fire safety laws such as the Fire Precautions Act 1971 and the Fire Precautions (Workplace) Regulations 1997. During the 1980s and following the Woolworths fire, the union led the national campaign on polyurethane foam furniture. Additionally it worked with the National Association for Safety in the Home (NASH), which included Ian McCartney MP, to campaign against exempting nursery furniture from match test requirements. FBU publications such as 'Who will pick up the pieces?' and 'Cutting the lifeline' (1994) made the case for fire safety regulation, and stood out against deregulation.[16]

After firefighters suffered deaths and major injuries at large fires during the 1990s, the officers' section of the union wrote a Fire Safety Bill to consolidate over 100 different statutes containing fire safety requirements. This influenced the government and informed the Regulatory Reform (Fire Safety) Order 2005. While welcoming the consolidation of fire safety law enacted by the Order, the union raised concerns about its approach to risk assessment, which was left to the 'responsible person' (i.e. the employer or building owner). Thus instead of fire certificates being issued by professionals within fire brigades, risk assessments could be undertaken by people without any expertise in fire safety. Similarly, the FBU argued for greater enforcement to ensure compliance with the law.

The FBU consistently warned politicians about the likely impact of deregulation on fire safety. It warned that the abolition of the CFBAC and the lack of guidance on fire safety enforcement would have dire consequences for fire safety. In 1999 the union warned MPs about the dangers of cladding 'providing a vehicle for assisting uncontrolled fire spread up the outer face of the building'. The union advocated that 'all cladding used on multi-storey buildings over 25 metres in height and the fixing systems should be completely non-combustible'.[17]

Mike Fordham recalls that after the 1979 Woolworths fire in Manchester he wrote a report for the FBU which recommended sprinklers in all public buildings:

> We still haven't got that all these years later. And if Grenfell had have had them, it wouldn't have been as bad as it was… what it would have done is give a safe route out. It's as simple as that. It would have put that first fire out quicker, if it had been in the flat, but it would also protect the route out.

Had all the FBU's warnings been heeded, the tragedy at Grenfell Tower could have been avoided.

Breathing apparatus

The breathing apparatus provided to firefighters across the UK has come a long way in terms of its appearance, weight, communications and other features, with far stricter procedures and guidance. Whilst the FBU still has criticisms about the way this is implemented on the fireground, few doubt that these advances make firefighters safer. Breathing apparatus is probably the best example of the FBU's contribution to firefighters' health and safety since the war. Matt Wrack remarked that the union had a 'proud record' of campaigning on 'the provision of sets, on proper training and on procedures'. Strathclyde official Rab Chalmers recalled:

> Sometimes we go back to the old days, the old smoke eaters, when BA [breathing apparatus] sets were put on as a kind of tokenistic thing, or get a bellyful of smoke first and then put the set on and go on along those lines. I remember those days myself, 1971. We had a Mark IV Proto set with goggles and a nose clip, and throwing up in the process, you know.[18]

The FBU raised issue of the inadequacy of breathing apparatus immediately after the Second World War. Manufacturers Siebe Gorman had a virtual monopoly on producing firefighter breathing apparatus, using a design originally developed for deep sea divers and miners.[19] Breathing apparatus sets were not available on every fire appliance, nor for every firefighter. Barnsley FBU official Norman Greenfield submitted proposals to modernise breathing apparatus as early as 1951, after firefighters died while wearing it. Although the CFBAC agreed to the FBU's demands to investigate, only after further tragedies, culminating in the deaths of two firefighters at a fire at Smithfield Market, London, in 1958 did the body establish a sub-committee to bring forward the necessary changes.[20] The FBU kept up the pressure by seeking members' views on breathing apparatus, arguing that those who do the job know what is needed. The union received 134 detailed proposals, which were fed into the CFBAC discussion. The immediate result was a national standard of control procedures, issued through a fire service circular and intended to keep a better record of firefighters wearing breathing apparatus, including identification tallies and control board procedures. The standard was necessary to ensure no confusion would arise with incidents involving more than one brigade. Assistant general secretary Tom Harris made it clear:

> As far as the control procedure is concerned, whether it be retained men that are using it or full time men, it has to be put

into effect and made obligatory. The life of a retained man to us
is just as important as the life of the full time man, and has to be
safeguarded by correct procedure when using BA.[21]

Firefighters' complaints throughout the 1950s about the basic
technology led the FBU to enter into an innovative engagement
with University of London academic Dr Bernard Lucas and the
Vickers manufacturing firm. In 1963, after two years of experiment
and hard work, the joint effort produced a one-hour self-contained
breathing apparatus set. It was an impressive achievement for a
small union to produce the first major step forward in breathing
apparatus for half a century.[22]

The FBU persevered with improvements in the design of
breathing apparatus, as well as in the training and procedures
associated with it. From the early 1970s it became evident that the
use of plastics and other new materials were producing a 'sticky
smoke' that generated a range of unquantified acute, chronic and
cumulative effects for firefighters and the public. The problem was
illustrated by the Woolworths fire in 1979, when 10 people died
due to the inhalation of toxic fumes. The FBU response concluded
that all crew members should have a breathing apparatus set.
Wiltshire's delegate to the FBU conference, Roger Rowling,
argued that 'in this day and age it is a must for every member
of an appliance to have a BA set for our protection... The cost is
irrelevant: the price of a life for a fireman.'[23]

In 1980 the FBU produced a pamphlet, written by Mike
Fordham, 'Today's fires – Today's protection', setting out the case
for universal provision, at a time when there was an average of
only one set of breathing apparatus for every four firefighters. In
the early 1980s, the FBU fought disputes in Northern Ireland and
London as part of its campaign to ensure all firefighters had a
set of breathing apparatus set. An FBU ultimatum successfully
resolved the issue of faults on the Aga Spiro breathing apparatus
set, with a valve freezing. The union imposed a deadline on
the manufacturers and the Home Office to fix the problem or
withdraw the set. During this period the FBU also fought for the
right of retained firefighters to go on breathing apparatus courses
equivalent to those taken by wholetime firefighters, and for
successive improvements to the technical bulletins (TB 1/77, TB

1/89 and TB 1/97) dealing with breathing apparatus procedures.[24]

At the CFBAC's request, the Home Office commissioned a study of the physiological effects of wearing breathing apparatus, which started in 1990 but took five years to complete. The research found that temperatures encountered by some firefighters meant training needed to be reviewed, as well as command and control at incidents. Researchers also feared that improved equipment could add to risks on the fireground, because 'firefighters may perceive themselves to be immune from danger and dwell longer than advisable in hazardous environments'.[25]

In 1996, the deaths of two firefighters in Blaina, Gwent, and the death of the first female firefighter in peacetime, Fleur Lombard, in Avon, prompted further agitation for improved breathing apparatus. South Wales official Dick Pearson highlighted breathing apparatus procedures and the initial attendance mobilised as being critical to the Blaina deaths. The upsurge of firefighter fatalities at the beginning of the 21st century also showed that breathing apparatus procedures, training and guidance had contributed to those deaths. The FBU was highly critical of the revised guidance on breathing apparatus produced by the English chief fire and rescue advisor, which it believes is not fit for purpose,[26] and it continued to press for improvements.

Personal protective equipment

Firefighters' personal protective equipment is intended to ensure a minimal level of protection from hazards – the last line of defence – although it is the lowest item in the safety hierarchy. The FBU has fought for improvements to firefighters' personal protective equipment throughout its history, helping to secure significant advances in the kit provided.

The FBU began campaigning for better standards for firefighters' uniforms after the end of the Second World War. The union's report, 'Give Me a Uniform of Which I Can Be Proud', demanded 'no more cast-offs from army, navy and post office', calling instead for lightweight fitted clothing with a high degree of water and heat resistance. Vice president Arthur Coupe said, 'We are out to get the best uniforms that we possibly can for the firemen of this country.' Bournemouth delegate George Gale told the 1958 FBU conference that the firefighters' uniform was a throwback to the days when horses pulled tenders: 'The whole lot is out-of-date and should be scrapped.' The FBU agitated for standardised uniform and personal equipment on the CFBAC. Bedfordshire delegate Harry Ruis expressed the point succinctly: 'What we want is a bit of standardisation... "uniform" is the last thing it is.'[27]

During the 1960s and 1970s the CFBAC oversaw improvements in personal protective equipment, such as Teled and Nomex tunics, iconic bright yellow leggings made of plastic, latex rubber gloves and the Cromwell county fire helmet. However the FBU was dissatisfied with these changes, which were shown to lead to burns and other problems. Strathclyde official Dave Patton denounced Nomex as a 'self-destruct tunic' and the fact that 'some poor lad had to lose his hands practically before they came across with gloves for us'. The rising indignation was well summed up by South Yorkshire delegate John Gilliver at the 1987 FBU conference:

> Let's get down to the wet legs. It is scandalous that firefighters in Britain are still suffering from burns to legs by having to wear the plastic leggings... What an insult to firefighters to protect your feet with wellies guaranteed to retain all the heat when wearing them, guaranteed, if you come into contact with a sharp object, to [allow it to] penetrate your leg.[28]

The shortcomings in firefighters' personal protective equipment were drawn into sharp focus by the Kings Cross fire in 1987, when 31 people, including a London firefighter, were killed and many others injured. The FBU gave evidence to the Fennell Inquiry, which made recommendations that included a review of the brigade's personal protective equipment and radio communications. London FBU safety rep Roger Sutton explained: 'This tragedy highlighted many problems associated with our protective equipment and uniforms. Leggings... became extremely hot and were actually burning our members' legs. Tunics were not giving the protection that they were designed to give.'[29]

The FBU became intimately involved with the intricate work of domestic and international standard-setting. Dave Matthews represented the union on British Standards Institution (BSI), European (CEN) and world (ISO) bodies setting specifications for firefighters' clothing and equipment. Although these committees were dominated by manufacturers, test houses and government officials, the FBU's intervention bore fruit in improved standards of personal protective equipment. Similarly, the union used the EU Personal Protective Equipment (PPE) Directive, which came into force in 1995, to achieve improvements in firefighters' kit.[30]

The FBU widened the battle on personal protective equipment during this period, to ensure that particular sections of the membership were suitably equipped. Avon rep Helen Hill spoke out against the practice of retained crews wearing fire tunics without integral cuffs to protect the wrists and arms. She told the 2001 conference, 'There can be no second class members, no second rate fire service'.[31]

Women were recruited as operational firefighters in greater numbers during the 1980s (see Chapter 7). However, they were supplied with personal protective equipment designed for male firefighters – a failing the FBU set out to correct. At the 1993 FBU conference, Fife delegate Linda Shanahan argued: 'It is time to look to the future and to design uniforms specifically for men and women. Too many women members are and have been struggling on in uniforms which were designed for men. We have been remiss on this issue for too long.'[32]

The complaint about the design of personal protective equipment was relevant to every firefighter, even though women suffered the greatest detriment. Personal protective equipment tested on generic male manikins exposes real-life wearers to the risk of injury when donning kit. So-called 'unisex' workwear was identified as not suitable for the variety of shapes and sizes of firefighters, compromising the safety of all. As London official Sally Harper argued, '[W]e must fight to defend properly fitted PPE [personal protective equipment] and properly fitted workwear uniform. It's not about cost, it's about lives.'[33] The FBU continued to campaign for improvements in personal protective equipment for all firefighters.

Safety equipment, appliances and training

Safety on the fireground requires much more than suitable personal protective equipment. Safe systems of work include standards on training, equipment and appliances. In the early post-war period, the FBU complained about deaths and injuries to members incurred by the use of hook ladders[34] and rescue drills that used live firefighters to act as people needing to be rescued rather than dummies, mostly during training on fire stations. Between 1948 and 1961, the union estimated that 17 firefighters had been killed and many more injured on hook ladders and performing live rescue drills.[35] The FBU instigated campaigns that took until the 1980s to succeed in removing these outdated practices.

The FBU pressed the CFBAC to abolish hook ladders, which had been introduced at the beginning of the 20th century after a serious fire in Queen Victoria Street, London, where nine people lost their lives. The victims were trapped at windows above pavement level and a public outcry lamented the lack of a means to reach the higher floors of buildings. However, by the mid-20th century, many brigades did not use hook ladders or did so only rarely at operations – particularly after aerial ladder platforms were introduced. Nevertheless the hook ladder and live rescue drills continued to be employed as a form of training for firefighters.[36]

It was direct action by firefighters that brought the issues to a head. In 1962, some 90 members of Bootle brigade refused to comply with a Home Office inspector's request to carry out the drill. FBU rep Wally Charters argued:

> It is not the fire authority's decision. It is the firemen's decision. You make the decision... All the firemen in Bootle agree with me on this. We have got rid of the live carry down and the hook. The way to get rid of it is this: you are the firemen; we control the live carry down.[37]

Vigorous activity by members in brigade committees pushed brigades to scrap hook ladders. Although the union pressed the CFBAC for their abolition nationally, it was unsuccessful. The executive feared a national ruling might undo the gains made locally to get rid of the equipment and drill. The union also worked with the Royal Society for the Prevention of Accidents to campaign for the use of realistic dummies as a substitute for actual firefighters during training.[38]

In August 1965 two London firefighters were killed doing

live rescue drills. The union took the issue directly to Labour home secretary Frank Soskice. However, instead of banning the practice, the government introduced regulations allowing drills to continue with the Everest safety anchor, a harness device and more supervision by officers. Delegates at the 1966 conference were critical of the national union's approach. One delegate felt the Executive Council should have issued instructions to all members to stop all live drills after the fatalities. Another bluntly stated that 'men have died doing a job that could equally have well have been done by a sack of potatoes'. FBU president Enoch Humphries concluded the debate by making it clear that 'if drills are going to be carried out which are not going to be within the framework of safety, then we will not carry out drills at all'.[39]

The FBU refused to concede on the issue. In 1974 the union persuaded the CFBAC to review the use of live bodies in rescue drills and secured an agreement that this practice would no longer be part of the training of operational firefighters. It still took until the mid-1980s to remove the practice, which coincided with the final demise of the hook ladder, but eventually amendments to the drill book and the modernisation of training put paid to these arcane and unsafe practices.[40]

Crew cab safety

The FBU has taken up safety concerns over appliances, raising the issue of safety standards for fire service vehicles with the CFBAC in the 1970s. Loughborough University researchers were commissioned to examine the ergonomics of fire appliances. London safety rep Trevor Jones reported that appliances had caught fire because of electrical defects, while one had a coffee jar lid for a petrol cap. By the late 1970s the FBU was demanding national standards on crew cab safety, including safety belts to prevent members going through windscreens en route to incidents.[41]

The fight for safety in relation to cabs continued in the 1980s. Gwent official Mike Smith moved the proposal for appliances to have an audible warning device fitted to sound automatically when they were in reverse gear. The FBU argued within the CFBAC for inserting seat belts into the rear crew compartments. The union managed to ward off a proposed Department of Transport exemption for firefighters from wearing seatbelts. Dave Matthews argued: 'It was the union, through resolutions at this conference, which moved the safety cab on appliances which was agreed by the Home Office a number of years ago and that went out in a 'dear chief officer' letter with the necessary changes to specifications.'[42]

In the 1990s, crew cab safety again came to the fore after a series of incidents, near misses and serious injuries. In particular, a Greater Manchester firefighter fell from an appliance en route to an incident and was killed. The union's Executive Council set up a working party to examine all aspects of crew cab safety. Greater Manchester official Kevin Brown reported that a union investigation had found cases around the country of 'cab doors opening with alarming frequency'.[43] Humberside delegate Sean Starbuck warned: 'We still find members in our brigade riding older appliances with lap belts, no belts, basic stowage methods and interiors that Fred Flintstone would turn his nose up at. We are letting first class firefighters ride on second class machines.'[44]

A related area of appliance safety is the FBU's long struggle to defend drivers subjected to the inconsistencies of road traffic law. As early as 1957, the Executive Council reported an 'unduly large' number of cases of drivers charged under the Road Traffic Act. The union's Safety At Work Sub-committee considered the issues and thereafter the FBU opposed Westminster government proposals to give fire service drivers discretion to ignore road traffic rules. The 1968 conference argued that drivers should comply with the law at all times and resolved that legal aid would no longer be provided by the union for drivers prosecuted for deliberately driving across traffic lights at red or halt signs. Instead the union supported crews who refused to ride behind drivers who deliberately ignored the road traffic regulations. Members took direct action on the policy, which resulted in a High Court case and a Court of Appeal judgment. The FBU was unhappy when the Labour government imposed new regulations in 1975, which the union described as treating 'a red light signal as if it were a "give way" sign'.[45]

The FBU remained sceptical of technologies that enabled fire appliances to control traffic lights, particularly after people were killed during trials. In the first decade of the new century the union reaffirmed its policy advising drivers to observe the traffic signals. National officer John McGhee told the 2010 conference that while the leadership understood the concessions that are made under road traffic regulations, 'quite simply the safest thing for our members to do is to stop at red traffic lights... that should be the guidance we continue to give our members'.[46]

Firefighters' health and welfare

Alongside pressing for safety provision, the union has simultaneously taken up health and welfare issues, to protect members in their work and wider lives. In the 1950s the FBU published research on firefighters' occupational health from the North American firefighters' union, the IAFF. This identified mental health, tuberculosis, lung cancer and cardiac diseases as principal concerns for firefighters, proposing annual medical examinations to help firefighters improve their health. John Horner told the 1960 FBU conference that the union's representatives were meeting with 'eminent Harley Street consultants' to discuss the creation of an occupational medical service.[47]

The FBU was constrained by the lack of systematic research on firefighters' health in the UK. During the 1970s, working through the CFBAC, the union embarked on a major campaign to rectify this. The FBU promoted the work of Dr Frederick Moran of Glasgow Royal Infirmary on blood and respiratory diseases. The union persuaded the Home Office to fund research on the health hazards to firefighters, including research on lung function involving London firefighters and a long-term study of the causes of death among firefighters, led by Professor Stuart Donnan.[48]

The FBU also pioneered the investigation of ill health among fire control staff, taking the issue to the CFBAC in the 1980s. When requests for research stalled, the union commissioned the Robens Institute at the University of Surrey to undertake a pilot. The study examined a range of health issues facing control staff, including 'sick buildings', air quality, lighting, seating, noise and the organisational structure of the job.[49] Stress experienced by control staff has also been tackled by the union (see pp 271-2).

Fitness and medicals

Operational firefighting is rightly regarded as a physically arduous occupation, requiring sustained levels of fitness to carry out a wide range of tasks on the fireground. In 1968 the FBU worked with the CFBAC and Home Office medical adviser George Godber to review the medical entry standards originally laid down after the war. The group recommended that operational firefighters should be medically re-examined at three-year intervals from the age of 40. The FBU also supported the CFBAC's conclusion that fitness training should be encouraged on fire stations, to ensure physical fitness and protect firefighters from injury. At the union's 1979 conference West Midlands delegate Pete Bilson moved a resolution to extend triennial medicals to all personnel, although the union was still demanding medicals for retained and control staff into the 1990s.[50]

The FBU backed research into firefighters' fitness training needs. In 1981 the CFBAC contracted Chelsea College, University of London, to carry out the work, which included physiological testing of new recruits and serving firefighters. The final report was produced during 1986. It found that one-third of fire service personnel were over their desirable weight and advocated at least 30 minutes' fitness training per shift.[51] On the basis of the results of the research, the FBU worked to revise the Godber standards, including on eyesight, height and the two-inch chest expansion test, which the union argued was not scientifically based and discriminated against women firefighters. The FBU accepted that firefighters should have a maximum oxygen uptake (VO_2 max) of 45 ml per kilogram of body weight per minute, or greater. The union also asked London member and sports expert Bill Jenkins to draft a fitness training syllabus. The recruitment regulations were amended to reflect the research and the joint conclusions.[52]

Firefighter fitness continued to trouble delegates at FBU conference into the new century. FireFit, an organisation consisting of academics and chief officers, argued for a national fitness standard of 42 VO_2 max on safety grounds. However, Derbyshire FBU rep Helen Tooley argued that the FireFit proposals threatened 'to entrench discrimination for not only female firefighters but also our older male colleagues'. The union was forced to confront the fitness issue as a result of the Westminster government's imposed pension scheme, which forced firefighters to work until they were 60 (see Chapter 6). The FBU accepted research by academics and occupational physicians that fitness standards were necessary, but it argued that these should be assessed using typical on-the-job tasks such as hose running, to ensure firefighters were fit to work. National officer Sean Starbuck worked with chief officers to produce a procedure to keep firefighters fit and on the run, issued through NJC best practice guidance.[53]

Mental health

Alongside the physical health of firefighters, the FBU has increasingly had to consider the protection of members' mental health. By the late 1980s, the issues ranged from PTSD arising from particular incidents to stress faced by officers and control staff. Staffordshire official Johnny Summerfield argued at the 1988 FBU conference that 'stress is an occupational hazard to all members of the service', while Control Staff National Committee delegate Linda McCartney said that work in control rooms also caused a type of stress, which she called the 'goldfish reaction', which resulted from rushing around in a high-pressure environment. Subsequent research found that over 100 officers had had to leave the service within the previous five years because of stress and that only eight of the UK's 63 fire authorities provided any kind of stress counselling. FBU publications advised members on how to tackle stress at work.[54]

PTSD was brought into sharp focus by firefighter fatalities and injuries during this period. In 1989 the FBU successfully pursued a medical appeal on behalf of a Hampshire firefighter, establishing for the first time that PTSD was a qualifying injury under the firefighters' pension scheme. In 1991 the FBU and the NUPE health union organised a joint one-day seminar on PTSD and emergency workers. In 1998 the FBU's campaign was frustrated by a Law Lords ruling that members of the emergency services were ineligible for compensation following PTSD. Greater Manchester official Kevin Brown said, 'We do fire gear when we attend incidents, not superman suits. We do not need Law Lords to lecture to us about mental trauma.'[55]

The FBU proposed that the CFBAC commission research into the causes of stress in the fire service and demanded Home Office guidance. When the government refused, the union commissioned Nottingham Trent University to investigate stress across its membership. The survey considered the issues affecting the wholetime, retained and control sections of the membership, and subsequent research examined the pressures affecting officer members.[56]

In the 21st century, firefighters' mental health was made worse by cuts to fire and rescue services and the spike in firefighter fatalities, as well as the expanding role of firefighters. In 2016, a survey by Mind, mental health charity, highlighted high levels of stress, anxiety and depression among firefighters. The union published 'Mental Health at Work – An initial guide for FBU reps', as part of its strategy to tackle mental health issues for firefighters.[57] Firefighters' mental health continued to be a concern in the context of emergency medical response (see Chapter 5) and the Grenfell Tower fire.

The FBU has also tackled the issue of violence towards firefighters. Northern Ireland members suffered throughout the troubles, with three firefighters killed by terrorist attacks in the early 1970s. However assaults against firefighters throughout the UK became more visible from the 1990s. The union commissioned the Labour Research Department in 2005 to investigate the extent of the problem and suggest solutions, which included prevention work with young people and legal action against perpetrators.[58] The FBU feared that police and crime commissioners taking over fire authorities in England (see Chapter 1) would jeopardise firefighters' neutrality and upset this kind of work.

Cancer

Cancer is a health concern that has preoccupied firefighters for many years. In the 1950s Executive Council member Les Hill raised fears of lung cancer in firefighters. During the 1970s the union began campaigning on the dangers from asbestos during damping down after a fire and from the use of asbestos fire blankets. In 1992, the FBU proposed that the CFBAC conduct a national cancer study, but the Home Office argued that the union had not made the case for this. Instead FBU representatives persuaded civil servants to extend Professor Donnan's mortality research. However, the study found no elevation of risk from diseases thought to have a possible association with smoke and other hazards of firefighting. Rather it stated that firefighters had less cancer than would be expected from national cancer registration rates.[59]

FBU reps were not so easily put off. Drawing on international research, in particular from the United States, Canada and

Australia, successive conferences demanded both the investigation of cancer risks and measures to tackle exposure to toxins on the fireground. Merseyside official Mark Rowe gave a few examples of the range of risks identified by available research: '[It is] 2½ times more likely a firefighter will develop testicular cancer compared to the general population; skin cancer – 1.3 times greater; leukaemia 1.2 times greater; non-Hodgkin's lymphoma 1.5 times greater'. He also referred to recent research on breast cancer among firefighters.[60]

Northumberland official Ian Dick referred to the advice given by American firefighters to their probationers after their first fire call: 'Don't swallow your snot for three days.' The FBU published guidance on respirators and on contaminants to highlight basic principles that members should follow to try and prevent unnecessary contamination before, during and after incidents.[61]

Infection

The FBU has sought to reduce the risks of infection at incidents. In the mid-1980s, FBU conferences carried resolutions demanding 'a procedure of medical assistance' including vaccination free of charge to the firefighters, because of the increase in tetanus, HIV and hepatitis B. The FBU subsequently produced a 'Viral hazards' booklet for members.[62]

In 1995 the union secured a 'dear chief officer' letter on the funding for hepatitis B vaccines. The Department of Health did not have a prescribed policy, but erred towards employers bearing the costs of vaccine. As Lothian and Borders conference delegate Karen Hunt put it: 'The approximate cost of a vaccination equates to two pairs of firefighting gloves.' However as the new century progressed, FBU officials still complained that no immunisation programme had been implemented.[63]

The FBU made progress on its HIV/AIDS policy, thanks to its LGBT activists. Although the union had had a policy on HIV since the mid-1980s, at the turn of the century this was revised with the involvement of national LGBT Committee members – for example, by adding advice on taking post-exposure prophylaxis within 72 hours of exposure. This was an important step, which benefited all members. Bedfordshire official Pat Carberry described how the guidance also assisted members diagnosed with HIV: 'They wanted to know if they needed to resign, they wanted to know if it could mean that they would be sacked, they wanted to know if they had to tell their employer. All of those questions are contained within this document.'[64]

The environment

The FBU's health and safety work includes addressing environmental hazards. Firefighters have long dealt with these hazards, which range from grassland fires to floods and storms. One of the principal environmental issues the FBU has addressed has been the risk from nuclear energy. In the 1950s the union applied the precautionary principle to radiation hazards, addressing 'the new dangers that are facing our service arising out of the proper and peaceful uses of nuclear energy'. The FBU worked with Association of Scientific Workers and the TUC to formulate a policy on radioactive materials used in industry, hospitals and other areas of the economy. As John Horner put it, 'All of us... face this immense new hazard arising from the misuse of nuclear energy.'[65]

During the 1980s the FBU took a firm stand against the use of nuclear power to generate electricity and the attendant hazards, such as the transportation of nuclear waste. The union joined the Anti-Nuclear Campaign and the consortium of trade unions opposed to the proposed pressurised water reactor at Sizewell 'B' in Suffolk. Executive Council member Terry Segars argued that nuclear power was 'unnecessary, uneconomic and unsafe', with the union submitting evidence to the public inquiry.[66]

In 1986, following the Chernobyl nuclear accident, the FBU conference called for 'the phasing out of all present nuclear plants and installations and a ban on all future expansion of the nuclear industry in the UK'. It condemned nuclear secrecy in both East and West. General secretary Ken Cameron spoke at the Labour conference debate the same year, which voted strongly to phase out existing nuclear plants. Cameron intervened repeatedly at successive TUC congresses, helping to win over the wider labour movement (at least temporarily) to an anti-nuclear stance. He argued: 'There is no use in talking about green issues unless we are prepared to call now for the phasing out of nuclear power.' In 1989 the FBU gave evidence to the public inquiry objecting to the proposed nuclear power station at Hinkley Point in Somerset.[67]

Responding to flooding has become a growing part of a firefighter's job. Firefighters played a heroic role in the worst flooding to affect the UK in the last century, the 'Great Flood' of 1953, in which over 300 people were killed in the East of England and Scotland. The press paid tribute to the work of firefighters, who swam for hours through icy waters to save lives. The 2007 summer floods were a turning point in the FBU's policy on flooding. During these floods, firefighters rescued over 3,000 people and salvaged vital national infrastructure. Gloucestershire official Mike Tully reported that firefighters 'worked well beyond the hours stipulated, adherence to safe work and water policy was abandoned and in general crews exposed themselves to increased risk, all in a noble cause'. Humberside delegate Dave Collingwood added: 'Two of our members were hospitalised, one of which is still receiving treatment and is yet unable to return to work. Doctors have now put this down to a waterborne viral infection.'[68]

As a result, the FBU demanded that fire and rescue services should have a clear statutory duty to respond to major flooding, with the resources to intervene. This was accepted by the Pitt Review into the 2007 floods. The Scottish government had already made such provision and FBU campaigning led to legislation in Northern Ireland and Wales, with only the Westminster government resisting a statutory duty for fire and rescue services in England.[69]

Responding to major incidents increased firefighters' awareness of the impacts of climate change. In 1976 the home secretary, Merlyn Rees, praised 'the manner in which wholetime and retained members of the fire service fought the unprecedented spate of fires during the recent dry weather', which, he said, 'has deservedly earned widespread public gratitude'. This century the union produced a report on the risks of climate change, which called for a UK fire and rescue service climate change adaptation strategy, with guarantees on staffing, Integrated Risk Management Plans, training, equipment and health and safety. The FBU supported the 'One Million Climate Jobs' campaign and worked within the TUC to support climate campaigns. As Executive Council member Tam McFarlane told the TUC Congress, 'Climate change is a political issue. It is an issue for every single trade union and every single working person.'[70]

Organising for safety

The history of the FBU's health, safety and environment work illustrates how trade unions can effectively organise to tackle matters of immediate concern for members. The FBU has established a 'safety culture' at every level of the fire and rescue service, from fire stations to central government, according to the union's fire safety and risk management advisor, Dave Sibert. A number of themes reoccur that deserve scrutiny.

To achieve this culture of safety, the FBU has critically engaged at all levels on health and safety issues, with government, employers and local management, which has required an effective structure of organisation throughout the union. At national level the CFBAC proved to be an effective standards body for over half a century, and this chapter has shown the many advances made by the union through that mechanism. Terry Parry was central to the Health and Safety Commission (now known as the Health and Safety Executive) immediately after it was founded in 1974 and Matt Wrack was only denied a seat at this table by government caprice in 2013 (see Chapter 9).[71] Dave Matthews played a vital role in standards-setting for decades, helping to improve the personal protective equipment firefighters now take for granted. The FBU succeeded in getting health and safety into the Grey Book in 2004, which enabled discussion on key matters such as fitness. Crucially, local FBU safety reps have sat through hours of joint health and safety committees, seeking to wring the smallest improvements from management and ensure its members are properly protected.

The FBU's approach to health and safety organisation has developed since the late 1950s, when the Executive Council established a sub-committee to oversee this work. In 1979 it held its first health and safety seminar, to discuss how to implement the new legislation on safety reps. Since the late 1970s a national officer has held responsibility for health and safety at head office as their primary role. Since 1996, the union has had a formal structure of regional health and safety coordinators to oversee the work.

The organisation of safety reps at regional, brigade and branch level has been paramount to the FBU's influence. Following the new safety at work legislation in the 1970s, the union sought to have safety reps in every workplace where it organised. However, even in the 1980s and 1990s, head office was still appealing to brigades to appoint more safety reps and to organise more training. Despite attacks from government and chief officers, many brigades can still take pride in having scores of active, trained safety reps able to pursue the health and safety issues that matter to members. Coroners have highlighted the importance of FBU safety reps in preventing injuries and ill health, their desire to learn lessons from earlier tragedies and their eagerness to ensure that safety measures are implemented at stations and on the fireground.[72] The union has made judicious use of legal action over fatalities, road traffic incidents and civil liability to secure further rights for firefighters.[73]

The organisation of safety reps also paved the way for the effective mobilisation of members around health and safety issues. When confronting civil servants and chief officers on breathing apparatus, hook ladders, training and other matters, the capacity of FBU members to refuse to comply and to contest diktats has been vital to establishing the safety culture on the job. The willingness of firefighters to take action to force governments, employers and chief officers to manage risks has been a crucial part of defending themselves.

Conclusion

The FBU's longstanding prioritisation of safety and health is illustrated by its pamphlets 'What kind of fire service?' (1943) and 'A service for the sixties' (1960), and a host of publications since then. The union has sought to define the shape and scope of the fire and rescue service, so that firefighters are central to their own destiny. FBU debates on hook ladders, live rescue drills, crew cab safety, personal protective equipment and other matters have gone on for decades, with many twists along the way. FBU activists have demanded accountability from the Executive Council and promoted a democratic culture.

The FBU has consistently championed the interdependence of public safety and firefighter safety, pointing to the fact that adequate funding, fire cover, crewing levels and resources are crucial to serving communities, while simultaneously protecting firefighters. The union's emphasis on risk assessment and safe systems of work has consistently aligned the interests of firefighters with those of the fire and rescue service and the public.

The FBU has been willing to learn from scientists and base its arguments on the best evidence available, drawing on expert advice to improve policies and provision relating to breathing apparatus, personal protective equipment, stress, cancer and fitness, and in order to investigate fatalities. It has campaigned alongside a range of safety organisations to advance its aims. The FBU has drawn inspiration from safety campaigners and other trade unions to augment its own work, including firefighters across the globe.

However, health, safety and environment matters remain unfinished business for the FBU. Firefighters continue to die on operational duties in alarming numbers, while horrific injuries continue to blight the lives of firefighters and their families. The FBU has struggled to resist the tide of deregulation imposed by successive governments and to rebuild its workplace safety rep network. Health and safety remains at the core of the FBU's mission. The union's history shows how improvements can be won and how further successes are achievable.

Matt Wrack and Jeremy Corbyn at Durham Miners' Gala in 2017

© Alamy

SUPPORT THE DURHAM MINERS' GALA

© FBU

Ken Cameron presents Nelson Mandela with life membership of the FBU, 1991

9

'Beyond the fire station doors': the labour movement and international solidarity

The Fire Brigades Union recognises that workers, however employed, can only improve their lot by their own endeavours and organisation. A richer and fuller life can be achieved only by similar means. To this end the Fire Brigades Union is part of the Working-Class Movement and, linking itself with the International Trade Union and Labour Movement, has as its ultimate aim the bringing about of the Socialist system of society.

Foreword to the FBU Rule Book, 1944

The FBU's explicit commitment to socialism has been in its rule book since 1944, a political stance that has at times brought it into conflict with the Labour Party, although for most of its 100 years the FBU has been a national affiliate to Labour. A notable exception occurred in recent times, with disaffiliation in 2004, which lasted for 12 years until re-affiliation in 2016, as this chapter explains. Earlier histories attest to the union's generally left-wing character and orientation, with significant association of the leadership with the Communist Party, particularly between 1939 and 1956.[1] As Chapter 2 suggests, subsequent individual political affiliations have been more varied, but all the FBU's leaders have shared a commitment to socialism. Devolution in Scotland and the creation of the Welsh Assembly have changed the political landscape, with some regional officials supporting the Scottish National Party (SNP) and Plaid Cymru, and the FBU pragmatically working with members of the Scottish government and the Welsh Assembly. In Northern Ireland the FBU needed to maintain a non-sectarian position to protect the safety of all its firefighters, and this neutrality allowed it to play a unique role in the peace process which resulted in 1998 in the Good Friday Agreement.

Despite being one of the smaller unions affiliated to the TUC, the FBU has played an important role in that body, not only raising fire and rescue service issues, but also providing wider labour movement solidarity. This chapter outlines how earlier periods of tension between the two organisations have given way to more positive relations. The FBU's equality sections have made significant contributions to the TUC Women's, Black Workers and LGBT conferences since the 1990s. Both through the TUC and independently, the FBU has been prominent in many national campaigns for social justice and in activities against far-right organisations. Crucially, in keeping with its political stance, the union has proudly maintained its internationalist outlook, initially under the leadership of John Horner, but even more so during Ken Cameron's leadership through its support for the anti-nuclear movement, its consistent opposition to apartheid in South Africa, its solidarity with Cuba and Palestine and its stand against the repression of trade unionists in Colombia. It has forged strong links with firefighter unions in other countries, including those in Greece and Spain, which faced severe austerity programmes following the financial crash of 2007-08. The chapter also highlights solidarity missions to deliver practical support to firefighters in Iraq and Palestine. The union's involvement in wider political issues, particularly the prominence it has given to international solidarity campaigns, has, at times, brought criticism from some members, who have believed that the union should pay greater attention to internal fire and rescue service matters. Nevertheless, the FBU's commitment to international trade union solidarity endures.

The Labour Party

The FBU affiliated nationally to the Labour Party in 1926, and several prominent FBU officials have become Labour MPs,[2] but tensions in the union's relationship with the Party have frequently arisen. The first stark example of conflict occurred in the late 1970s, when government pay policy eventually led to the 1977 strike. The 1977 conference motion over cuts in public expenditure opposed the policies of the Labour government. Following the 1977-78 dispute, many members felt frustration and anger with Labour, with the president reporting to the 1978 conference that many had requested to opt out of the political levy.[3]

The FBU remained affiliated to Labour after the 1977-78 pay dispute, but the sense of betrayal resonated when the union once again came into conflict with a Labour government in 2002-04. Kevin Brown, Executive Council member for the North West region, recalled: 'There's a recognition that the wider FBU membership felt betrayed by the previous Labour government they'd been out on strike under. We'd been on strike twice now, on national strike, under Labour governments. So there was a significant disillusionment amongst the wider membership.'

The disillusionment with the Labour government's actions and language during the 2002-04 dispute led to calls for disaffiliation from the party. The issue was brought to the union's Bridlington conference in June 2004. Writing in *Firefighter* in May, former political editor of the *Daily Mirror* Kevin Maguire predicted – with a possible nod to Joe Strummer's role in supporting the 2002-04 dispute (see Chapter 4) – that the unofficial anthem would be the Clash song 'Should I stay or should I go?' This question articulated the dilemma facing many members over whether to stay and fight within Labour or whether to seek alternatives outside it. Despite the anger towards Blair's New Labour party and the expulsion of the RMT (the railworkers' union) from Labour for providing support for other left-wing parties, Maguire observed that a majority of 'the newly awkward unions believe the party is reclaimable, that it can be shifted back to a recognisable, traditional Labour agenda and have opted to stay and fight rather than leave and shout'. In this vein, Tony Woodley, general secretary of the Transport and General Workers' Union, urged the FBU in *Firefighter* April 2004[4] not to walk away but, instead, to fight from within to 'dump New Labour's third-way one-nation dogma' and to 'return Labour to its basic values and principles'. This position was the substance of the Executive Council statement presented to conference which recommended continued affiliation.

However, a composite motion on disaffiliation was proposed by Northern Ireland and seconded by Strathclyde. Tony Maguire, in proposing the motion, expressed the sentiments of many:

Our party, the party who trade unionists like ourselves give millions and millions of pounds to – and for what? To be stabbed, not in the back, but stabbed in the heart. Our members have been betrayed by this party and our class have been betrayed by this party and yes, they are angry, and yes they are bitter and they want this mirage of a relationship with New Labour completely and utterly severed.[5]

In an emotive debate, delegates expressed huge disappointment with New Labour, but some argued against disaffiliation, wanting to retain influence within party. However, the majority voted to break the 78-year link, with 35,105 votes in favour and 14,611 against this resolution: 'The aims and objectives of the Labour Party no longer reflect those of the Fire Brigades Union. Therefore, this Conference demands that the FBU disaffiliates from the Labour Party nationally. This Conference withdraws the authority given under Rule 29 for Labour Party national affiliation.'

Matt Wrack, at the time a London official, spoke in support of the resolution to disaffiliate but expressed concern that the union proposed no alternative political strategy, calling for further debate on the use of the political fund, and recommended the development of a parliamentary group made up of sympathetic Labour MPs, as the RMT had done. National Officer John McGhee concurred that the momentous decision left the union's political strategy unclear, but reported that 'what was plain from the conference debate was that no-one was saying we should switch allegiance to another political party, although it is clear that this would be welcomed in some quarters'.[6] Individuals did subsequently support other left parties or groupings, such as the Socialist Alliance or Respect, in specific local or national elections. At the same time, links with Labour continued at local level, with FBU members and officials taking on roles as local councillors and fire authority members. The union also formed alliances with local Labour councillors to oppose cuts to the fire and rescue service; for example, through the organisation Councillors Against the Cuts.

At national level the FBU continued to work with the Labour Representation Committee, chaired by John McDonnell MP, to pursue socialist, trade union agendas within the Labour Party and in 2005 the FBU Parliamentary Group was founded in collaboration with McDonnell and Jeremy Corbyn MP.[7]

The question of national re-affiliation to Labour regularly reappeared on the conference agenda, but the moment of change occurred after the 2015 general election, which was won by a Conservative Party committed to further public sector austerity and which triggered a leadership contest in the Labour Party. To the surprise of many, left-wing candidate Jeremy Corbyn was elected Labour leader with 59.5 per cent of first round votes, defeating the three other candidates. Wrack recognised, given Corbyn's long history of supporting firefighters, that re-affiliation to the Labour Party was now an urgent imperative. He gained support for a recall conference to debate the issue. Former president Alan McLean reflected:

> I always felt that it was time to get back into the Labour Party. I firmly believe that you need to ride a horse to steer it. I don't believe you can steer a horse from the sidelines and I think that's what we were trying to do. I think we were punching above our weight while we weren't re-affiliated. We have a parliamentary group which has yielded us the leader of the opposition, Corbyn, and also the shadow chancellor, John McDonnell. They were both massive parts of our parliamentary group and I think that when they were given the office, I think it was incumbent on us, and right and proper, that we should re-affiliate to that party.

In November 2015 the union held a recall conference in Blackpool to discuss its political strategy in the aftermath of the general election. The Executive Council argued that the union would be more effective resisting attacks on firefighters' pay and conditions and combating the government's broader austerity programme from within the Labour Party:

> An affiliation to the Labour Party now gives the FBU a once-in-a-generation opportunity to help set the wider political debate on fire and rescue service funding, firefighters' pay and conditions, fire service governance, national standards, firefighter safety and the whole range of wider issues faced by our members. It also gives us an opportunity to counter the wider attacks of austerity, privatisation and the anti-union laws that directly affect our members and our ability to defend ourselves.[8]

For many, the election of Jeremy Corbyn as Labour leader awakened, or renewed, support for Labour, as expressed by London organiser Steve White:

> So when we got that change at the top of the Labour Party with Jeremy Corbyn and John McDonnell, all of a sudden that was the obvious thing to do because these were people that backed the FBU and they always had backed the FBU and they'd always worked for us when we were in the Labour Party, when we were outside the Labour Party. So re-affiliation made sense.

The conference supported the Executive Council's resolution on re-affiliation, which noted the union's role in the change of Labour leadership and in the direction of the party:

> The FBU was among the first trade unions to pledge support for Jeremy Corbyn in the Labour leadership race, even before he had reached the required number of MPs to join the contest. The union supported Corbyn from the beginning because of his record of support for our union and its members. The union provided material support to his campaign, including our FBU fire engine that was visible at many rallies. The FBU and many of our officials, whether individual members of the Labour Party or not, contributed actively to the success of his campaign.[9]

In proposing to re-affiliate to Labour, the Executive Council recognised the different political contexts of Northern Ireland and Scotland, making it clear that the decision did not mean affiliation to the Labour Party in Northern Ireland or Scotland. Although the Executive Council had expected some opposition to the proposal, particularly from members in Scotland, Wrack noted that this did not really materialise.

Links with Labour were strengthened when Corbyn addressed the FBU conference in May 2016:

> On behalf of the Party, welcome back and I'm delighted you're part of the Party and delighted to look forward to FBU resolutions coming up to annual conference and the huge contribution this union has always made, not just on behalf of the

industry obviously, but also on behalf of so many international issues over many years. All general secretaries have been great supporters of the Party and its international work. So thank you very much, all of you, for that re-affiliation.[10]

The FBU then played a prominent role in Corbyn's second leadership campaign, which was prompted by a vote of no confidence by the Parliamentary Labour Party on 27 June 2016. Corbyn addressed over 10,000 supporters in Parliament Square from the fire engine, which Simon Green, the former Hampshire branch chair, dubbed 'the movement's truck'. As Wrack recalled:

I think I was the only general secretary who came out very, very clearly and I was on the news quite a lot as defending Corbyn. I'd raised the idea of having some public events and that ended up being that rally in Parliament Square... The aim of the MPs' attack was to destroy the Corbyn leadership, and in reality, to kill off the left, therefore, in the Labour Party for the next generation, and that to me was what that was about. And I think the Corbyn leadership offers an opportunity to, if we do it right, create a sort of renaissance for the labour movement, you know, on lots of levels – politically, in the unions, at a local level in the Labour Party. You know, it's still a long shot in a lot of ways, everything's stacked against it, but, it's the only game in town.

In September 2016 Corbyn was re-elected Labour leader, with an increased vote of 62 per cent, against the 38 per cent for Owen Smith, the only challenger. Corbyn's leadership was then put to the public vote in the surprise 2017 general election, called by Conservative prime minister Theresa May. The FBU strongly supported the Labour Party manifesto, which for the first time made commitments to recruit more frontline firefighters, also promising to give fire and rescue services in England a statutory duty to tackle flooding. Corbyn's leadership encouraged the Cambridgeshire brigade secretary, Cameron Matthews, to stand as a parliamentary candidate in Suffolk:

Following the election of Jeremy as leader and his progressive politics, I was inspired to become more involved in the Party. This led to being contacted to inquire if I would stand in the General Election. After deliberations and late-night phone calls of encouragement from our general secretary, I applied and was subsequently chosen as the candidate for Suffolk Coastal. It was a uniquely busy time as we were also engaged in local shift negotiations. However, it was a wonderful experience. Getting out and speaking to people about their aspirations, challenges and political perspectives – leading the debate. Whilst I did not win the long-held blue seat, we made great progress in seven weeks, increasing Labour votes from 10,013 in 2015 to 17,701 in 2017, the second-highest for Labour in the constituency's history. Next time we will win!

Against polling predictions, the Labour Party increased both its share of the vote and the number of Labour MPs in Westminster (by 30), leaving the Conservative Party without an overall majority.

Wales

In 1997 a referendum was held on devolution of powers to a Welsh assembly, a campaign which the Welsh region of the FBU had supported through the Labour Party in Wales. Former Executive Council member for Wales Mike Smith remembered:

Over numerous years at Wales Labour Party conferences leading up to the devolution referendum in 1997, we tabled resolutions supporting devolution and urging the Wales Labour Party Executive to move forward. Grudgingly they did so, eventually, thanks to Ron Davies, the secretary of state for Wales. In the campaign itself we produced posters for noticeboards in fire stations and control rooms all over Wales urging our members to vote 'yes' in the referendum.

The result was a narrow majority in favour of devolution. The Welsh National Assembly held its first elections in 1999, giving Welsh FBU members a different relationship to the Westminster government from their English counterparts. Responsibility for the fire and rescue service in Wales was devolved to the Welsh government in 2004. Disaffiliation by the FBU from the Labour

Party in 2004 also freed Welsh FBU members to become actively involved with other parties. Welsh regional secretary Cerith Griffiths, for example, stood unsuccessfully as a Plaid Cymru candidate in the 2015 General Election, and for the Welsh Assembly in May 2016. Beci Newton also stood for Plaid Cymru in Caerphilly in 2015 but, similarly, was not elected. Griffiths explained his personal support for Welsh independence:

> Plaid Cymru want the best for Wales and I'm not saying that Labour don't, but I think because of the ties to Westminster it just doesn't seem that the best has been done for Wales. I'd like to see an independent Wales in my lifetime, simply because I think people in Wales know what's best for Wales.

Others believed that the FBU in Wales had a positive working relationship with the Labour Party in the Welsh Assembly, which had resulted in improvements in firefighter terms and conditions when compared to England. Executive Council member for Wales Grant Mayos explained:

> Clearly Welsh Labour assisted eventually during the pensions campaign, and we ended up with a better deal, which meant that we didn't go on strike with the English members for the last three strike periods. They are people we can do business with. We've done business with them over the pay issue of late. Over the medical response trials, they've been quite supportive of the FBU stance, but they've also been quite supportive of the fact we've now ceased the trials – they understand why.

A pensions advisory board was established in Wales in 2015 to provide oversight of the local brigades, with two seats reserved for the FBU.

In April 2017 fire and rescue services in Wales were given a statutory duty to respond to flooding emergencies, following a long campaign led by the FBU to have flooding recognised as a core element of fire and rescue service work. Mayos recalls that the union had been campaigning on the issue for about nine years, but eventually the Welsh Assembly agreed to provide funding:

There was some opposition to it as there was going to be funding involved. But we managed to secure £1.8m of capital funding as well, to assist with new equipment, boats, dry suits, etc, so basically our members will be better equipped to go out and deal with flooding incidents.

This decision left England as the only nation in the UK with no statutory duty on fire and rescue services to respond to flooding.

Scotland

The establishment of the Scottish Parliament in 1999 changed the political landscape, particularly when the SNP became the largest party at the 2007 election, winning 47 seats and becoming the leading party in a minority government. In 2011, it won 69 seats and formed a majority government. According to Scottish regional chair Gordon McQuade, for the FBU, disaffiliation from the Labour Party in 2004 meant 'freedom in Scotland to support candidates, not parties, who had the FBU and firefighters' best interest at heart'. McQuade suggested that adopting this course of action had been unpopular with the Scottish TUC, which was strongly of the view at that time that trade unions should only give financial support to the Labour Party. Some FBU members and activists joined the SNP, regarding it as offering more progressive policies than Scottish Labour, while others joined the Scottish Socialist Party, particularly after the 2003 Holyrood election, at which it won six seats, although its attractiveness ended abruptly after internal crisis in 2006. Others still remained with Labour but nevertheless acknowledged the opportunities that an SNP government might present. Scottish regional secretary Denise Christie, a Labour Party member, said:

> The SNP has got its faults like everybody else, but certainly they're not a right-wing Tory government that's union-bashing. So we've got access to senior ministers, senior justice secretary Michael Matheson, but at the SNP conference we'll meet with the justice secretary, talking about issues in the fire service as well. So we're much more accessible to politicians and to managers sitting down and picking up the phone... So for example, the control members of staff, some of them are being

displaced. If a control room is shut down in Aberdeen and they can't go to Dundee control room, they're being displaced. So there wasn't a lot of job opportunities in that era so – we picked up the phone to the chief and says, 'Look, you need to make jobs for these people. Right, how can we resolve this?' So that's the relationship that you've got.

The FBU's relationship with the Scottish government was important in bringing changes to the structure of the Scottish fire and rescue service. Some SNP-supporting officials were eager to endorse the Scottish government's plans for a single national service, despite the implied job losses and redeployments. Eight brigades were merged into a single fire and rescue service in April 2013. In the year following reorganisation, 297 frontline firefighter jobs were lost in addition to emergency control room posts.

The union developed a 'partnership working' agreement with the Scottish fire and rescue service. While, on the positive side, it might enable access to senior officials in the Scottish government and to brigade chiefs, on the negative side it has been a way of locking the union into management decisions. Christie reported: 'We meet regularly with the chief fire officer. We meet regularly with senior management. We mightn't always get what we want, but at least there's a dialogue there. We work together to try and resolve some of the disputes before they've escalated.'

The 'partnership' was to be severely tested by proposals for extensive reforms intended to 're-balance firefighter numbers' and review the service's 'station footprint'.[11] Newspaper reports suggested that decisions might be taken to shift city-centre-based firefighters to on-call rotas similar to those of retained firefighters in rural areas in the context of a further reduction in full-time posts, a momentous change, for which the SNP government and not Westminster would be responsible. On 23 November 2017 hundreds of FBU members protested outside the Scottish Parliament against the proposed cuts. The newly-elected regional secretary, Denise Christie, made clear the union's opposition to Scottish government policy, which had resulted in the loss of '700 frontline firefighters in Scotland since 2013' and the inevitable increase in emergency response times.[12]

Northern Ireland

In Northern Ireland the FBU inevitably had a distinctive experience during the troubles, with firefighters facing extreme situations on a daily basis. Former Executive Council member Jim Barbour described an attack on the central fire station in Belfast during an FBU meeting:

> When one particular night there had been a lot of activity, probably 1986-ish, we had called an emergency branch meeting because of the amount of gun attacks. We were sat in the room – it was on the first floor, central fire station – and lo and behold the glass came flying through. It was a gun attack in the middle of a branch meeting, and we were all diving to the floor and all that sort of stuff. But very quickly we got ourselves picked up and finished the bloody meeting.

Tony Maguire, former regional secretary, similarly recalled:

> We had incidents where the fire engine and the driver were taken away at gunpoint and on that particular branch the members were talking about having one appliance for Catholics and one appliance for Protestants, to serve respective areas. And the union bounced that one right away, and it's good, thankfully, they did. We could never have afforded to have gone down that road; apart from the morality of it, the damage it would have done to union unity would have been disastrous. But sometimes, when in a fraught situation, people can knee-jerk very quickly.

The divided nature of the north had necessarily engendered impartiality in a union with members from both communities, particularly after the influx of Catholics in the 1980s, as Executive Council member Jim Quinn recounted:

> We were traditionally very apolitical in our union terms. The brigade were even more so and that was to do with keeping neutral. The key tenet of the brigade in the '70s and '80s and even up to the '90s was for people to gain access to all areas and to do that you had to show no partiality, you had to be

impartial completely. So we didn't have chief officers making statements or complaining about x, y and z... the union was similar in political terms. Don't forget, our people were at the sharp end of bombs going off and so on. But very rarely did you hear us making any sort of political statement – and that was understandable. But some of us younger people then started to say, 'You know what? Maybe it's time to do something a little bit different. Maybe it's time.' And on the political landscape it changed as well. We started to engage with people. I'm jumping probably ahead into the '90s. But certainly the end of the '80s saw a new crowd of – on our committee – younger, more politically aware [people]... wanting to move things on. The dynamics started to change – more outward and less insular. And then the Good Friday Agreement. We had the opportunity at that point to engage with local politicians because they were setting up assemblies, they were setting up local fora, and so we could engage for the first time ever.

Former regional secretary Jim Hughes also described how the union 'had to be extremely careful and had to walk the tightrope', adding, 'It was very hard as union officials to remain on that tightrope so that we were welcomed as a fire brigade, we were welcomed everywhere we went, usually.'

The non-sectarian nature of the union allowed it to play a unique role in the peace process which resulted in the Good Friday Agreement. In June 1998 the FBU organised a seminar for its members, inviting representatives of both sides of the divide. Jim Barbour remembered:

So we had Sinn Fein. We had David Irvine from the DUP [Democratic Unionist Party]. We had someone from the Ulster Unionist Party, I think it was Ken McGuinness; he was an ex-UDR [Ulster Defence Regiment] major. We also had, I think, Mark Durkan, who was leader of the SDLP [Social Democratic and Labour Party] and we had an Irish MP. We also had a group called Different Drums, who played music from different backgrounds, and we had the then general secretary, Ken Cameron. We were in close contact with the police about potential threats to the event and so on. But we took a risk as a trade union and we were one of the first to do that and that was a massive step. It was the politicisation of the FBU in Northern Ireland really and it was the first real tangible move that we made. So we were agitating for a number of years, and we managed to get in a position of power. Once we got into a position of power we then pushed on.

The union had been strengthened by a dispute in the 1980s to prevent new recruits being brought in on new contracts with less annual leave, and later by the successful defence of the Northern Ireland allowances (Chapter 3). The legacy of politicisation and greater engagement with the national union was evident in the 2002-04 strike, where Northern Ireland had a 95 per cent vote in favour of industrial action. During the strike there was a cross-community walk up the Shanklin and down the Falls Road in support of firefighters, and both Alex Maskey from Sinn Fein and David Irvine from the DUP joined picket lines. The balanced engagement in politics produced a vote in the Northern Ireland Assembly in support of the £30k claim and later resulted in agreement to retain the retirement age of 55 compared to 60 across the UK. Summing these achievements up, former Executive Council member Jim Quinn said, 'We have moved the fire brigade from a silent service to a service which is part of the community.'

The TUC

Although the FBU affiliated to the TUC in 1923, it was not until the union grew in the post-war period that it took a more active role, becoming involved in three main areas: fire service conditions and safety, incomes policies and international affairs. While during the Cold War period the FBU's participation was limited by its connection with the Communist Party, by the 1970s the FBU had 'progressed from being a weak and relatively insignificant part of the organised trade union movement to the position of an important, though still small, section with elected officers in strategic positions in both the TUC and the STUC [Scottish Trades Union Congress].'[13] The union used its position in the TUC to make representations to the government on fire safety and to be consulted on matters such as the draft British Standards for fire service equipment.[14] The FBU opposed the UK joining the

European Community in 1973 and advocated voting to withdraw in the 1975 referendum.[15] The FBU had come into conflict with the TUC over the latter's support for Labour government incomes policies in the 1960s, and when the Callaghan government's policy of pay restraint finally resulted in the 1977-78 pay dispute, the TUC continued to support the government's pay policy and did little to support the firefighters' cause (see Chapter 1). During Ken Cameron's leadership, relations with the TUC grew far more positive and remained so thereafter. Cameron was on the TUC General Council between 1981 and 1984 and from 1991 to 2000, and when he died TUC general secretary Frances O'Grady paid tribute: 'A committed socialist and internationalist, he inspired respect from fellow union leaders, employers and politicians of all stripes alike. I will always be grateful to Ken for the support and encouragement he gave me and many others.'[16]

Matt Wrack warmly welcomed Frances O'Grady to the FBU's 2013 conference, noting the significantly improved relationship:

There's been ups and downs over the years in the FBU's relationship with the TUC. There are some famous pictures from 1977 of a quite angry picket outside Congress House of firefighters frustrated at the strike and at what they perceived as the role of the TUC. People will remember that there was a great deal of support from the TUC in 2002-03 with Brendan Barber and Frances playing a role in that, and Frances has assisted us since then in a number of our local disputes on a whole number of fronts.[17]

The respect shown by the TUC towards the FBU and Wrack's leadership was underlined by the TUC's nomination of Wrack for one of the employee seats on the Health & Safety Executive (HSE). O'Grady described Wrack as 'a man whose knowledge and commitment to health and safety, in my experience, is quite simply second to none', expressing her great disappointment that the HSE and the government failed to appoint him.[18]

The FBU has played an important role in the TUC not only through its international work (see page 293), but also through involvement in committees for women, race relations and LGBT members. In 1991 control member Lynne Harding was elected onto the TUC Women's Committee as the first FBU representative[19] and the FBU National Women's Committee has continued to play an active part in the TUC Women's Committee and conference since, regularly sending delegations and putting forward motions. Similarly, the FBU B&EMM section has participated regularly in the TUC Black Workers Conference, including the 2003 conference in Liverpool, which was co-chaired by B&EM member Garrett Brooks, whose closing speech remembered the thousands of slaves who had arrived in Liverpool in the 17th and 18th centuries.[20] The FBU LGBT section has also worked extensively with the TUC's LGBT Committee and has been heavily involved with its international work.

National campaigns

The FBU has a long history of challenging racism and fascism. In 1978 Mick Shaw, later FBU president, formed Firemen against the Nazis in response to the National Front's local election successes, and in 1979 the union hosted an Anti-Nazi League fringe meeting at the TUC conference in 1979, addressed by general secretary Terry Parry.[21] Mick Shaw's obituary in 2012 noted the FBU's prominent role among trade unions in fighting the National Front, and Gerry Gable, editor of anti-fascist magazine *Searchlight*, recalled Shaw's role: 'He was much admired for taking a strong stand against racism, despite being physically threatened. His entire life was dedicated to his fellow workers and combating fascism and racism.'[22]

The union's continued activism against far-right parties has brought it into conflict with fire service employers. When Southern regional B&EMM rep and brigade chair Lud Ramsey heard that a retained firefighter in Hampshire (not an FBU member) was standing in the 2004 European elections for the British National Party (BNP), he was supported by the regional committee to take action. Following an initial meeting, at which Hampshire fire and rescue service claimed there was nothing they could do, Ramsey, together with local activists, organised a demonstration outside the fire authority's headquarters and a petition. Together with B&EMM section officials, Ramsey contacted the Commission for Racial Equality (CRE) and a meeting was called with Hampshire fire and rescue service, representatives of the Office of the Deputy

Prime Minister and union lawyers. Ramsey recalled his anger during the meeting:

> The HR guy got up and said, 'Look, I've interviewed him and I just think he's a little bit naïve.' And I jumped up and said, 'No, I'm not having this. Look, how many people in this organisation do you know who are racist?' And he went quiet. I said, 'You don't know any. You think everybody is all great.' I said, 'I know every single one because I had to − I make it my duty. The people who are racist are the ones who are going to attack me. That's what I'm talking about.' And he just went silent. And he wanted the room to swallow him up and get away.

The CRE used the occasion to demonstrate that the authority had not complied with its obligation to publish its race equality scheme, leaving it liable to significant fines. Ramsey recounted how the chief fire officer was scared into action: 'So he got £200,000 out of the budget from nowhere to start an equality team in Hampshire and he said, "Oh could you help us?" I said, "Of course I can help you."' Eventually the BNP member left the brigade, facing pressure from the brigade and the press when he tried to stand again for the BNP.

The union's rules prohibit membership of racist or fascist organisations, and union education programmes address the threat posed by the far right to the labour movement and to democratic rights nationally and internationally. In 2008 a leaked BNP membership list exposed a small number of fire service employees who were possibly members, prompting a conference resolution calling on the fire and rescue service to make a clear statement that members of extremist organisations were not welcome.[23]

The FBU has been prominent in campaigns for racial justice, for example, in the battle to bring to justice the murderers of Surjit Singh Chhokar, stabbed in a street in North Lanarkshire in 1998. This case is often compared to the Stephen Lawrence case, and the failure of two prosecution cases in 1999 and 2000 led to a public outcry, followed by two official inquiries, with one finding the legal system guilty of institutional racism. The FBU and the STUC raised funds to support the family's campaign for justice, and joined voices calling for an independent public inquiry.[24]

It was not until October 2016 that a conviction was secured for Chhokar's murder, following a retrial and a change in the double jeopardy law.[25] Similarly the union, and in particular the B&EMM Committee, has been active in campaigns for those killed in police custody and in supporting the families of victims, including Ricky Reel, Michael Menson and Roger Sylvester, for many years joining the United Friends and Family Campaign marches to Downing Street and Trafalgar Square.[26]

Given the FBU's prominent political campaigning, it is not surprising that it was revealed as one of the unions that had been spied upon by the police, alongside Unite, UNISON, UCATT, NUT, NUM and CWU. Evidence presented to the House of Commons in March 2015 showed that Matt Wrack was subjected to illegal surveillance during the 1990s while a London FBU official, as was Ken Cameron while general secretary during the 1980s. An inquiry into undercover policing led by Lord Pitchford was established in 2015, with the FBU as a 'core participant', giving the union the right to question witnesses and gather evidence, although progress was initially slow.[27]

International solidarity

The FBU has long had an internationalist approach, as set out in its rule book commitment to socialism, which dates from John Horner's leadership in the 1940s and 1950s. Ken Cameron's leadership enhanced the internationalism of the union, a contribution Matt Wrack highlighted in his obituary:

> Arguing the case for solidarity at home and abroad was central to Ken's politics and trade union beliefs. Building on the traditions of the FBU, he urged the union to take up international causes which, at the time, were sometimes controversial. As a result, the FBU often pioneered the case for solidarity with those struggling against apartheid or fighting for the rights of the Palestinian people.[28]

Opposition to South Africa's apartheid regime was a cornerstone of the FBU's international work, the union being a founder member of the Anti-Apartheid Movement in 1960, when campaigners in Britain and globally rallied to support the struggle in South

Africa.[29] On Nelson Mandela's release from prison in 1990, and the start of the dismantling of the apartheid regime, Cameron wrote him a letter saluting his 'courage and integrity which have inspired all opponents of apartheid'.[30] The 1990 FBU conference, recognising 'the supreme sacrifice made by Nelson Mandela over many years', made him an honorary member.[31] The honour was presented by Cameron to Mandela in 1991 in the presence of African National Congress (ANC) president Oliver Tambo and Mrs Adelaide Tambo.[32] Tony Maguire recalled how political education in the union exposed him to wider debates, including events in South Africa at the time, and Ken Cameron's role in these:

> I always considered myself to be political but my politics would have been focused on what was happening on the doorstep. But [as regards] a raising of political consciousness to the bigger issues, the wider labour movement, I remember Ken Cameron saying – and I had great regard for Ken Cameron – on more than one occasion 'There's a world outside the fire service doors' and I found myself using that expression at various times in my own service. Ken was a small man – softly spoken, soft Scottish accent – and he took a personal interest in everybody. And he remembered you. He was everything that a good leader should be, I think, and I do remember having discussions with him about things that he mightn't necessarily have agreed with, to do with the Northern Ireland situation. But in a few well-chosen sentences, he had pointed me in a better direction. And I remember there was a fellow from the Confederation of South African Trade Unions, when apartheid was still up and running, who'd given a spectacular presentation on the injustice of apartheid. And I said to him something like, 'It's terrible what's happening in South Africa but should you not take a more political aim rather than the violence of the ANC?' And he pointed out, 'We've tried all of that for generations.' And I said, 'Look, it's just I don't believe in violence and terrorism.' And he said, 'Well I'm prepared to die for what I believe.' So from that time I stopped buying any produce from South Africa.

The union supported work on the democratic reconstruction of South Africa after the end of apartheid through backing for

On Ken Cameron's retirement

When Cameron retired in 2000, Mandela wrote to thank him for the FBU's support, saying: 'The FBU under your leadership campaigned unselfishly against the evil of apartheid' and 'Our liberation from the darkness of apartheid was in no small measure due to people like you.' Mandela added: 'The solidarity among your members, born out of their work experience and tempered by their own struggles, was the solid basis on which you lent your weight to a struggle by people you didn't know, some 6,000 miles away in another continent. It was therefore a great honour for me when I learned that I have been made an Honorary Member of the Fire Brigades Union and had so become a brother of so many wonderful brothers and sisters.'[33]

Action for Southern Africa (ACTSA). A Scottish union delegation to South Africa in 2000 included officials from Unison, the EIS (a Scottish teaching union) and the STUC, as well as Alan Campbell, then the FBU's Scottish regional chair, and national officer John McGhee, with the aim of consolidating and strengthening trade union links.[34]

The FBU for many years supported the Cuba Solidarity Campaign, with the Scottish region FBU office hosting the Scottish branch of the campaign. Senior officials, including former presidents Ruth Winters and Mick Shaw, playing a prominent role, and undertaking a week-long study tour in 2008.[35]

HIV and AIDS campaigns are further examples of the many international campaigns in which the union's equality sections have been involved, supporting B&EM workers, women's rights or LGBT issues around the world. Through his role on the TUC LGBT Committee, Stewart Brown represented the UK unions at the International Labour Organisation (ILO) in Geneva for four years and worked on the ILO Recommendation on AIDS and the World of Work, the adoption of which was celebrated at a TUC seminar on World AIDS Day, 1 December, in 2010.[36]

The international solidarity work of the FBU and its members continues to take a number of forms and many members get involved in international rescue work (for example, after the Armenian earthquake in 1988 and the Haiti earthquake in 2010), although these activities are not directly linked to the FBU.[37] Former Lancashire brigade secretary Steve Harman explained:

> I used to be part of the international team that went abroad to earthquakes and things like that, but that was nothing to do with the FBU. I just volunteered within Lancashire and that came about for some odd reason that we had a firefighter whose parents were Russian and in the Armenian earthquake, years and years ago. He asked our brigade could we send out a team to help and that's how it started but then it got more formalised. And in Lancashire we had volunteers to go out to do rescue, say in the Indian earthquake. I went to the Indian earthquake and to a couple in Turkey, but we also had charities that sent old fire engines out; we went to Bosnia, Croatia. I've been to Tanzania.

At times, the international focus of the union has been questioned by members, in the form of letters to *Firefighter* arguing that the union and the journal should be spending its resources on local and national issues affecting the working lives of members, with 'more on the fire service and a bit less on the politics'.[38] In responding to such objections, former West Midlands regional secretary Chris Downes explained how everyday discussions can help members to make connections between local and international trade unionism; for example, through questions about where someone's T-shirt was made and by whom:

> It's all about education and knowledge about supporting trade unionists and workers' rights in other countries. Once you read and understand what's going on, at that moment you then pass it on to someone else and you say, 'That's not really fair. You wouldn't want your daughter/son/wife/husband/partner to be going through that, would you, at work? That's the whole reason we do this – so we can support each other.' And then the light bulb comes on.

A review of the union's international work was undertaken during 2007 and 2008, which sought to relate it more directly to members' concerns and to make links between austerity measures facing firefighters at home and abroad, while taking account of

301

the union's own budgetary constraints. The review suggested that resources be 'targeted to initiatives where we can raise issues directly related to the fire and public services, and those where we can help others in need of assistance and support'.[39]

However, the international contribution of the FBU continues to be recognised within the labour movement and was praised by Frances O'Grady in her speech to the FBU conference in 2013:

> I also want to pay tribute to everything that the FBU has achieved as a powerful and principled voice of firefighters, as a staunch defender of our public services, and as a great champion of internationalism, because from Colombia to Cuba, be in no doubt your commitment to global solidarity is quite simply second to none.[40]

The union has historically made links with firefighters around the world, as a means of sharing best practice on industrial matters, as well as to offer solidarity and more recently to build political resistance to austerity. In an example of practical and political support to firefighters and the trade union movement in Iraq and Iraqi Kurdistan, in 2006 six FBU members drove two fire appliances on a 10-day trip to Iraq, with a special supplement documenting the journey published in *Firefighter* in June 2007 (see box overleaf).[41]

There have been long-standing associations with the North American firefighters' union, the IAFF, with dialogue including fact-finding delegations to the US to learn more about their approach to preventing firefighter fatalities, cancers and burns, improving fitness and dealing with emergency medical response.[42]

In Europe, the FBU has been central to the development of a European Firefighters Network through the European Public Sector Unions organisation (EPSU) since 2006, with the aim of sharing information on EU health and safety directives, working time regulations, pensions and other industrial issues. Additionally, the EPSU link has enabled the union to build connections with worker organisations across Europe that are opposed to austerity measures.[43] The FBU's increased solidarity action with unions in Europe since the 2008 financial crisis reflects the changed international context facing the union and

The road to Iraq

On 24 September 2006 six FBU members set out from the UK to Iraq, after eight months of preparation and fundraising. The team was composed of three serving and retired West Midlands members, Mick Henn, Phil Goalby and Norman Brackenridge, who were the drivers, with Brian Joyce (former South West Executive Council member), Val Salmon (Executive Council member for Control) and Duncan Milligan (FBU head of research and communications). Brian Joyce had visited Iraq on several occasions, and had taken much-needed fire kit, uniforms and protective equipment and felt that delivering appliances was 'the next logical step'. He said:

Firefighters are firefighters. There is a bond which connects us, we do the same job and take the same risks wherever we are in the world. In Iraq I found firefighters were trying to tackle fires wearing only sandals, T-shirts and boiler suits and suffering horrific burns as a result. Like firefighters all over the world all they were trying to do was save lives and help their people, but they were doing that in appalling and dangerous circumstances.

Milligan, in *Firefighter*, recounts the adventurous trip, including bribing officials to get into and out of Turkey, detention overnight in 'no man's land' on the border with Iraqi Kurdistan and the warm welcome offered by Iraqi and Kurdistan trade unionists once over the border. They finally handed the appliances over in Duhok in Kurdish Iraq after a journey of 3,000 miles, with one appliance destined for Erbil and the other for Baghdad. Delays had left only a day for meetings and hospitality with the president and 26 officials of the Kurdistan Workers Syndicate Union, who expressed their thanks for the support shown by the FBU to the union movement and firefighters of their country, expressing the hope that strong bonds would continue.

its European neighbours. The FBU participated in a delegation to Greece in 2013 that visited firefighters facing substantial cuts in wages and pensions as a result of austerity cuts demanded by the European Commission, the European Central Bank and the International Monetary Fund. National officer Dave Green describes the union's support for the Greek Solidarity Campaign:

The delegation took over medicine, mainly because the health service was collapsing. Hospitals were being closed down, schools had been closed down. We went to a school and they were having to work in shifts. So some kids went in the morning, some kids went in the afternoon. It's just unbelievable really. And all because, you know, [of] the banking crisis which had nothing to do with Greek people and certainly nothing to do with Greek firefighters.

In resisting austerity, Spanish firefighters adopted the slogan 'We rescue people, not banks', emanating from the refusal of Coruña firefighter, Roberto Rivas, to evict an elderly woman from her home in February 2013, which inspired Spanish firefighters to refuse to cooperate in the growing number of evictions resulting from increased economic hardship. Firefighters, too, had been facing cuts, closures and attacks on pay and pensions. Overnight the slogan '*Rescatamos personas, no bancos*' appeared on fire stations all over Spain. Soon afterwards, firefighters in Barcelona produced a T-shirt bearing the slogan in Catalan, and the FBU followed suit with its own English version of the 'We rescue people, not banks' T-shirt, worn widely on pickets and demonstrations.[44] Solidarity was cemented when Spanish firefighters travelled to the FBU march and rally in October 2013, and when Rivas spoke to the union's 2014 annual conference:

After I felt really sad and deeply emotional about what happened that day when I got called by the police to break that door, to get this 85-year-old lady out, the solidarity shown around the country and outside the country, and all the people shouting 'We rescue people, not banks', it gave me an immense happiness. I am glad to be here today to tell you that this is our duty. We have to help people out there, we have to help our communities and we have to be on their side, not on the other side.[45]

A further example of the union's long-standing and continuing international work is its support for Palestinian firefighters. Solidarity included raising funds to buy two fire engines in 2011 and driving them to Palestine, and developing courses for the Palestinian civil defence fire service, run in Scotland in a collaboration between the FBU, the Scottish government and the Scottish fire and rescue service. Former Scottish official Jim Malone described a visit to Palestine in 2015 to see whether the training had fulfilled its goals:

> When we visited Hebron, it was an eye opener beyond belief. Although it's a big wealthy city – it's the biggest city in the West Bank, 360,000 people almost – their fire service is decrepit. The guys had no PPE [personal protective equipment], no jackets, no leggings, no helmets, no boots. They'd put out a fire in basically overalls. One of the fire engines is, like, 53 years old – absolutely ridiculous.

Following the visit, a consignment of personal protective equipment and other kit was sent to the West Bank in 2016 to help firefighters in their work. Welsh firefighter Ciaran Gibbons's film, *Firefighters Under Occupation*, documenting the dangerous and under-resourced conditions facing Palestinian firefighters, won the runner-up documentary award at the Respect Human Rights Film Festival in 2017.[46]

The EU referendum

On 23 June 2016, a referendum was held on whether the United Kingdom should remain in the European Union. While some trade unions chose to remain neutral, the FBU decided to take a stance, and in 'one of the most important debates of 2016 conference' backed a decisive 'remain' position. This decision put it among the majority of TUC affiliates, with 13 unions supporting remain, 11 taking a neutral position and only three (RMT, ASLEF, BFAWU) supporting leave.[47] National officer Dave Green explains why it was important for the union to take a side:

> Within the fire service if we look back historically, you know, we are a safety-critical industry. We're an industry that needs to provide 24-hour cover and therefore our members need protection whilst at work. And that protection in my view has come through a lot of European legislation. So the working time regulations, part-time workers' regulations, for example.

> And certainly health and safety legislation. And some of my concerns over all of that is that they might all be stripped away.

The Executive Council had concluded that the union should take a position in the interests of workers' rights. Matt Wrack's impassioned speech to conference in favour of remain was nevertheless strongly critical of the EU status quo, arguing that 'it was not created with workers in mind. It was, and still remains, a bosses' club'. However, he argued, Brexit would jeopardise workers' rights, and he urged members to reject the anti-immigration arguments of those advocating Brexit:

> We have an economic recession. It was sparked by the banks, not by migrants. There are housing shortages in the UK. They are caused by the failures of the market, not by migrants. We have stretched public services in the UK. They are caused by the austerity policies of this government, not by migrants. We have low wages in this economy. They are caused by rip-off bosses, not by migrants. Our answer to all that is solidarity, not the division that is promoted by that sort of argument.[48]

The London region put a motion to support the leave campaign, with Paul Embery arguing that the EU was 'a pro-capitalist, pro-austerity, pro-privatisation institution' that does not represent workers' interests. This position was overwhelmingly rejected as delegates backed the Executive Council's position to support a 'remain' vote. Conference took place only four weeks before the referendum, so the period of campaigning for the union's position was limited. However the union website carried full details of the Executive Council and general secretary's position, together with a cost-benefit analysis produced for the union, urging all members to vote in 'the most important decision voters will have for a generation'.[49]

Following the referendum result in favour of leaving the EU, the FBU vowed to protect the interests of firefighters and the fire and rescue service and to work with the labour and trade union movement to protect working people. It also called for unity, highlighting that the FBU represents members across the UK, including Scotland and Northern Ireland, where votes to remain were at odds with those in many English regions.[50]

Conclusion

The FBU's long tradition of global solidarity work endures, albeit with a shift in emphasis towards international support focused more closely on firefighter issues, while it continues its support for campaigns for political and social justice. Former Strathclyde brigade chair Stewart Kinnon explained the significance of the union's explicit commitment to socialism:

> One of the proudest things I always remember is the opening of the FBU rule book – the creation of a socialist society for all. And I always thought that was dead important, being part of the rule book, because trade unions can be elitist, a bit narrow-minded and 'we just want to look after our own'. You think about the reasons trade unions were set up. They were of the working classes.

Following the FBU's break with Labour after the 2002-04 pay dispute, re-affiliation in 2016 has led to the union playing a key role in Jeremy Corbyn's leadership on its centenary, as Matt Wrack concluded:

> Jeremy Corbyn has shifted the political debate decisively in favour of working-class people by working towards what is fair and just. It seems that the Tory party's austerity agenda may have had its day... Millions have rejected the endless attacks on living standards and public services. People are sick of seeing their wages cut, facing a future where young people cannot get a decent job or a decent home. Theresa May now has no mandate to continue with the policy of endless cuts that put the safety and health of the public at risk... The FBU wholeheartedly welcomes the rapid change of direction that is needed to make our country a safer, fairer place.

TABLE 1 The respondents

* Roles are given for January 2018 or, for former officials, their most senior position held.

Name	Role*
NATIONAL OFFICERS	
Matt Wrack	General secretary
Andy Dark	Assistant general secretary
Ian Murray	President
Dave Green	National officer
Sean Starbuck	National officer
Ken Cameron	Former general secretary
Mike Fordham	Former assistant general secretary
Alan McLean	Former president
Ruth Winters	Former president
John McGhee	Former national officer
SCOTLAND	
Chris McGlone	Executive Council (EC) member
Denise Christie	Regional secretary
Seona Hart	Regional organiser
Roddy Robertson	Former EC member
John Paul McDonald	Former EC member
Kenny Ross	Former regional secretary
Gordon McQuade	Former regional chair
Alan Paterson	Former regional chair
Ronnie Robertson	Former regional chair
Jim Malone	Former regional official
Alex Miller	Former brigade secretary
Alan Campbell	Former brigade chair
Stewart Kinnon	Former brigade vice-chair
NORTHERN IRELAND	
Jim Quinn	EC member
Jim Barbour	Former EC member
Tony Maguire	Former regional secretary
Jim Hughes	Former regional secretary
NORTH EAST	
Andy Noble	EC member
Karl Wager	Brigade chair
Holly Ferguson	Brigade organiser
Darren Lane	Branch representative

Table 1

YORKSHIRE & HUMBERSIDE	
Pete Smith	Regional secretary
Neil Carbutt	Regional treasurer
Nicola Brown	Brigade chair
John Gilliver	Former brigade secretary
Graham Wilkinson	Former brigade chair
NORTH WEST	
Les Skarratts	EC member
Ian Hibbert	Brigade chair
Kevin Brown	Former EC member
Steve Harman	Former regional official
EAST MIDLANDS	
Phil Coates	EC member
Dave Limer	Former EC member
Marc Redford	Former regional chair
WEST MIDLANDS	
Barry Downey	EC member
Pete Goulden	Regional secretary
Rose Jones	Former EC member
Chris Downes	Former regional secretary
Marcus Giles	Former regional official
WALES	
Grant Mayos	EC member
Cerith Griffiths	Regional secretary
Mike Smith	Former EC member
EASTERN	
Jamie Wyatt	EC member
Riccardo La Torre	Regional secretary
Brian Hooper	Regional chair
Cameron Matthews	Brigade secretary
Alan Chinn-Shaw	Brigade secretary
Gary Critch	Brigade chair
Andy Findlayson	Branch representative
Keith Handscomb	Former EC member
Graham Noakes	Former brigade secretary
LONDON	
Paul Embery	EC member
Gareth Beeton	Regional chair
Lucy Masoud	Regional treasurer
Steve White	Regional organiser

Ian Leahair	Former EC member
Joe McVeigh	Former regional secretary
Linda Smith	Former regional treasurer
Khaled Haider	Former regional committee representative
SOUTH EAST AND SOUTHERN	
Danni Armstrong	Former EC member
Ricky Matthews	Former EC member
Simon Green	Former branch chair
SOUTH WEST	
Tam McFarlane	EC member
Trevor French	Regional secretary
Gary Spindler	Brigade chair
Bob Walker	Former brigade chair
SECTIONS	
Micky Nicholas	B&EMM section secretary
Lynda Rowan O'Neill	Control section secretary
Pat Carberry	LGBT section secretary
Peter Preston	Retained section secretary
Yannick Dubois	LGBT section chair
Rod Barrett	B&EMM national committee representative
Emma Turnidge	Control representative
Stewart Brown	Former EC member for LGBT
Tam Mitchell	Former EC member for retained
Vicky Knight	Former EC member for women
Kerry Baigent	Former women's section secretary
Dave Beverley	Former officer's section secretary
Lud Ramsey	Former B&EMM section chair
Carl St Paul	Former B&EMM section chair
Sian Griffiths	Former women's section representative
Joy Bingham	Former control representative
OTHER	
Brian Hurst	FBU Union Learning Fund project manager
Terry Segars	Former EC member
Trevor Cave	Former director of education
Philippa Clark	Former research officer
Mary Davis	Former tutor for FBU
Roger McKenzie	Former tutor for FBU

NOTES

Chapter 1

1 V Bailey (ed), *Forged in Fire: The history of the Fire Brigades Union*, London: Lawrence & Wishart, 1992, pp 289-90

2 Ibid

3 FBU, Executive Council Annual Report (ECAR) 2017, p 87

4 L Peterson, 'The one big union in international perspective: Revolutionary industrial unionism 1900-1925', *Labour / Le Travail*, Vol 7, No 1, 1981, pp 41-66

5 J McIlroy, *Trade Unions in Britain Today*, Manchester: Manchester University Press, 1995

6 FBU, ECAR 2017, p 87; Home Office, Scottish Fire and Rescue Service, Welsh Government, Northern Ireland Fire and Rescue Service workforce statistics

7 R Seifert and T Sibley, *United They Stood: The story of the UK firefighters' dispute 2002-2004*, London: Lawrence & Wishart, 2005

8 S Ewen, *What Kind of Fire Service?*, London: FBU, 2016

9 The terms fireman/firemen are used on occasion in this chapter to reflect the terminology of the time.

10 M Wrack, 'Firefighters' history appeal', *Firefighter*, December 2016/January 2017, p 13

11 Bailey, *Forged in Fire*, p 5

12 Ibid, p 18

13 Ibid, p 18

14 Ibid, pp 13-14 and 23-24

15 H Hague, 'Austerity 1920s style', *Firefighter*, April/May 2017, p 15

16 Bailey, p 40; S Ewen, *Fighting Fires*, Basingstoke: Palgrave Macmillan, 2010; Ewen, *What Kind of Fire Service?*

17 J Horner, 'Recollections of a general secretary', in Bailey, p 281

18 Ibid, p 293

19 Bailey, p 43

20 Ibid, p 45

21 Ibid, p 52

22 Ibid, p 53

23 Horner, p 325

24 T Segars, 'Women, war and the FBU', in Bailey, pp 139-57

25 Bailey, p 83

26 Ibid, p 159

27 Horner, p 353

28 Bailey, p 173

29 Horner, Appendix I, p 443

30 Ibid, p 355

31 R Holroyd, *Report of the Departmental Committee on the Fire Service*, London: HMSO, May 1970; C Cunningham, *Report of the Cunningham Inquiry into the Work of the Fire Service*, London: HMSO, November 1971

32 *Firefighter*, February 1978, cited in Bailey, p 240

33 J Flockhart, 'The Glasgow strike', in Bailey, p 401

34 J Saville, 'Terry Parry: A profile', in Bailey, p 273

35 P Kleinman, 'The strike in London', in Bailey, p 406

36 Bailey, p 256

37 Cameron, Foreword, in Bailey, p xvii

38 F Burchill, 'The UK Fire Service dispute, 2002-2003', *Employee Relations*, Vol 26, No 4, 2004, p 405

39 A Spence, 'Fighting a Labour government', in Bailey, p 429

40 Saville, p 271

41 R Carter, A Danford, D Howcroft, H Richardson, A Smith and P Taylor, '"All they lack is a chain": Lean and the New Performance Management in the British civil service', *New Technology, Work and Employment,* Vol 26, No 2, 2011, pp 83-97

42 S Bach and I Kessler, *The Modernisation of Public Services and Employee Relations,* Basingstoke: Palgrave Macmillan, 2012, p 7

43 J Webb, 'Work and the new public service class?', *Sociology,* Vol 33, No 4, 1999, pp 747-66

44 I Fitzgerald, 'The death of corporatism? Managing change in the fire service', *Personnel Review,* Vol 3, No 6, 2005, pp 648-62

45 FBU, *The Fire Safety Bill,* 1997

46 FBU, *Facing Reality – The need for a fully-funded fire and rescue service.* FBU submission to the Spending Review 2013 and initial response to Ken Knight's Review, June 2013

47 J Newman, *Modernising Governance: New Labour policy and society,* London: Sage, 2001

48 Bach and Kessler, p 153

49 Fitzgerald, 'The death of corporatism?'

50 Seifert and Sibley, p 58

51 A Gilchrist, 'A vision for the future', *Firefighter,* July 2000, pp 2-3

52 Fitzgerald, 'The death of corporatism?'

53 HM Fire Service Inspectorate, *Managing a Modernised Fire Service: Bridging the gap,* 2001, p 3

54 G Bain, *Independent Review of the Fire Service,* 2002, p vi

55 Fitzgerald, p 659

56 S Ewen, 'Grenfell lessons', 15 September 2017, www.fbu.org.uk/blog/grenfell-lessons

57 FBU Executive Policy Statement, *A Service for the 21st Century,* Annual Conference 2009

58 Local Government Association, *Fire and Rescue Services in England: A guide for Police and Crime Panel members,* 2017, p 13

59 Ewen, *What Kind of Fire Service?*

60 FBU, 'Matt Wrack elected general secretary', *Firefighter,* June 2005, p 4

61 HM Treasury, *Spending Review 2010,* October 2010, www.gov.uk/government/publications/spending-review-2010

62 FBU, 'Almost one-in-five frontline firefighter jobs cut since 2010', *Fire and Rescue Service Matters,* July 2017

63 FBU, 'Cuts to fire safety inspectors put the public at risk', *Fire and Rescue Service Matters,* July 2017

64 Home Office, *Fire Statistics: England April 2015 to March 2016,* 27 April 2017 www.gov.uk/government/statistics/fire-statistics-england-april-2015-to-march-2016

65 FBU, 'Firefighters rescue more people than ever before', *Fire and Rescue Service Matters,* September 2016

66 D Hencke, 'Profiting from the fire service', *Firefighter,* March 2011; D Hencke, 'AssetCo shows the folly of privatisation', *Firefighter,* October 2011

67 FBU, *Facing Reality – The need for a fully-funded fire and rescue service,* June 2013, p 5

68 FBU, *Losing Control? Cuts, closures and challenges in UK fire controls,* April 2017

69 Scottish Fire and Rescue Service, *Fire Safety and Organisational Statistics 2016-17,* Table 1a

70 A Thomas, *Independent Review of Conditions of Service for Fire and Rescue Staff in England,* 2016, p 5

71 FBU, 'FBU: Thomas Review an attack on all firefighters', *Firefighter,* April 2015, p 4

72 Home secretary speech on fire reform, 24 May 2016

73 FBU press release, 'FBU reacts to Theresa May's first speech on the fire and rescue service', 24 May 2016

74 FBU 'Police, fire and crime commissioners', *Fire and Rescue Service Matters*, February 2017

75 FBU, 'A very expensive mistake', *Firefighter*, February/March 2016, p 7

76 FBU press release, 'Fire service in crisis as 10,000 firefighter jobs axed', 13 September 2016 www.fbu.org.uk/news/2016/09/13/fire-service-crisis-10000-firefighter-jobs-axed

77 L Passerini, *Fascism in Popular Memory: The cultural experience of the Turin working class*. Cambridge: Cambridge University Press, 2009

78 A Portelli, 'The peculiarities of oral history', *History Workshop Journal*, Vol 12, No 1, 1981, pp 96-107

79 E P Thompson, *The Making of the English Working Class*, Harmondsworth: Penguin, 1981

80 A Pollert, *Girls, Wives, Factory Lives*, Basingstoke: Palgrave Macmillan, 1981

81 H Beynon, *Working for Ford*, Harmondsworth: Penguin, 1973

82 D Lyddon, 'Writing Trade Union History: The case of the National Union of Public Employees, *Historical Studies in Industrial Relations*, Vol 38, 2017, pp 221-54

83 Former general secretary Andy Gilchrist was invited to participate, but declined.

84 This chapter provides a longer-term perspective than that provided by Seifert and Sibley's account *United They Stood*, which was published shortly after in 2005. While presenting different perspectives of the dispute, based on the testimonies, we have not sought to adjudicate on developments and the outcome or adopt a partisan political stance, which Seifert and Sibley tend towards.

Chapter 2

1 Seifert and Sibley characterise the FBU as 'a closed craft union' but concede it has elements of industrial unionism. R Seifert and T Sibley, *United they Stood: The story of the UK firefighters' dispute 2002-2004*, London: Lawrence & Wishart, 2005, p 36

2 The decline of UK trade union membership in the decades following the Thatcher Conservative government in 1979 has been well documented. In 2016 there were 6.2 million employees in trade unions, compared to 13.2 million in 1979. While public sector trade union membership has been more resilient than membership in the private sector, trade union density in the public sector fell to 53 per cent in 2016 – a decline from 84 per cent in 1980. While in 1996 three-quarters of public sector employees were covered by collective agreements, by 2016 this had declined to 59 per cent. Department for Business, Energy & Industrial Strategy, *Trade Union Membership 2016*, 2017.

3 Excepting London and West Midlands, which have no retained firefighters.

4 The exception is action over pensions where control staff belong to a different pension scheme (LGPS).

5 Record of Decisions, FBU 88th Conference, Blackpool, 12-15 May, 2015

6 M Martinez Lucio, S Marino and H Connolly, 'Organising as a strategy to reach precarious and marginalised workers: A review of debates on the role of the political dimension and the dilemmas of representation and solidarity', *Transfer*, Vol 23, No 1, 2017, pp 31-46

7 London regional organiser Steve White suggested that a branch secretary in London would represent around 50 members.

8 W Murphy, 'Strong roots, strong union', *Firefighter*, April 2017, p 16

9 S Moore and S Tailby, 'The changing face of employment relations: Equality and diversity,' *Employee Relations*, Vol. 37, No 6, 2015, pp 705-19.

10 Record of Decisions, FBU 88th Conference, Blackpool 12-15 May, 2015.

11 'Marion is first woman on EC', *Firefighter*, July 1979, p 2

12 FBU, Executive Council Annual Report (ECAR) 1980, p 94.

13 'More delays to FiReControl project after government admits major technical problems', *Firefighter*, November/December 2008, p 9

14 The film was part-funded by the FBU and nominated for a BAFTA (www.operatorshortfilm.com).

15 In Cornwall, staff were even required to monitor Council CCTV.

16 M Wrack, 'A firefighter is a firefighter is a firefighter', *Alerter*, August 2005, p 6.

17 Bailey describes rifts opening up in the 1977-78 national strike. The RFU gained trade union recognition in 2005. See *Forged in Fire*.

18 'Union in court fight for retained pensions justice', *Firefighter* June 2004, p 8

19 Butterfield had been a retained firefighter and FBU member since 1978 at Burntisland fire station in Fife. He was elected branch secretary in 1985 and subsequently retained brigade chair and then region 1 retained representative in 1993.

20 In 2004 Butterfield reported that there were only three wholetime stations in the Highland and Islands, an area the size of Belgium (*Firefighter*, June 2004).

21 Bailey, p 62

22 T Sibley, 'Anti-Communism: Studies of its impact on the UK labour movement in the early years (1945-50) of the Cold War', PhD thesis, University of Keele, 2008

23 Swabe reports that NAFO was originally called the National Fire Service Officers Association and sponsored by Herbert Morrison to counter the danger of role conflicts arising from firefighters and their officers being in the same union; A I R Swabe, 'Multi-unionism in the fire service', *Industrial Relations Journal*, Vol 14, No 4, 1983, pp 56-69

24 J B Smethurst and p Carter, *A Historical Directory of Trade Unions: Volume 6*, Farnham: Ashgate, 2009. The FOA was granted a Certificate of Independence in 1995.

25 M Wrack, 'Imperative for the union to unite', *Firefighter*, June 2005, p 2

26 Bailey, p 10

27 This was reflected in the British Airways cabin crew dispute; p Taylor and S Moore, 'Cabin crew collectivism: Labour process and the roots of mobilisation in the British Airways dispute 2009-11', *Work, Employment and Society*, Vol. 29, No 1, 2015, pp 79-98

28 I Fitzgerald and J Stirling, 'A slow burning flame? Organisational change and industrial relations in the fire service', *Industrial Relations Journal*, Vol 30, No 1, 1999, p 57

29 Record of Decisions, 88th FBU Conference, 2015

30 These costs rose from approximately £125,000 in 2001 to £1.3 million in 2007.

31 Under the Trade Union Act 2016, unions must provide workers with other means through which to pay subscriptions (such as direct debit) and must pay for the check-off systems themselves.

32 T Redman and E Snape, 'Kindling activism? Union commitment and participation in the UK fire service', *Human Relations*, Vol 57, No 7, 2004, pp 854-69

33 Ibid

34 Fitzgerald and Stirling, *A slow burning flame?*

35 R Darlington, 'Workplace union resilience in the Merseyside Fire Brigade', *Industrial Relations Journal*, Vol 29, No 1, 1998, p 71

36 S Moore, *New trade union activists – Class consciousness or social identity?* Basingstoke: Palgrave Macmillan, 2011

37 FBU, ECAR 2016, p 72

38 G Daniels and J McIlroy, *Trade unions in a neoliberal world: British trade unions under New Labour*, London: Routledge, 2009

Chapter 3

1 Labour Research Department, *Bringing the Formula into the 21st Century – A report for the Fire Brigades Union on the fire fighters' pay formula,* 2002
2 V Bailey (ed), *Forged in Fire: The history of the Fire Brigades Union*, London: Lawrence & Wishart, 1992
3 M Smith, 'Swansea national demo Sept 18', *Firefighter,* October 1987, p 4
4 FBU Report of Annual Conference Proceedings, 1988
5 F Burchill, 'The UK fire service dispute, 2002-2003', *Employee Relations*, Vol 26, No 4, 2004, pp 404-21
6 Fire Cover Review Report of the Task Group to the CFBAC, 2002
7 FBU, 'Academic's findings prove unity is strength', *Firefighter,* July 1998, pp 4-5
8 T Maguire, 'If Merseyside falls we all fall', *Firefighter,* December 1996, p 8
9 R Darlington, 'Workplace union resilience in the Merseyside Fire Brigade', *Industrial Relations Journal*, Vol 29, No 1, 1998, pp 58-73
10 S McNeil, 'Derbyshire dispute comes to an end', *Firefighter,* January/February 1997, p 4
11 K Handscomb, 'The will to win', 1998 Arthur Charles Memorial Essay, *Firefighter,* July 1998, pp 20-23
12 K Handscomb, 'Essex County Council backs down – Strikes off!', *Firefighter,* July/August 1996, pp 4-5
13 General secretaries of the Transport and General Workers Union and the TUC respectively
14 The ridership factor determines how many people are required to crew an appliance made up of total availability (shifts per year a person is available for work, minus leave, sickness and training). Altering the amount of training achieves a reduction of 20 posts.
15 K Handscomb, 'A tribute to Ken Cameron', *Firefighter,* January/February 2000, pp 16-17
16 The Merseyside Dockers' dispute lasted 28 months, resulting from the sacking of union members employed by the Merseyside Docks and Harbour Company when they refused to cross a picket line organised by dockers who had been sacked by docks company Torside. Strikers and supporters wore a customised Calvin Klein T-shirt incorporating the CK into 'dockers'.
17 J Faulkner, 'Suffolk wins fight to save retained jobs', *Firefighter*, May 1995, p 14
18 L Hammond, 'Surrey ballot for strike action', *Firefighter*, August 1998, p 14
19 Burchill, 'The UK fire service dispute'
20 J P McDonald, 'Smash 'n' Grab: Outmoded and unjustified actions of employers', *Firefighter*, October 1999, pp 8-9
21 Burchill, 'The UK fire service dispute'
22 R Seifert and T Sibley, *United they Stood: The story of the UK firefighters' dispute 2002-2004*, London: Lawrence & Wishart, 2005
23 Burchill, p 407
24 J McDonald 'A Vindication of Smash and Grab, *Firefighter,* July 2000, p 4
25 Burchill, 'The UK fire service dispute'
26 'FBU supports London's suspended members', *Firefighter,* January/February 2000, p 4
27 A Gilchrist, 'So what's the Merseyside dispute got to do with me?', *Firefighter*, July/August 2001, pp 2-3
28 L Ball, '81% vote for action', *Firefighter*, April 2001, p 3

Chapter 4

1 V Bailey, 'The first national strike' in Bailey (ed), *Forged in Fire: A history of the Fire Brigades Union,* London: Lawrence & Wishart, 1992; R Seifert and T Sibley,

United They Stood: The story of the UK firefighters' dispute 2002-2004, London: Lawrence & Wishart, 2005

2 K Marx, *The Eighteenth Brumaire of Louis Bonaparte*, New York: International Publishers Co, 1852/1994

3 'Iraq war illegal says Annan', BBC news, 16 September 2004, nin.tl/Annanquote

4 Labour Research Department, *The Fire Service Pay Formula 1979-1995: A report for the FBU,* London: LRD, 1996

5 Andy Gilchrist became associated with the so-called 'awkward squad' of left-wing leaders, including Bob Crow (RMT), Mick Rix (ASLEF), Mark Serwotka (PCS) and Derek Simpson (Amicus).

6 Seifert and Sibley, p 64. The draft was not progressed to the White Paper stage and was dropped following the sacking of Mike O'Brien as the responsible minister.

7 A Gilchrist, *Pay, Reorganisation, Mobilisation,* pre-conference tour, 2002

8 In his speeches, Gilchrist acknowledged the legitimacy of criticisms of new Labour but expressed his fervent opposition to FBU disaffiliation which 'would be a monumental mistake'.

9 A Gilchrist, 'For a new improved pay formula', *Firefighter*, January/February 2002, pp 2-3; A Gilchrist, 'Time to revisit our fire service pay formula', *Firefighter*, March 2002, pp 2-3

10 FBU Executive Council Emergency Resolution No 1, 14 May 2002

11 Ibid

12 Labour Research Department, *Bringing the Formula into the 21st Century – A report for the Fire Brigades Union on the Fire Fighter's pay formula*, London: LRD, 2002

13 Ibid, pp 18-19

14 Ibid, pp 30-39

15 S Hastings, *The Changing Role of the Firefighter,* London: FBU, 2002

16 Incomes Data Services, *Pay in the Public Services*, 2002-03, London: IDS, 2002

17 FBU, *Fire Service Pay Campaign: Key comparators,* May 2002

18 *The Guardian*, 'Firefighters willing to delay strike', 17 November 2002

19 S Bach, 'Public-sector employment relations reform under Labour: Muddling through on modernisation', *British Journal of Industrial Relations*, Vol 40, No 2, 2002, pp 319-39; J Waddington, 'Heightening tension in relations between trade unions and the Labour government in 2002', *British Journal of Industrial Relations*, Vol 41, No 2, 2003, pp 335-58

20 This conclusion was drawn by Mike Fordham, FBU assistant general secretary, one of three members of the union negotiating side, alongside Ruth Winters (president) and Andy Gilchrist (general secretary). (Seifert and Sibley, pp 92-93).

21 FBU Annual Report, 2004, p 4

22 Employers' Organisation for Local Government, 'Pay performance and modernisation', *Pay Advisory Bulletin*, No 3, 2002

23 Bain was vice-chancellor of Queen's University (Belfast), and chair of the Low Pay Commission; Lyons was professor of public policy at the University of Birmingham and chief executive of Birmingham City Council; Sir Anthony Young was trade union liaison officer of the Ethical Trading Initiative and TUC president

24 G Bain, *The Future of the Fire Service, The independent review of the fire service,* 2002, pp 1-2

25 Letter from Andy Gilchrist to John Prescott, 14 October 2002.

26 Subsequent evidence confirms FBU scepticism of the inquiry's ostensible independence and its distrust of Bain. Alistair Campbell, press secretary for prime minister Tony Blair, recounts the detail of communication between Bain and Blair on 16 November 2002: 'Bain called to speak to him to say in his view the FBU didn't deserve much at all, and he was worried JP [John Prescott] saw

it as an old-fashioned split-down-the-middle negotiation'. A Campbell, *The Burden of Power: Countdown to Iraq, The Alistair Campbell diaries, volume 4*. London: Arrow, 2013, p 365

27 T George, *Evening Standard*, 17 October 2002, cited in Seifert and Sibley, p 116

28 P Blyton and P Turnbull, *The Dynamics of Employee Relations* (3rd edition), Basingstoke: Palgrave Macmillan, 2004, p 323

29 Hansard, 21 November 2002, pp 885-86

30 I Fitzgerald and J Stirling, 'A slow burning flame? Organisational change and industrial relations in the fire service', *Industrial Relations Journal*, Vol 30, No 1, 1999, pp 46-60

31 A Campbell, *The Burden of Power*, p 379

32 Seifert and Sibley claimed Executive Council members were now reporting 'disquiet' by some at the sustainability of long strikes. This author's preference is for these claims to be evidenced by actual developments and interviewee testimony.

33 Letter from Andy Gilchrist to Charles Noida, 13 January 2003.

34 *Daily Telegraph*, 17 March 2003

35 F Burchill, 'The UK fire service dispute, 2002-2003', *Employee Relations*, Vol 26, No 4, 2004, pp 404-21

36 The recall conference also supported a brigade motion to call off strikes in the event of war.

37 Seifert and Sibley, p 181

38 Ibid, p 185

39 Reports from local newspapers. Seifert and Sibley, *United They Stood,* p 192, cite examples from Coventry and East Yorkshire where firefighters over-whelmingly rejected the offer, were preparing to strike and did not want action suspended.

40 The qualification was the 'sunset clause', whereby the Act's powers would cease after two years.

41 R Martin, *Bargaining Power*, London: Clarendon Press, 1992

42 Given the intensity of member concerns, the seriousness of the issues and the degree of psychological and material commitment to action, it is demeaning to participants to trivialise internal disagreement and caricature the challenge to the leadership as the conspiratorial work of ultra-left groups, as Seifert and Sibley repeatedly do.

43 Seifert and Sibley, pp 204-05

44 *The Guardian*, 6 November 2003, p 6

45 Seifert and Sibley, p 204

46 *The Times*, 20 May 2004, p 2

47 FBU, *Pay Campaign Update*, No 1, 2004

48 FBU, *Pay Campaign Update*, No 2, 2004

49 FBU, *Pay Campaign Update*, No 3, 2004; Mike Fordham's interviews (7 June, 27 June 2017) delivered an equally graphic and embittered account that had not been tempered by the passage of 13 years.

50 FBU, *Pay Campaign Update*, No. 3, 2004

51 FBU, *The Truth About Monday's NJC Meeting – In their own words*, 2004

52 FBU, 'FBU says employers are lying over claims the union has been invited to talks and that it is refusing talks or delaying modernisation', fbu.org.uk/news, 20 May 2004.

53 FBU, 'Union bans Grassroots FBU', *FBU Bulletin No. 12*, 11 October 2004

54 Barbour recalls it was Mike Smith who raised the 40 per cent figure. Other participants said it was Mick Shaw. The minutes do not record the contributions.

55 Following compassionate leave.

56 FBU, 'Poll reveals strong public backing for firefighter pay claims', 2 September 2002

57 M Bedford, 'A sound clash: Revising Joe, remembering Strummer', *Vertigo*, Vol 3, No 7, 2007; G Binnette, *Last Night London Burned*, London: George Binnette, 2003

58 theclashorg.uk/new_page_1_htm

59 See also a lengthy account by Mike Fordham in Seifert and Sibley, pp 139-40

60 The then responsible government minister.

Chapter 5

1 M Wrack, 'Imperative for the union to unite', *Firefighter*, June 2005, p 2

2 Ibid, p 3

3 Essentially how many fire engines and firefighters are needed, and response times.

4 Executive Policy Statement, 'A service for the 21st century', Annual Conference 2009

5 I Fitzgerald, 'The death of corporatism? Managing change in the fire service', *Personnel Review*, Vol 3, No 6, 2005

6 M Wrack, 'Let's move forward together', *Firefighter*, June 2010, p 2

7 Mick Shaw, introduction to Executive Council Annual Report (ECAR) 2007, p 9

8 The government project to promote fire and rescue service resilience and capability to respond to national catastrophic incidents using urban search and rescue, mass decontamination and high volume pumping equipment; P Matthewman and P Goulden, 'Future fears, welfare worries', *Firefighter*, June 2007, pp 12-13

9 The two firefighters who died were Michael Millar, 26, from Stevenage, and Jeff Wornham, 28, from Royston.

10 The largest explosion since the Second World War at the Buncefield fuel depot in Hemel Hempstead.

11 BBC news, 20 May 2006, nin.tl/strikeovercutbacks

12 'Cleveland members help stop cuts', *Alerter*, Winter 2005-06, p 4

13 'Autumn of discontent', *Firefighter*, October 2009, pp 12-13

14 FBU press release, 'Union reveals confidential letters at centre of "gagging-order" storm – and makes formal complaints', 21 June 2011

15 www.fbu.org.uk/news/2017/09/22/fire-service-increase-crew-sizes-after-union-outcry

16 'FBU members' campaigning pays off', *Firefighter*, April/May 2017, p 7

17 M Wrack, 'Imperative for the union to unite', *Firefighter*, June 2005, p 2

18 FBU/IFE, *Independent Review and Comparison of Full Business Case for the FiReControl Project*, September 2007; FBU/IFE, *Independent Review of Regional Business Case for the FiReControl Project*, Autumn 2008; FBU/IFE, *Independent Review of National Business Case (November 2008) for the FiReControl Project*, February 2009

19 Later on, after FiReControl was scrapped, Scotland went from 8 to 3 after the creation of the single service. See *Losing Control? Cuts, closures and challenges in UK fire controls*, FBU Report, April 2017.

20 'Defend Control jobs', *Firefighter*, June 2008, pp 10-13

21 J Drake, 'Privatisation Mapped out', *Firefighter*, July 2008 p 8,

22 'Defend Control jobs', pp 10-13

23 Committee of Public Accounts report into FiReControl project, 29 September 2011, nin.tl/PublicAccounts

24 T McFarlane, 'Exposing the shambolic Regional Fire Control project', FBU blog, 2 August 2017

25 FBU press release, 'Cumbria fire union demands action over axing fire control as it launches save Cumbria fire control campaign', 4 November 2011

26 *Losing Control? Cuts, closures and challenges in UK fire controls*, FBU Report, April 2017

27 Whereby the administration of leave is devolved to watch managers, with additional work for operational staff.

28 FBU press release, 'Chronic staff shortages at North Yorkshire fire control leave public at risk, say firefighters', 28 July 2017

29 'Modern times', *Firefighter,* June 2006, p 11

30 'Hard times ahead?', *Firefighter*, July/August 2006, pp 10-11

31 'South Yorks members up action', *Firefighter,* August/September 2009, p 5

32 I Murray, 'Lessons from the South Yorkshire dispute', *Firefighter,* July 2010, p 15

33 Circular: 2008HOC0472MW, 14 July 2008

34 In 2015 members in Essex took strike action on 14-16 January, 1-2 March, 10-19 March, 12-15 June, 6 August, 17 August, 19 August, 21-26 August, 28 August and 1 September.

35 Essex FBU press release, 26 February 2015

36 L Hudson, S Moore, K Tainsh, P Taylor and T Wright, 'The only way is Essex': Gender, union and mobilisation among fire service control room staff', *Work, Employment and Society,* 2017, online first: journals.sagepub.com/doi/pdf/10.1177/0950017017728613

37 FBU press release, 'Fury at plans to sack Greater Manchester's entire firefighter workforce', 19 September 2016

38 'Irrational and perverse', Firefighter, November/December 2015, pp 14-15

39 'Merseyside dispute: Determined action gets results', *Firefighter,* November 2006, pp 14-15

40 Constructive dismissal is the legal term used to describe circumstances in which an employee is not formally dismissed, but forced to resign because of their employer's unlawful behaviour.

41 'United we stand', *Firefighter,* October 2006, pp 14-15

42 ECAR, 2016, p 83

43 ECAR 2008, p 67

44 FBU press release, 'London firefighters vote yes in industrial action ballot', 27 April 2004

45 FBU press release, 'Court rules firefighters cannot be forced to attend 999 medical emergencies on behalf of the Ambulance Service', 23 October 2006

46 Report of Proceedings, 89th Annual Conference, 11-13 May 2016

47 L Wallis,' Wanted: Agreement on our pay, safety and health', *Firefighter*, April/May 2017, pp 12-13

48 P Hampton, 'Time to end the pay freeze', *Firefighter*, April/May 2017, pp 10-11; In 2010-11, the Westminster government imposed a two-year pay freeze on firefighters, followed ever since by a 1 per cent pay cap on public sector pay.

49 'Pay: Mind the gap', *Firefighter,* July 2010, p 17. In 2010 it was calculated that chief officers were earning as much as six times the pay of a regular firefighter, with their pay increasing twice as fast.

50 Hampton, pp 10-11

51 FBU press release, 13 September 2018

52 T Redman and E Snape, 'Industrial relations climate and staff attitudes in the fire service: A case of union renewal?' *Employee Relations*, Vol 28, No 1 2006, pp 26-45

Chapter 6

1 M Peel, 'Is the pension scheme safe?', *Firefighter*, May/June 2001, p 31. Malcolm Peel, chair of Region 4, citing the opening paragraphs to the Pensions Commentary in the FPS.

2 The need for a full review of the FPS was identified by the Home Office and the Treasury in the course of a fundamental review of fire service expenditure in 1993. The review began in 1994 but the report of the review, and its recommen-

dations were not published before the general election in May 1997 intervened. *The Fire Service Pensions Review: Consultation* document was published in 1998.

3 M Wrack, 'Imperative for the union to unite', *Firefighter*, June 2005, p 2

4 General unions UNISON, AMICUS, the TGWU and the GMB, building workers' union UCATT, youth workers' union CYWU, probation service union NAPO and the teaching union NUT balloted their members. At that stage the Local Government Association proposed to cut pension rights but refused to agree protection for existing members of the LGPS.

5 Circular: 2006HOC0175GE

6 From December 2005 the FPS was amended to provide benefits (based on service after 5 April 1988) for surviving civil partners on the same terms as would apply to widow(er)s. Executive Council Annual Report (ECAR), 2007, p 121

7 'Same job, same pension', *Firefighter*, March 2006, pp 14-15

8 ECAR, 2007, p 83. ECAR 2013, p 83

9 FBU press release, 'Retained firefighters: FBU wins eight-year legal battle, 11 September 2007

10 Under the Part-time Workers (Prevention of Less Favourable Treatment) Regulations 2000, part-time workers are protected from being treated less favourably than equivalent full-time workers.

11 M Peel, 'Is the pension scheme safe?', *Firefighter*, May/June 2001, pp 31-32

12 ECAR 2009, p 55

13 Ibid, p 55

14 Ibid, p 56

15 Under CARE schemes, pensions are based upon averaged pensionable earnings over time in the scheme. Final salary schemes are based upon final pensionable salary in the years immediately before the pension is taken.

16 T Cutler and B Waine, *Pension Schemes in the Fire Service and the Independent Public Service Pensions Commission*, 2011, p 4

17 R Hammond, *Impact of Government's Proposals for Members of the FPS and NFPS*, First Actuarial Consultants, 2011

18 With the exception of the LGPS, public sector schemes are unfunded. This means that pension benefits are paid out of current income as and when they become due. Funded schemes mean that members' pension rights should be covered by assets held under trust: Pensions Policy Institute, *Occupational Pension Provision in the Public Sector*, 2005

19 A Williams, D M Wilkinson, V Richmond and M Rayson, *Normal Pension Age for Firefighters - A review for the Firefighter's Pension Committee*, 2012

20 Hilary Benn, in the debate triggered by the Labour Party in December 2014, noted: 'Under the Government's proposals, firefighters will lose 21.8 per cent of their pension at the age of 55, yet the Government Actuary has shown that there are two different ways of calculating that reduction: one that seems fair to firefighters, and another that is not, which is the one that the Government have chosen. This issue of the reduction is where negotiations in Scotland and Wales have made most progress. Scotland is not proposing a 21.8 per cent reduction, as in England, but a 9 per cent reduction, and in past weeks, Wales has also moved to consult on 9 per cent.' nin.tl/Hansard15Dec2014

21 ECAR, 2015, p 92

22 Emergency Shorts, 11 October 2013, nin.tl/emergency

23 ECAR, 2015, p 93

24 Ibid, p 93; 45 per cent of those returning ballot papers voted against on a 38 per cent turnout

25 Ibid

26 Ibid

27 See Chapter 5.

28 'FBU: Fitness research has destroyed government claims on retirement at 60',

Firefighter, November/December 2015, p 4

29 ECAR, 2017, p 40

30 'Union lawyers report on fight for firefighters' pensions', *Firefighter*, Feb/Mar 2017, p 7

31 Those who joined the 1992 FPS aged 18-20 had to contribute for up to 32 years to receive a 30-year pension at the earliest age of 50 – since the accrual cap was 30 years they were paying two years' contributions more than they should have.

32 A complaint to the Pensions Ombudsman that the Government Actuary's Department (GAD) failed to review the commutation factors within the 1992 FPS from 2001 to 2006 was upheld. Commutation is a procedure where a member of a pension scheme gives up a part of their pension in exchange for an immediate lump sum payment. The test case found that the GAD had failed to identify its responsibility to calculate appropriate commutation factors – the amount that needs to be given up in order to provide a lump sum – and that they should compensate the member for the loss of money and any tax liability. This decision should be applied to all affected firefighters in the 1992 scheme.

33 'Thousands raised for pensions fighting fund', *Firefighter*, February/March 2016, p 6

34 'Pension scheme imposed but campaign continues', *Firefighter*, May/June 2015, p 4

35 ECAR, 2016, p 26

Chapter 7

1 M Wrack, 'Farewell, Ken Cameron', *Firefighter*, June/July 2016, p 2

2 L Wallis, 'Women blazing a trail', *Firefighter*, June/July 2017, p 12

3 T Segars, 'Women, war and the FBU', in Bailey (ed), *Forged in Fire: The history of the Fire Brigades Union*, London: Lawrence & Wishart, 1992, p 142

4 Hicks was one of the three women appointed staff officers at the National Fire Service headquarters at the Home Office (one of the first three women 'brass hats'). In 1943 she was promoted to deputy chief woman fire officer and she ended the war in Cambridge as regional woman fire chief for the eastern region; P Clark, 'Hidden from history – Joyce Hicks OBE', *Firefighter*, March/April 2000, p 2

5 T Segars, 'Women in WW2', *Firefighter*, August 1986, p 10

6 L Wallis, 'Women blazing a trail', *Firefighter*, June/July 2017, pp 12-13

7 Segars, 'Women, war and the FBU', p 146

8 Segars, 'Women, war and the FBU', p 147

9 Segars, 'Women, war and the FBU', p 150

10 'Britain's first woman fire-fighter joins the East Sussex brigade', *Fire* magazine, October 1976, p 232

11 'UK's longest serving woman firefighter retires' *Siren*, Winter 2007, p 4; J Reynolds, *Fire Woman: The extraordinary story of Britain's first female firefighter*, London: Michael O'Mara Books, 2017. In Norfolk Josephine Reynolds joined the 'junior firemen' training scheme in July 1982 aged 17 and started work at Thetford in March 1984.

12 'First mother and daughter whole-time firefighters, *Siren*, Summer 2016, p 2

13 Her Majesty's Chief Inspector of Fire Services (HMCIFS) reports

14 Home Office, *Equality and Fairness in the Fire Service: A thematic review*, September 1999, p 3

15 Home Office, *Fire Statistics Table 1103: Staff headcount by gender, fire and rescue authority and role, England*, 2015-16

16 Scottish Fire and Rescue Service, *Fire Safety and Organisational Statistics Scotland 2015-16*

17 *Fire and Rescue Service Operational Statistics for Wales*, 2010-11

18 HMCIFS reports

19 Home Office, *Fire Statistics Table 1103*; Scottish Fire and Rescue Service, *Fire Safety and Organisational Statistics Scotland 2015-16*
20 *Fire and Rescue Service Operational Statistics for Wales*, 2010-11
21 W Murphy, 'A pioneer honoured', *Firefighter*, October/November 2016, pp 16-17
22 London Fire Brigade, *In Our Own Words: A history of people of colour in the London Fire Brigade*, 2007
23 M Nicholas, 'Frank Bailey obituary', *The Guardian*, 26 January 2016
24 Executive Council Annual Report (ECAR), 2007; 2008; 2016
25 *Rise to the Challenge*, by Alan Miles and Simon Green, with the support of the FBU and B&EMM section, youtube.com/watch?v=UWVDikdKZMo&feature=youtu.be
26 D Vaux, 'Equal opportunities', *Firefighter*, May 1989, p 14
27 HMCIFS 1992-93, p 14
28 Home Office, *Fire Statistics Table 1104: Staff headcount by ethnicity, fire and rescue authority and role, England*, 2015-16
29 Home Office, *Fire Statistics Table 1104*; BBC News, 'Fire brigades "must do more to improve racial diversity" – minister', 12 March 2016
30 *Fire and Rescue Service Operational Statistics for Wales*, 2010-11
31 Home Office, *Fire Statistics Table 1103*; Scottish Fire and Rescue Service, *Fire Safety and Organisational Statistics Scotland 2015-16*
32 D Baigent, 'Gender relations, masculinities and the fire service: A qualitative study of firefighters' constructions of masculinity during firefighting and in their social relations of work', PhD thesis, Anglia Polytechnic University, 2001; F Colgan, C Creegan, A McKearney and T Wright, 'Lesbian, gay and bisexual workers: Equality, diversity and inclusion in the workplace', London: Comparative Organisation and Equality Research Centre, London Metropolitan University, 2006; J Ward and D Winstanley, 'Watching the watch: The UK Fire Service and its impact on sexual minorities in the workplace', *Gender, Work & Organization*, Vol 13, No 2, 2006, pp 193-219; T Wright, 'Lesbian firefighters: Shifting the boundaries between "masculinity" and "femininity"', *Journal of Lesbian Studies*, Vol 12, No 1, 2008, pp 103-114
33 Home Office, *Thematic Review*, 1999, p 26
34 Wright, 'Lesbian firefighters'
35 Home Office, *Fire Experimental Statistics Table 1107: Staff headcount by sexual orientation and role, for England, 2015-16*
36 W Murphy, 'Bravery of a different kind', *Firefighter*, February/March 2016, pp 12-13
37 'Successful seminar to launch FBU equal opportunities policy', *Firefighter*, April 1987, p 6
38 'Conference '92: Equal opportunities policy must be implemented', *Firefighter*, June 1992, pp 6-7
39 'Conference '95: Call for action on equality', *Firefighter*, June 1995, p 11
40 'Conference '96: "Fairness at Work"', *Firefighter*, June 1996, p 14
41 ECAR, 1999, pp 159-60
42 ECAR, 1997, pp 111-15
43 ECAR, 1999, pp 163-66
44 ECAR, 2016, p 76
45 N Jewson and D Mason, 'Theory and practice of equal opportunities policies: Liberal and radical approaches', *Sociological Review*, Vol. 34, No 2, 1986, pp 307-34
46 F Colgan and S Ledwith, 'Sisters organising - Women and their trade unions', in S Ledwith and F Colgan (eds), *Women in Organisations: Challenging gender politics*, Basingstoke: Palgrave Macmillan, 1996, pp 152-85
47 ECAR, 1993, pp 202-04

48 ECAR, 1998, p 157; 'First National FBU Women's Meeting', *Firefighter*, Jan/Feb 1998, p 11
49 ECAR 1997, p 115; 'Steering Committee elected for Black and Ethnic Group', *Firefighter*, March 1997, pp 8-9
50 ECAR 1997, pp 116-18
51 ECAR 2009, p 72
52 Report of Proceedings 2016, p 125
53 'Lesbian and gay rights – Why do we need a lesbian and gay rights group?', *Firefighter*, June 1997, pp 23-25
54 ECAR, 2000, p 93
55 'First ever elected member for women', *Firefighter*, January/February 2002, p 2; 'First Executive Council Member for Black & Ethnic Minority Members', *Firefighter*, March 2002, p 2; 'Election of officials for gay and lesbian section', *Flagship,* Summer 2006, p 4
56 J McGhee, 'What impact has the organisation of women's groups in the Fire Brigades Union had on the participation of women, the culture and the effectiveness of the organisation?', MA thesis, London Metropolitan University, 2011, p 64
57 Report of proceedings 2016 pp 90-91
58 '25 years ago in Firefighter', *Firefighter*, December 1994, p 23
59 ECAR 1997, p 126
60 'Control staff victory', *Firefighter*, July 1979, p 13
61 'Action call on racism and sexism, *Firefighter*, June 1985, p 7
62 'Record damages for sexual harassment – won with union support', *Firefighter*, May 1988, p 13
63 'FBU and Tanya Clayton achieve resounding victory in sex discrimination case', *Firefighter*, May 1995, pp 4-5
64 'Bully boy tactics defeated – Decency prevails', *Firefighter*, December 1996, p 2
65 'Racial abuse led to firefighter being "sent to Coventry"', *Firefighter*, July 1997, pp 5-6
66 'FBU Annual conference 1986: Equality', *Firefighter*, June 1986, p 9
67 ECAR, 1993, p 167; ECAR, 1994, p 187
68 ECAR, 1994, p 187
69 ECAR, 1999: p 40
70 Home Office, *Thematic Review*, 1999, pp 14-15
71 ECAR, 1999, p 162; ECAR 2000, p 31
72 'A conspiracy of silence', *Firefighter*, April 1999, pp 6-7
73 'FBU – Fighting for you! A letter to all members from the general secretary, Ken Cameron', *Firefighter*, November 1999, pp 22-23
74 'Women speak out on thematic inspection', *Firefighter*, January/February 2000, p 11
75 FBU circular 2008HOC0440JM, 1 July 2008
76 ECAR, 2009, p 106
77 ECAR, 2011, p 135
78 ECAR, 2015, p 155
79 ECAR, 2008, p 73
80 ECAR, 2013, p 165
81 ECAR, 2004, pp 122-23
82 ECAR, 2008, p 85
83 ECAR, 2011, p 115
84 ECAR, 2010, p 90; 'Fire minister: Homophobia not acceptable in the workplace', *Flagship*, Spring 2009, p 5
85 ECAR, 2008, p 118; ECAR 2009, p 76, p 121
86 Local Government Association, *An inclusive service: The twenty-first century fire and rescue service*, 2017

Chapter 8

1 Written by Paul Hampton, FBU Head of Research and Policy. Thanks particularly to Pete Goulden, Keith Handscomb, Brian Hooper, Dave Matthews and Dave Sibert for expert advice on FBU safety, health and welfare.

2 FBU, Record of Proceedings, 2013, pp 29 and 33

3 Department of Communities and Local Government, *Fire Statistics, United Kingdom, 2007*, 2009, p 95; Home Office, *Fire Statistics: England April 2015 to March 2016*, Table 0501; Northern Ireland Fire and Rescue Service (NIFRS), *Annual Report 2015/2016*

4 The causes of the deaths of the 200 others were mostly heart attacks, road traffic collisions or appliance crashes. Some of them involved rail or water rescue.

5 The Labour Research Department (LRD) report for the FBU, *In the Line of Duty*, 2008, found at least 122 firefighter deaths in the line of duty between 1978 and 2007, including at least 44 at fires. The Firefighters Memorial Charitable Trust and Institute of Fire Engineers have records for a much longer period. These figures record fatalities in incidents and training but are patchy on deaths at work from heart disease and do not include work-related causes such as suicide and cancer.

6 FBU, Executive Council Annual Report (ECAR) 1948, pp 221 and 240, pp 217-19

7 F Radford, *Fetch the Engine*, London: FBU, 1951, p 174. An advisory council was envisaged under the Fire Brigades Act 1938 and taken up by the FBU in its wartime pamphlet, 'What kind of service', 1943, pp 4-5, p 10

8 ECAR, 1964, p 13; ECAR, 1968, p 40; FBU, Record of Proceedings 1994, p 211; ECAR 2004, p 31

9 FBU, 'Whoa now, Jim, you can't go back on that one', *Firefighter*, February/March 1977, p 10

10 FBU, *The 'ONLY' union campaigning on behalf of the fire service since 1918*, 1983, p 11

11 ECAR, 1980, p 54; ECAR, 1981, p 76; Record of Proceedings, 1992, p 157, p 159; Record of Proceedings, 2011, p 115

12 D Matthews, 'Health and safety', *Firefighter*, June 1990, p. 19; Mike Fordham, 'European Union – A firefighters' charter', *Health and Safety Bulletin No.5*, July 1995, p 4

13 Record of Proceedings, 1991, p 132

14 S Ewen, *Fighting Fires*, Basingstoke: Palgrave Macmillan, 2010, p 158

15 H Richardson, 'Less spit and polish – More fire prevention', *Firefighter*, December 1954, p 14; FBU, Report of Proceedings, 1964, p 144; ECAR, 1972, pp 42-43

16 D Matthews, 'Many questions begged', *Firefighter*, January 1989, p 16; ECAR, 1990, p 17; ECAR, 1996, p 62; ECAR, 2007, p 49

17 FBU Memorandum, Select Committee on Environment, Transport and Regional Affairs, 1999; FBU Memorandum to the House of Commons Office of the Deputy Prime Minister: Housing, Planning, Local Government and the Regions Committee, 2006

18 Record of Proceedings, 1993, pp 52 and 54

19 ECAR, 1960, p 33

20 FBU, 'Technical committee wants breathing apparatus on all stations', *Firefighter*, July 1951, p 10; FBU, 'New BA Committee at Work', *Firefighter*, March/April 1958, p 5

21 FBU, 'Members' ideas on safety', *Firefighter*, July/August 1958, pp 22-23; ECAR, 1960, p 37; Report of Proceedings, 1958, pp 90-91

22 ECAR, 1963, p 30

23 Record of Proceedings, 1979, p 63

24 M Fordham, *Today's Fires – Today's Protection*, 1980, pp 2 and 7; ECAR, 1981, p 79;

Record of Proceedings, 1981, p. 179; FBU, 'Retained', *Firefighter*, June 1985, p 8

25 ECAR, 1995, p 33; ECAR, 1996, p 31

26 Record of Proceedings, 1996, p 260; Record of Proceedings, 1998, pp 89-91; LRD, *In the Line of Duty*, 2008; A Watterson, *Firefighter Fatalities at Fires in the UK: 2004-2013: Voices from the fireground*, 2015; ECAR, 2015, p 175

27 Record of Proceedings, 1951, p 137, p 140-41; Report of Proceedings, 1958, p 196; Report of Proceedings, 1960, p 112

28 Record of Proceedings, 1981, pp 168-69; Record of Proceedings, 1989, p 47; Record of Proceedings, 1987, p 63

29 Record of Proceedings, 1988, p 67

30 ECAR, 1991, p 23; ECAR, 1994, p 80; ECAR, 1998, p 25

31 Record of Proceedings, 2001, p 156

32 Record of Proceedings, 1993, p 28

33 Record of Proceedings, 2013, p 84

34 Hook ladders were meant to hook onto the building on fire (for example, onto window sills) but were very unstable, leading to falls from height.

35 Record of Proceedings, 1961, p 89

36 ECAR, 1957, p 91; Report of Proceedings, 1960, p 55

37 Report of Proceedings, 1962, p 107; Record of Proceedings, 1963, p 146

38 Report of Proceedings, 1965, p 94

39 ECAR, 1966, p 37; FBU, 'Firemen in determined mood over live rescue drills', *Firefighter*, June 1966, p 5; Report of Proceedings, 1966, p 116

40 ECAR, 1976, p 139-40; ECAR, 1995, p 29

41 Report of Proceedings, 1973, 166; FBU, 'Tighter safety standard bid', *Firefighter*, June 1973, p 19; Record of Proceedings, 1979, pp 82 and 83; FBU, 'Belt up', *Firefighter*, June 1979, p 9

42 FBU, 'Health, safety and warning devices', *Firefighter*, June 1986, p 4; ECAR, 1987, p 73; Record of Proceedings, 1993, p 23; Record of Proceedings, 1997, pp 29 and 31. A 'dear chief officer' letter was an instruction from the Home Office.

43 FBU, 'Working party on appliance cab safety', *Firefighter*, July 1998, p 15

44 Record of Proceedings, 2004, p 136; ECAR, 2009, p 125

45 ECAR, 1957, p 34; ECAR, 1961, p 79; ECAR, 1969, pp 33 and 42; ECAR, 1976, pp 158 and 160

46 Record of Proceedings, 2000, pp 51-52; Record of Proceedings, 2010: p 96

47 C Irwin, 'Occupational hazards of a fireman', *Firefighter*, February 1954, p 10; C Irwin, 'Occupational hazards of a fireman – Part 2', *Firefighter*, April 1954, p 6; FBU, 'A Service for the Sixties' (2nd edition), 1960, p 26

48 ECAR 1976, p 161; Report of Proceedings, 1977, pp 106-07

49 ECAR, 1990, p 58; ECAR, 1991, p 76

50 ECAR, 1969, p 73; ECAR, 1972, pp 77-79; ECAR, 1977, pp 54-56; FBU, 'More regular medical checks needed', *Firefighter*, June 1979, p 9; Record of Proceedings, 1994, p 125

51 ECAR, 1982, pp 35-36; ECAR, 1988, pp 31-32

52 Record of Proceedings, 1986, pp 63 and 64; FBU, *Joint Working Party on Appointment Provisions*, 1988, p 17; ECAR, 1991, p 54

53 FBU, 'Say NO to VO2 max 42', *Siren*, Spring 2010, pp 4-5; Record of Proceedings, 2010, p 139; ECAR, 2017, p 40

54 'Health and safety', *Firefighter*, June 1989, p 5; Record of Proceedings, 1988, p 69; FBU, 'Treat stress', *Firefighter*, June 1988, p 10; 'Stress gaining more attention', *Firefighter*, June 1991, p 6; ECAR, 1993, p 98

55 ECAR, 1992, p 82; D Matthews, 'Coping with PTSD five years on', *Health and Safety Bulletin No.2*, July 1994, p 9; Record of Proceedings, 1999, p 103

56 ECAR, 1997, p 42; Record of Proceedings, 1999, pp 63 and 65; ECAR, 2002, p 104; Centre for Trauma Studies, *An Audit of Organisational, Operational and Traumatic Stressors in Firefighters and Fire Control Staff*, 2001; L Hawkins,

An Audit of Organisational, Operational and Traumatic Stressors in Officers in the UK Fire Service, 2005.

57 ECAR, 2017, p 38; University of Hertfordshire, *Broadening Responsibilities: Consideration of the potential to broaden the role of uniformed fire service employees*, 2017

58 LRD, *Attacks on Firefighters*, 2005; LRD, *Easy Targets? Tackling attacks on fire crews in the UK*, 2008

59 L Hill, 'Health service must be comprehensive and free', *Firefighter*, February 1954, pp 12-13; ECAR, 1977, pp 41-42; ECAR, 1993, p 80; ECAR, 1994, p 23; ECAR, 1998, p 31

60 Record of Proceedings, 2015, p 118

61 Record of Proceedings, 2013, p 61; ECAR, 2015, p 177; ECAR, 2017, p 39

62 'Free jabs for firemen', *Firefighter*, July 1979, p 3; FBU, 'Health and safety policies', *Firefighter*, June 1988, p 7; ECAR, 1989, p 49

63 ECAR, 1996, p 26; Record of Proceedings, 2002, pp 14-15

64 Record of Proceedings, 2010, p 38; FBU, *HIV and Aids: A workplace policy*, June 2009.

65 Record of Proceedings, 1959, p 173; ECAR 1960, pp 56-57

66 ECAR, 1984, p 85; T Segars, 'Danger! Sizewell', *Firefighter*, January 1984, p 5; ECAR, 1985, p 93

67 Record of Proceedings, 1986, p 115; FBU, 'Labour Party conference', *Firefighter*, November 1986, p 8; FBU, 'End nuclear power', *Firefighter*, October 1989, p 13; ECAR, 1990, p 90

68 Record of Proceedings, 2008, pp 173-75; Record of Proceedings, 2010, p 145; FBU, *Inundated: The lessons of recent flooding for the fire and rescue service*, 2015

69 ECAR, 2013, p 37; ECAR, 2017, p 52

70 ECAR, 1977, p 76; Record of Proceedings, 2009, p 147; FBU, *Climate Change: Key issues for the fire and rescue service*, 2010; TUC, Report of Congress, 9 September 2014, p 128

71 'General secretary on new Health-Safety Commission', *Firefighter*, October 1974, p 2; Record of Proceedings, 2013, p 92

72 FBU, *Oldham Street Incident July 2013: The death of Stephen Hunt*, 2016, p 45

73 ECAR 1960, p 70; ECAR, 2002, p 72; ECAR, 1980, p 55; Record of Proceedings, 1989, pp 165 and 167; D Matthews, 'Annual meeting of education officers and regional health and safety co-ordinators', *Health and Safety Bulletin* No.7, April 1996, p 4

Chapter 9

1 G Johnson, 'The FBU, the TUC and the Labour Party', in Bailey (ed) *Forged in Fire: The history of the Fire Brigades Union*, London: Lawrence & Wishart, 1992; J Saville, 'The Communist Party and the FBU' in Bailey (ed) *Forged in Fire*

2 John Horner was a Labour MP from 1964 to 1970. Other prominent FBU officials who became MPs include Jim Sillars (1970-79); Terry Fields (1983-92) and Jim Fitzpatrick (1997 to date).

3 Bailey (ed), p 219

4 T Woodley, 'Defending political unity', *Firefighter*, April 2004, p 7

5 Report of Proceedings 2004, p 119

6 J McGhee, 'What is to be done now?', *Firefighter*, July/August 2004, p 12

7 'First meeting of FBU parliamentary group', *Firefighter*, June 2005, p 5

8 Recall conference, 27 November 2015, 'FBU Political Engagement Strategy', ECAR, 2016, p 65

9 ECAR, 2016, p 65

10 Report of Proceedings 2016, pp 145-50

11 *Glasgow Herald*, 25 October 2017; BBC Scotland News, 25 October 2017, nin.tl/firestationsclose

12 nin.tl/Scottishfirefighters

13 Johnson, in Bailey (ed), p 202

14 Ibid, p 203

15 Record of Proceedings 1962, p 118; TUC, *Report of the 104th Annual Trades Union Congress*, September 1972, p 449; 'Use FBU funds to counteract press campaign', *Firefighter*, May 1975, p 4

16 TUC press release, 'TUC pays tribute to former FBU General Secretary Ken Cameron', 17 May 2016

17 Report of Proceedings 2013, p 95

18 Ibid, p 92

19 'Conference elects FBU member to TUC Women's Conference', *Firefighter*, May 1991, pp 10-11

20 ECAR 2004, p 112

21 'Stamp out all racism in the fire service', *Firefighter*, October 1979, p 8

22 P Steel, 'Obituary Mick Shaw: Firefighter, union leader and anti-racist', *Independent*, 4 May 2012

23 ECAR 2010, p 80

24 'Chhokar Family Justice Campaign', *Firefighter*, July 2000, p 27; 'All they want is truth and justice', *Firefighter*, March 2001, pp 8-9

25 L Brooks, 'Man found guilty of murdering Surjit Singh Chhokar after retrial', *The Guardian*, 5 October 2016

26 ECAR 2000, p 109; ECAR 2002, p 133; ECAR 2009, p 50

27 ECAR 2016, p 86

28 M Wrack, 'Farewell, Ken Cameron', *Firefighter*, June/July 2016, p 2

29 R Fieldhouse, 'Anti-apartheid: A history of the movement in Britain: A study in pressure group politics', Merlin, 2005

30 'Declaration on the release of Nelson Mandela', *Firefighter,* April 1990, p 2

31 ECAR 1991, p 84

32 'Honour to Nelson Mandela', *Firefighter*, June 1991, p 20

33 'Nelson Mandela', *Firefighter*, August 2000, p 31

34 'ACTSA Scotland delegation to South Africa', *Firefighter*, February 2001, pp 13-16

35 ECAR 2009, p 52

36 TUC Briefing, 3 December 2010, https://www.tuc.org.uk/international-issues/countries/nigeria/human-rights/unions-celebrate-adoption-ilo-recommendation

37 ECAR 1990, p 94; M Nicholas, 'What now for Haiti?', *Advisor*, Spring 2010, pp 10-11

38 'The debate on politics rages: Members attack the journal others back it to the hilt', *Firefighter*, January 1984, pp 10-11

39 ECAR 2008, p 43

40 Report of Proceedings 2013, p 93

41 'The Road to Iraq', Special Pull-out, *Firefighter*, June 2007

42 ECAR 2016, p 66

43 ECAR 2007, p 73; ECAR 2015, p 77

44 M Wrack, 20 July 2014, https://www.fbu.org.uk/blog/rescatamos-personas-no-bancos-we-rescue-people-not-banks-inspiration-firefighters-spain

45 ECAR 2015, p 91

46 youtube.com/watch?v=PX7IuNEqWls and facebook.com/FirefightersUnderOccupation/

47 *Labour Research*, June 2016

48 Report of Proceedings 2016, p 66

49 fbu.org.uk/eu-referendum

50 EU referendum result, Circular: 2016HOC0329MW

INDEX

Page numbers in **bold** refer to boxed text and glossary terms, and those in *italic* refer to illustration captions.